Reflective Practice in Mental Health

Advanced Psychosocial Practice with Children, Adolescents and Adults

Edited by Martin Webber and Jack Nathan

Forewords by James Blewett and Alan Rushton

Jessica Kingsley *Publishers*
London and Philadelphia

MT

Figure 4.1 reprinted with permission from Taylor & Francis
Chapter 4 prologue reproduced with permission from PCCS Books (Fleischman 2009)

First published in 2010
by Jessica Kingsley Publishers
116 Pentonville Road
London N1 9JB, UK
and
400 Market Street, Suite 400
Philadelphia, PA 19106, USA

www.jkp.com

Library of Congress Cataloging in Publication Data
Reflective practice in mental health : advanced psychosocial practice
with children, adolescents and adults / edited by Martin Webber and
Jack Nathan ; forewords by James Blewett and Alan Rushton.
    p. cm.
Includes bibliographical references and index.
ISBN 978-1-84905-029-6 (alk. paper)
1. Psychiatric social work--Great Britain. 2. Mental health services--Great Britain. 3.
Child mental health services--Great Britain. 4. Psychiatric social work--Great Britain-
-Case studies. 5. Mental health services--Great Britain--Case studies. 6. Child mental
health services--Great Britain--Case studies. I. Webber, Martin. II. Nathan, Jack, 1954-
HV690.G7R44 2010
362.2'04250941--dc22
                                          2010006848

British Library Cataloguing in Publication Data
A CIP catalogue record for this book is available from the British Library

ISBN 978 1 84905 029 6

Printed and bound in Great Britain by
MPG Books Group

6/27/11

Reflective Practice in Mental Health

Reflective Practice in Social Care Series
Edited by James Blewett, King's College London, UK

This series takes a practice-led, reflective approach to key areas of work in social care. Books in the series tackle the complexities and dilemmas that practitioners face every day, by using a series of case examples. Each book focuses on a different area of social work, including vulnerable children, looked after children and mental health. The discussion within each book is built around case studies, in order to give clear examples of how an integrated knowledge base can be applied to practice. This series is essential reading for all post-qualifying social work students and social work practitioners. **James Blewett** is a registered social worker with 25 years' experience in the care field. He is currently national chair of the research dissemination network Making Research Count, based at the Social Care Workforce Research Unit, King's College London.

other books in the series

Reflective Practice with Vulnerable Children and their Families
James Blewett
ISBN 978 1 84310 931 0

Reflective Practice in Care Proceedings and with Looked After Children
Anna Gupta
ISBN 978 1 84905 033 3

of related interest

A Multidisciplinary Handbook of Child and Adolescent Mental Health for Front-line Professionals
2nd Edition
Nisha Dogra, Andrew Parkin, Fiona Gale and Clay Frake
ISBN 978 1 84310 644 9

The Social Worker's Guide to Child and Adolescent Mental Health
Steven Walker
Foreword by Stephen Briggs
ISBN 978 1 84905 122 4

Social Perspectives in Mental Health
Developing Social Models to Understand and Work with Mental Distress
Edited by Jerry Tew
Foreword by Judy Foster
ISBN 978 1 84310 220 5

Mental Health Interventions and Services for Vulnerable Children and Young People
Edited by Panos Vostanis
Foreword by Richard Williams
ISBN 978 1 84310 489 6

This book is dedicated to Andrea, Caitlin and Freya
who endure my long hours at the keyboard (Martin)

This book is dedicated to Jill Thompson, my
soulmate and mentor, and my children, Jess and
Lily, who ensure I remain grounded (Jack)

Acknowledgements

Martin Webber would like to thank Andrea for her perseverance and his daughters Caitlin and Freya for their creative contributions to the manuscript. He would also like to thank his co-editor, Jack Nathan, who has provided a critical review of each Chapter and has helped Chapter authors to work to their brief and keep to their deadlines. He is very grateful for the contributions of all authors in this volume; their wisdom and expertise have immensely enriched this book. Finally, he would like to acknowledge the inspiration of his predecessor, Alan Rushton, without whom the MSc in Mental Health Social Work with Children and Adults and this book would, quite simply, not have been.

Jack Nathan would like to begin by acknowledging Alan Rushton, a young social worker in the late 1970s determined to cultivate a culture of research in our profession. As the founding father, Alan developed the MSc in Mental Health Social Work with Children and Adults in a way that brought together research as well as advanced practice long before the Social Care Institute for Excellence (SCIE) had been dreamt of. It goes (almost) without saying that I will remain ever grateful to the authors for giving so generously of their time and knowledge. Modesty forbids Martin Webber from taking credit for the energy, enthusiasm and skill that enabled this book to become a reality. I want to end by thanking our small but creative team at the Institute of Psychiatry. With Martin at its helm, ensuring we steer a forward-looking path, supported by Caroline Grimbly's quiet thoughtfulness and the no-nonsense intelligence that the Programme Administrator Julie Smith brings, I am lucky to be a member of this talented group.

Paul Godin would like to thank Jacqueline Davies, John Davis and Anne Nixson for their very useful comments on previous drafts of Chapter 2.

Pete Fleischmann would like to thank Professor Mike Fisher, Jolie Goodman and Dr Angela Sweeney for their comments on earlier versions of Chapter 4.

Contents

List of Tables, Figures and Case Studies

Table

Figures

Case Studies

List of Abbreviations

ACT	Assertive community treatment
ADHD	Attention deficit hyperactivity disorder
ASI	Attachment Style Interview
ASW	Approved Social Worker
ASWP	Advanced Social Work Professional
BPD	Borderline personality disorder
CBT	Cognitive behavioural therapy
CHW	Community Health Worker
CMD	Common mental disorder
CMHT	Community mental health team
CoLP	Cares of Life Project
CPD	Continuing professional development
CQC	Care Quality Commission
CRAG	Consumers Research Advisory Group
CRHT	Crisis resolution and home treatment
CSC	Children's Social Care
CSCI	Commission for Social Care Inspection
CTT	Community treatment team
DBT	Dialectical behavioural therapy
DES	Dissociation Experiences Scale
ECT	Electro convulsive therapy
GP	General practitioner
IFSW	International Federation of Social Workers
IoP	Institute of Psychiatry
LEDS	Life Events and Difficulties Schedule
LTPP	Long-term psychodynamic psychotherapy
MBT	Mentalisation-based treatment
MDD	Major depressive disorder

MDT	Multi-disciplinary team
MHSW	Mental health social worker
NICE	National Institute for Clinical Excellence
NES	Negative evaluation of self
NEWPIN	New Parent Infant Network
NHS	National Health Service
NQSW	Newly qualified social worker
NSF	National Service Framework
PET	Positron Emission Tomography
PQ	Post-qualifying
PTSD	Post-traumatic stress disorder
RCT	Randomised controlled trial
SCIE	Social Care Institute for Excellence
SFBT	Solution-focused brief therapy
SP	Supportive psychotherapy
SPN	Social Perspectives Network
SSRI	Selective serotonin reuptake inhibitor
STPP	Short-term psychodynamic psychotherapy
SUD	Subjective Unit of Distress
SURE	Service User Research Enterprise
TAIT	Traumatic Attachment Induction Test
TFP	Transference-Focused Psychotherapy
UFM	User-Focused Monitoring

Series Editor's Foreword

These are challenging times for practitioners who are delivering social care services. In a period when those in social care are experiencing contracting funding, high workloads and the demands of operating within complex bureaucratic systems, it is all too easy for professional values and identities to be diminished.

In recent years the idea of reflective practice has become increasingly influential in many fields as a way of supporting professional resilience. It is an approach that can make sense of the complexity of modern social work and social care practice. Although there are different approaches to what is described as reflective practice, overall it is a framework that seeks to enable the practitioners to understand and deal with uncertainty and ambivalence that is such a feature of contemporary practice.

This book is the first in the new Jessica Kingsley Publishers series, 'Reflective Practice in Social Care', which will seek to take a reflective approach to different key areas of practice in social work and social care. *Reflective Practice in Mental Health: Advanced Psychosocial Practice with Children, Adolescents and Adults* focuses on some of the key issues and debates within the mental health field, and there will be other forthcoming volumes on current areas of concern to students and practitioners, such as working with vulnerable children and their families. What will be common across the series will be a desire to bring the best available knowledge together with a critical approach to theory and professional values. It will have an applied approach with an explicit focus on practice. While this series will be a valuable resource for those engaged in professional training, it is hoped it will also be a useful tool for practice.

James Blewett
Making Research Count, Social Care Workforce Research Unit,
King's College London

Foreword

It is now 30 years since the 'Maudsley' course was founded by the social work staff at the Bethlem Royal and Maudsley Hospitals in conjunction with the Institute of Psychiatry. It was a continuation of the long-standing mental health social work training provided at the joint hospitals. The contents of this book capture the heart of the current MSc programme, even as it evolves in line with new developments.

The point of departure for the programme was recognition that basic training at the time was nowhere near adequate for competent mental health practice. It was a pioneering educational venture because, with a few notable exceptions, mental health teaching for social workers was afforded low priority. It was originally called a post-qualifying course with the term 'in mental health settings' appended to acknowledge that, although the programme was then largely hospital-based, mental health social work was also practised in clinic and community locations and in a range of child, adolescent and adult services. The programme has continued with this broad conception of mental health social work practice.

The programme also remains rooted in a human development approach to understanding the complex genetic, psychological and environmental factors that influence mental health over the lifespan. One of the most important and fascinating areas of contemporary psychological research is in discovering links between childhood adversity and adulthood. Such research benefits enormously from new longitudinal studies where it is apparent that adverse childhood experiences may not simply lead to disturbances in child development, but also contribute to enduring physical and mental health problems in adulthood. The social work role is therefore crucial in safeguarding children and promoting environments beneficial to their development as well as supporting adults suffering depression, anxiety and other major mental health problems.

In aiming to provide advanced, specialist education, the programme marked a new development in mental health social work. Theories then abounded on the nature of mental disorder and its appropriate treatment. As the notion of an advanced course was somewhat new, the programme was open to adopting a number of orientations. But out of many discussions in course management meetings came a clear idea of aims and ambitions and what should constitute the core curriculum and what values should underpin it. We struggled to make it a mental health social work course and not a course for social workers *about* psychiatry, as it was essential that it was anchored in the psychosocial domain. We considered how best to define advanced practice and how to assess it rigorously in 'real life' contexts. Essentially we wanted to encourage course members to develop 'reflective practice', to expand the range of techniques they used and to provide a genuinely relevant and effective service. Whatever the chosen mode of intervention, these core elements were stressed: careful psychological and social assessment, sensitivity to people in distress, and self-critical judgement by the practitioner. We encouraged them to work more within a framework of research-based evidence; to think independently; to challenge inequalities in service provision and to try to see the world through service users' eyes, not just those of professionals. This was a considerable set of ambitions, and it sometimes seemed like heaping all the expectations of the profession on the heads of the students!

Some years after the programme was established, we teamed up with the Goldsmiths' post-qualifying child care course to investigate the outcomes of the new post-qualifying ventures. A survey of opinion of former course members (Rushton and Martyn 1990) revealed two clear messages. First, a high level of satisfaction was recorded with the educational experience, especially with opportunities to absorb new research and to think more deeply about practice. Second, we found that, following completion of the programme, the transition back to the full rigours of the workplace often proved obstacle-strewn. We tried to address the question of how graduates of the programme could carry forward the wealth of newly acquired knowledge and skills and we looked forward to the development of new advanced practitioner roles through which good quality supervision and consultation could be available to front-line workers. This, we hoped, would promote the dissemination of new knowledge and drive forward a progressive model of mental health social work.

A new generation of advanced reflective practitioners will profit from the original contributions to be found in these chapters and it is gratifying that the learning on the programme will be made available to a much wider readership. It will reinvigorate psychosocial practice in mental health and will help social workers to articulate their role and expertise in mental health services, thus defining the discipline of mental health social work. At a time when the Social Work Task Force has set out a path as well as a vision for the profession as a whole, this volume's lifespan approach is timely and much-needed. With so much attention currently focused on reform and renewal in social work, this book is also an eloquent testament to the traditional strengths of the profession and the importance of advanced reflective practice in improving outcomes for users of services.

Alan Rushton
Visiting Professor, Institute of Psychiatry, King's College London
(Programme Leader of MSc in Mental Health Social Work with Children
and Adults from its inception in 1979 until 2006)

Reference

Rushton, A. and Martyn, H. (1990) 'Two post-qualifying courses in social work: the views of the course members and their employers.' *British Journal of Social Work 20*, 5, 445–468.

Introduction

Martin Webber

Most practitioners working with people with mental health problems – whether children or adults – use ideas, skills or intervention techniques associated with 'psychosocial practice'. Even those who hold a predominantly biomedical world view understand the need to make sense of the whole person within their social environment in order to make an accurate diagnosis and treatment plan. It is in the very nature of mental 'illness' that an individual's inner world (which refers to phenomena such as thoughts, feelings and cognitions) is inextricably connected with their external world (which refers to the social context of their life such as relationships with others or socio-economic status). Using the insights offered by the range of psychosocial perspectives, some of which are demonstrated in this volume, practitioners help people understand how their external environment affects their internal world, and how their internal world affects their environment.

Social workers are particularly skilled at intervening in complex social systems to promote change and, we suggest, are well placed to take a lead on psychosocial practice in agencies working with people with mental health problems and in child care settings. Because we recognise that psychosocial practice is by no means exclusive to the social work profession, this book is written with all practitioners in mind. Although this volume has a focus largely specific to social work, it is readily applicable to nurses, occupational therapists, psychologists, psychiatrists and other health and social care workers interested in learning more about advancing their skills, knowledge and expertise in psychosocial practice.

Social work

At the beginning of the second decade of the twenty-first century, social work has reached a new crossroads in its professional development in the UK. The publication of the Social Work Task Force (2009) report set in motion a reform programme with the potential to transform the professional status of social work. The introduction of a probationary year following qualification, a national college for social work, a reformed system of initial training, a renewed framework for continuing professional development, a single nationally recognised career structure and a programme of action on the public understanding of social work should help to make social work a profession we can be proud to be members of.

The reform programme followed the tragic death of Peter Connelly (known as 'Baby P') at the age of 17 months in 2007. He received 60 visits from health workers and social workers but was not adequately protected from the abuse inflicted by his carers. Lord Laming was commissioned to report on the effectiveness of the national plans for safeguarding children (Laming 2009) and the Social Work Task Force was set up to undertake a root and branch review of the profession.

The circumstances of the Baby P case highlight the complexity of the social work task and the need for advanced skills in psychosocial practice. His mother, Tracey Connelly, suffered from post-natal depression following his birth. She rarely got out of bed before lunchtime and was still asleep at the time of his death at 11.30am. Her boyfriend, Steven Barker, was left to care for Baby P and it appears that he physically abused him and caused him horrific injuries which went undetected by doctors. When visited by social workers, Tracey hid the fact that her boyfriend and his brother were living with her. She misled the authorities about her parenting abilities by signing up for a parenting group, but attended very few sessions, and she smeared Baby P's bruises in chocolate to disguise them.

Whilst it is widely recognised that systemic failures in health and social services in the local authority serving Baby P contributed to his death, confident practitioners trained in psychosocial intervention skills may have been able to safeguard him. Of course it is overly simplistic to make this point in retrospect, but the whole tragedy underlines the importance of practitioners working with children being able to recognise and ameliorate the impact of mental health or psychological problems just as effectively as specialist mental health social workers.

At the Institute of Psychiatry, King's College London, we have many years of experience in training social workers in advanced intervention skills with children and adults. As Alan Rushton mentioned in the foreword, this book is based on this experience and draws on many expert contributors to our MSc in Mental Health Social Work with Children and Adults programme. Within these covers we bring together insights from research, practice and theory-based knowledge of psychosocial mental health practice to help practitioners reflect on their own practice. Some sections may be quite demanding to read and will take some time to work through. We have purposely neither compromised on academic rigor nor relied on simplistic explanations of complex concepts in order to convey the complexity of the social work task and the need for advanced reflective practice. However, beginning with a lifespan approach that recognises the *core similarities* shared by all social workers, we have retained a focus on practice so that it is relevant for all practitioners on qualifying and post-qualifying programmes, in addition to being an essential resource for every team.

Psychosocial practice

Psychosocial practice is at the heart of what social workers do. This is reflected in the International Federation of Social Workers' definition of social work:

> The social work profession promotes social change, problem solving in human relationships and the empowerment and liberation of people to enhance well-being. Utilising theories of human behaviour and social systems, social work intervenes at the points where people interact with their environments. Principles of human rights and social justice are fundamental to social work. (International Federation of Social Workers 2000)

Psychosocial practice operates at the interface between an individual's external social world and their internal psychological experience. It requires practitioners to draw upon a range of theories, skills and knowledge to work effectively with individuals in order to bring about social change. Formerly known as a 'casework' (Hollis 1964), social work has a long tradition of psychosocial practice. However, it has recently been eroded by a creeping bureaucratisation and, in mental health settings, a 'bureau-medicalisation' of social work practice (Nathan and Webber 2010).

In mental health services, social work is in the process of rearticulating its role. As a result of the integration of social work into NHS mental health trusts, posts have been cut, roles have become blurred and morale within mental health social work has dropped. There have been ongoing debates about whether social work should retreat to its local authority base, join with other mental health professions in creating a generic 'mental health worker' role or merge roles within integrated settings whilst maintaining professional diversity (McCrae *et al.* 2004). We believe the future of social work in mental health services lies in the latter option with social workers taking the professional lead on psychosocial practice (Nathan and Webber 2010). With the statutory role of Approved Social Worker now open to other mental health professionals (in England and Wales), it is professional suicide for mental health social workers to argue that their only unique contribution is expertise in mental health law, though this is undoubtedly considerable and will remain so for the foreseeable future. Within this context, this book will articulate a vision for social work psychosocial practice that will enable practitioners to be confident about their role and provide an opportunity to reflect on and enhance their practice.

Book structure

This book complements, and builds upon, several important mental health social work texts that have been published in recent years. For example, Gould (2010) and Golightley (2008) have both written excellent introductions to the discipline which are worthy additions to any bookshelf. Edited collections by Tew (2005) and Reynolds *et al.* (2009) introduce a range of social perspectives and models for working with people with mental health problems. Specialist texts for Approved Mental Health Professionals (Brown 2009) and on evidence-based policy and practice for mental health social workers (Webber 2008) are also available. This volume builds on these texts by providing an authoritative articulation of advanced psychosocial practice as defining the discipline of mental health social work with children and adults.

The book is structured in three parts. It starts by discussing the context for psychosocial practice and highlights the need for social workers, armed with advanced practice skills and knowledge, to take a lead role in promoting social perspectives and interventions. In Chapter 1, Jack Nathan defines our understanding of an advanced practitioner in social work as someone capable of critically reflecting on their practice using relevant theory and research and also generating new forms of social work knowledge that can inform policy and practice. The concept of an advanced practitioner is not abstract or theoretical, but has been developed from our long experience of postgraduate post-qualifying education for social workers at the Institute of Psychiatry, King's College London. The Chapter is illustrated with examples of graduates' work, which sets the standard for aspirant practitioners.

Sociologist Paul Godin provides the historical context of mental health care for us in Chapter 2. He discusses the social nature of mental disorder and how sociological perspectives have influenced psychosocial practice in mental health care, with a particular focus on social divisions caused by class, ethnicity, gender and age.

This is followed in Chapter 3 by a summary of nearly 40 years of scholarship from the co-author of the epoch-defining *The Social Origins of Depression* (Brown and Harris 1978). Tirril Harris discusses the evolution of the Brown-Harris psychosocial model of depression through its series of empirical phases and highlights its relevance for contemporary psychosocial practice. She restates the value of emotional support and its critical importance in social interventions.

In Chapter 4, Pete Fleischmann outlines the epistemological challenge that mental health service users/survivors pose to the generation of mental health knowledge. Mental health service users/survivors are increasingly involved in, or leading, mental health research which they often approach from a different standpoint to professionals. In addition to having an emancipatory purpose, this research is steadily becoming an important corpus of knowledge in its own right that is influencing psychosocial practice in mental health.

Martin Webber follows this with a discussion of the evidence base for psychosocial mental health practice in Chapter 5. He focuses on the importance of randomised controlled trials (RCTs) in the generation of knowledge about intervention effectiveness and their strong influence in National Institute for Clinical Excellence guidelines. Although the study design is perhaps inimical to psychosocial practice, it is becoming increasingly apparent that without RCT evidence of effectiveness, psychosocial interventions may not be supported in contemporary health and social care settings.

The second part of the book uses case studies to explore how psychosocial theories and intervention models help to produce positive changes in the lives of people with mental health problems. The case studies provide a lens for practitioners to reflect upon their own practice and increase their knowledge about different intervention models. Each Chapter is written by an authority of each modality, all of whom use these theories and therapeutic techniques in their daily practice.

Jack Nathan begins by discussing the role of psychoanalytic theory and research in psychosocial practice in Chapter 6. Although somewhat out of favour in mental health care today, the enduring influence of psychodynamic perspectives in casework and the rich, unique insights it provides to relationship-based practice are undeniable. Understanding the psychodynamics of casework is an essential component of any psychosocial practitioner's toolkit.

Cognitive behavioural therapy (CBT) represents the *zeitgeist* of mental health practice, particularly in primary care settings. In Chapter 7, Florian Ruths connects the theoretical framework of CBT with that of social work and describes its basic principles. Using case examples, he demonstrates how practitioners can use CBT techniques in their everyday practice.

Social workers are often working amidst complex family dynamics and social systems, and it is essential to have a sound understanding of systemic approaches and interventions. In Chapter 8 Judith Lask uses a family therapy case study to highlight the importance of systemic approaches in promoting change in both families and individuals.

In Chapter 9 Felicity de Zulueta demonstrates how attachment theory informs her work with adults who have suffered abuse as a child or other traumas. She discusses the psychological and physical consequences of traumatic attachments and describes a method for helping people to be aware of them in order to promote change.

Psychosocial practice is often conducted in groups. Whether they are formal or informal groups, there are undoubtedly underlying dynamics which affect their functioning and may impact on their effectiveness in achieving their goals. In the final Chapter of this part of the book (Chapter 10) Caroline Grimbly uses insights from group analytic psychotherapy to understand group behaviour and promote effective group functioning.

The third part of the book explores advanced reflective psychosocial practice in action from a variety of perspectives. This section provides detailed examples of how practitioners can implement evidence-based psychosocial approaches in their routine practice.

It begins with three chapters written by advanced practitioners who are graduates of the MSc in Mental Health Social Work with Children and Adults at the Institute of Psychiatry, King's College London. First, in Chapter 11, Rebecca Peters provides two case studies of social work practice from the Children's Social Care Department of the London Borough of Hackney. Under the leadership of consultant social workers, practitioners implement evidence-based psychosocial interventions in close partnership with clinicians from the local child and adolescent mental health services. These case studies provide an important insight into the effectiveness of advanced social work practitioners.

Second, Tony West presents a case study drawn from his practice in community mental health services in Chapter 12. He draws on the social context of mental health discussed in Chapters 2 and 3, outlines a social model of mental disorder and illustrates how psychosocial practice can effectively promote recovery.

Third, Paul Richards provides an example of psychosocial practice within an inpatient mental health setting in Chapter 13. Using a case study from a medium secure unit he highlights the importance of practitioners engaging with complex social systems, being aware of the needs of both children and adults, and promoting a vision of holistic recovery.

Next, in Chapter 14, Don Brand and Sarah Carr reflect on their personal experiences of using mental health services. In their striking and honest accounts of their encounters with health professionals they describe the reality of living with mental distress and their struggle to maintain relationships and employment. They highlight the continuing dominance of medical models in mental health care and call for a stronger social dimension.

Finally, Martin Webber and Jack Nathan set out a vision for the future challenges and opportunities for psychosocial practice in mental health in Chapter 15. We argue that psychosocial practice defines the discipline of mental health social work and that these practitioners can develop the knowledge and skills to provide professional leadership in this field. We hope that this book has helped to articulate this vision.

A note on terminology

Health and social care professionals working in the mental health field use a plethora of terms to refer to people with mental health problems: service users, survivors, patients, clients, consumers, to name but a few. Contributors to this book have similarly used a variety of terms to refer to themselves or the people they work with. We have made an editorial decision to allow Chapter authors to use terms they are most comfortable using, as long as they convey respect, because there is no universally acceptable vocabulary. We acknowledge that the use of the term 'patient' conveys unequal power relationships in a traditional medical hegemony, but its inclusion in this book reflects its popularity amongst 'patients' (McGuire-Snieckus, McCabe and Priebe 2003; Ritchie, Hayes and Ames 2000; Simmons *et al.* 2010) and the reality that psychosocial practitioners are working in health settings and need to engage with its vicissitudes.

Conclusion

This book is for all practitioners – social workers and health workers working with children and/or adults – who wish to enhance their knowledge of psychosocial practice. It draws together an eclectic mix of theoretical and therapeutic practices which psychosocial practitioners can use in their daily work. In the context of the enduring threat of assimilation within a health-dominated mental health care system, this book provides mental health social workers with a means to define their disciplinary uniqueness. Whether read as individual chapters or the whole way through, we hope that it will inspire practitioners on their journey working alongside people, in services for children and/or adults suffering social, emotional and mental distress.

References

Brown, R. (2009) *The Approved Mental Health Professional's Guide to Mental Health Law.* Second edition. Exeter: Learning Matters.

Brown, G.W. and Harris, T.O. (1978) *The Social Origins of Depression: A Study of Psychiatric Disorder in Women.* London: Tavistock Publications.

Golightley, M. (2008) *Social Work and Mental Health.* Third edition. Exeter: Learning Matters.

Gould, N. (2010) *Mental Health Social Work in Context.* Abingdon: Routledge.

Hollis, F. (1964) *Casework: A Psychosocial Therapy.* New York: Random House.

International Federation of Social Workers (2000) *Definition of Social Work.* Available at http://www.ifsw.org/en/f38000138.html, accessed on 10 December 2009.

Laming, Lord (2009) *The Protection of Children in England: A Progress Report.* London: The Stationery Office.

McCrae, N., Murray, J., Huxley, P. and Evans, S. (2004) 'Prospects for mental health social work: a qualitative study of attitudes of service managers and academic staff.' *Journal of Mental Health 13*, 3, 305–317.

McGuire-Snieckus, R., McCabe, R. and Priebe, S. (2003) 'Patient, client or service user? A survey of patient preferences of dress and address of six mental health professions.' *Psychiatric Bulletin 27*, 8, 305–308.

Nathan, J. and Webber, M. (2010) 'Mental health social work and the bureau-medicalisation of mental health care: identity in a changing world.' *Journal of Social Work Practice 24*, 1, 15–28.

Reynolds, J., Muston, R., Heller, T., Leach, J., *et al.* (eds) (2009) *Mental Health Still Matters.* Basingstoke: Palgrave Macmillan.

Ritchie, C.W., Hayes, D. and Ames, D.J. (2000) 'Patient or client? The opinions of people attending a psychiatric clinic.' *Psychiatric Bulletin 24*, 12, 447–450.

Simmons, P., Hawley, C.J., Gale, T.M. and Sivakumaran, T. (2010) 'Service user, patient, client, user or survivor: describing recipients of mental health services.' *The Psychiatrist 34*, 1, 20–23.

Social Work Task Force (2009) *Building a Safe, Confident Future. The Final Report of the Social Work Task Force.* London: Department for Children, Schools and Families.

Tew, J. (ed.) (2005) *Social Perspectives in Mental Health: Developing Social Models to Understand and Work with Mental Distress.* London: Jessica Kingsley Publishers.

Webber, M. (2008) *Evidence-Based Policy and Practice in Mental Health Social Work.* Exeter: Learning Matters.

Part I
Context

Chapter 1

The Making of the Advanced Practitioner in Social Work

Jack Nathan

Introduction

This Chapter discusses the ways in which practitioners acquire advanced social work skills, a development given significant impetus by the Laming Report (2009) and the Select Committee's Report, *Training of Children and Families Social Workers* (House of Commons Children, Schools and Families Committee 2009). There is now an unambiguous acknowledgement that, 'obtaining a degree in social work must be only the starting point of career-long learning and development' (House of Commons Children, Schools and Families Committee 2009, p.65). Taking the lead from the Laming Report, the Select Committee goes on to assert the need for a practice-focused Master's degree as a pathway to the development of the advanced practitioner. There are parallel developments taking place in the delivery of adult services. In *The Roles and Tasks of Social Work in Adult Services* (Department of Health 2009), the consultation document identifies the *similarities* in the roles and requirements of practitioners working with adults, emphasising the need for ongoing professional development within a career framework and culture that promotes evidence-based practice, as well as practice-based evidence.

These reports share a common central message. If social work is to leave behind its historical status as a 'semi-profession' (Etzioni 1969) and join the ranks of the law, medicine and psychology, then there needs to be a step change in the training framework so as to produce a social work profession predicated on the taken-for-granted assumption of advanced practice. This Chapter will outline the core elements that support the professional journey of a newly qualified social worker through to the making of the advanced practitioner.

What is an advanced practitioner?

In the early 1990s at the Institute of Psychiatry Alan Rushton (author of our foreword) and I began to define what constituted an 'advanced practitioner'. Our definition was subsequently published in the *Journal of Practice Teaching in Health and Social Work* (Nathan 2002).

The work of Donald Schon (1987, 1992) was crucial in the evolution of these ideas through his conceptualisation of 'the reflective practitioner', which led to the innovation of the 'training hierarchy'. By this was meant a form of continuing professional development in which the practitioner begins with a basic knowledge as a newly qualified social worker and with experience, supervision and post-graduate training evolves to being an advanced practitioner.

Schon (1987) conceptualised this progress by suggesting that after qualification a practitioner can be properly regarded as using what he calls 'professional artistry'. At this point, after what is still only a three-year training programme, the newly qualified social worker (NQSW) will have trained in appropriate placements supported by the practitioner wisdom imparted by a competent practice supervisor. Buttressed by this support and having completed the degree programme, the practitioner will in theory be able to utilise a range of skills when confronted by what Schon (1992) refers to as situations characterised by 'uncertainty, complexity and uniqueness' (p.56) and I would add, at times, conflict. Schon views such practice as a more high-powered, esoteric form of competence that any reasonable lay individual may exercise in their everyday actions. His key point is that this form of practice competence does not depend on practitioners 'being able to describe what [they] know how to do or even to entertain in conscious thought the knowledge [their] actions reveal' (Schon 1987, p.22). In other words NQSWs demonstrate what has been called 'a tacit knowledge' (Nathan 2002).

At first glance this may seem an overly negative description of social work knowledge at point of qualification. In fact, sadly, it seems quite accurate. The Social Work Task Force (Department for Children, Schools and Families 2009), set up by the UK government to undertake a comprehensive review of front-line social work practice, gathered evidence that up to nearly six out of ten NQSWs in children's services and one in four in adult services did not feel prepared for the demands of the job.

Given both the enormity and complexity of the task, it seems that Schon was perhaps *over-estimating* the newly qualified professional's capacity to meet the challenges of the work. In fact this quite accurately tallies with our experience on our advanced level post-qualifying MSc programme at the Institute of Psychiatry. Practitioners with a wealth of experience, typically three to five years post qualification, apply to undertake our programme. During the interview they routinely give a coherent and fluent account of their workplace and offer rich material when asked to talk about a current case. What equally routinely happens when asked to give a reflective description, layering their work through the prisms provided by practice theories and/or any evidence base, is that many of these skilful improvisers become embarrassed and tongue-tied and struggle to do justice to the casework they have already demonstrated in their initial presentation.

To repeat, for this group of experienced practitioners, theirs is a 'tacit knowledge'. In Schon's (1987) terms their practice competence is predicated on a 'knowing-in-action' and/or a 'reflection-in-action' (see Figure 1.1 for a diagrammatic representation). According to Schon (1987), knowing-in-action reveals the practitioner's capacity to be professionally spontaneous, skilfully responding to the requirements of the task at hand in their work with an angry client, for instance. What is key to this form of knowledge is that the worker does not necessarily have the reflective capacity to make explicit the underlying assumptions dictating their actions. Similarly, as a function of increasing casework experience, the practitioner can develop reflection-in-action, a form of professional artistry based on years of first-hand experience which enables the practitioner to improvise, to think on their feet. What we are beginning to understand is that for too long far too much has been expected of NQSWs who, it seems, would struggle to give even the kinds of casework accounts, however unreflective, that their more experienced colleagues are able to convey at interview. But even this group have had to 'learn on the job' and have in general not been provided the educational space to develop a practice worthy of the term 'reflective'.

Schon (1987) summarised their current professional competence by claiming that 'it is one thing to be able to reflect-in-action and quite another to be able to reflect *on* our reflection-in-action so as to produce a good verbal description of it' (p.31). Our view is that it is only when this professional developmental point has been reached, that the reflective practitioner comes into being. Such a practitioner is no longer working from the realm of a tacit knowledge base or what one psychoanalyst appropriately termed 'the unthought known' (Bollas 1987). For the reflective practitioner, that which was previously non-conscious can now be thought about from within a range of practice paradigms and with a degree of research literacy. In other words, their work can be thought about and reflected upon from diverse perspectives (Schon 1987).

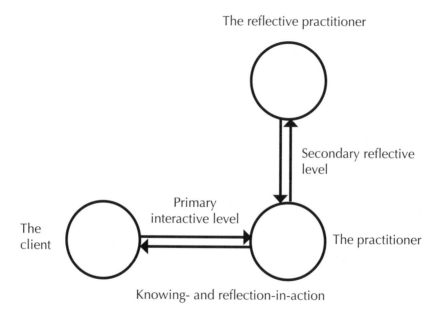

Figure 1.1 The reflective practitioner

We are now in a position to claim that what was previously a form of *tacit knowledge* can justifiably be termed *explicit knowledge*. This is often our experience at the end of the first year of the MSc programme when the practitioners present audio-taped case material at a viva examination. Anxiety-provoking as this experience often is, most students are able (in Schon's words) to reflect on their practice reflections-in-action and to give an articulate, consciously thought through verbal narrative that is faithful to the work they have brought to the panel. They meet the requirements of what constitutes the reflective practitioner defined in the following terms:

> A practitioner who has the capacity to translate the knowing- and reflecting-in-action from a tacit knowledge, based on learned intuition, into a form of practice knowledge that includes reflection on that practice, where that knowledge is explicit and articulated. What is termed explicit knowledge. (Nathan 2002, p.68)

It is important to clarify that a social worker armed with this complex, even sophisticated knowledge base, is not thereby able to claim omnipotent insight into all casework dynamics. Indeed the reflective practitioner may be more confident of that which remains unknown, especially in the realm of human emotional engagement. What the reflective practitioner can do, however, is work with a client at a primary interactive level based on knowing- and reflecting-in-action. Additionally, a reflective practitioner has a secondary reflective level that facilitates a capacity to explore other layers of the dynamic tensions inherent in work with highly disturbed or disturbing clients. This is illustrated by Case Study 1.1.

CASE STUDY 1.1 *WORKING AS A REFLECTIVE PRACTITIONER*

When I was an Approved Social Worker (in pre-Approved Mental Health Professional days) I undertook a Mental Health Act assessment of a woman with a history of violence whose mental health seemed to be deteriorating. The assessment took place at her home where the woman was screaming at the top of her voice for us to get out of her house, as she did not know why we (including two doctors) were all there. At a primary interactive level I attempted to explain in a rational manner that neighbours had been worried about her, especially after she had thrown a large fridge out of her first-floor window. The intention was to 'explain', using as many of the skills of spontaneity, partnership working and improvisation that I could muster. None of these seemed to make any difference as the woman quite rightly understood, however mentally disturbed she may have been, that we were threatening her literal as well as her emotional space.

As it was, it was only when I began to reflect on my *own* emotional experience at the secondary reflective level, using my counter-transference (see Chapter 6 for details about this concept), that I began to recognise that I was experiencing a profound sense of terror. At this point, I wondered to myself if this was how she was feeling. After all, strangers, mostly men, had forced their way into her house, leaving her powerless and out of control. I therefore suggested to her that she was terrified by our uninvited and frightening presence and suggested that we sat down. She was able to sit down and continue the interview in a much calmer manner. Although the outcome was that she was eventually placed on a section, I think the fact that her screaming had been heard, understood and put into words made a huge difference to the way in which the assessment was conducted. The police who were at hand in case violence erupted, did not need to be used. Alongside this woman's conscious fury that was so clearly being given voice to, there was a less conscious communication, which was being registered at the secondary reflective level by me as terror, mirroring the client's own internal emotional experience (see Figure 1.1 for a diagrammatic representation of these underlying dynamics).

What Case Study 1.1 highlights is that being a reflective practitioner is always a process. Any social worker's initial response will begin at the primary interactive level, utilising the learned intuitive dexterity associated with knowing- and reflection-in-action that Schon identified through the use of spontaneity and improvisation. As in this case, in situations replete with uncertainty, complexity and potential conflict, this will not be sufficient. At the secondary reflective level, the reflective practitioner will usually be able to draw on a knowledge base that stems from their understanding of different forms of practice paradigms and research. With this particular client I turned to my grasp of psychoanalytic concepts such as projection and counter-transference (see Chapter 6) as it is implicit in our definition of the reflective practitioner that the social worker is a key instrument of knowledge, not an outsider to proceedings 'delivering' a service to the inert service user.

It is perhaps stating the obvious to suggest that in the deeply troubling human stories we are asked to bear witness to we are inevitably, and sometimes profoundly, drawn into their drama. At the scene of the sometimes intensely emotionally charged engagement with the client, the practitioner has to evolve a capacity to contain anxiety sufficiently to create a space, internally, to think. Casement (1985) referred to this quality as akin to having an 'internal supervisor'. This form of internal supervision brings in its wake the possibility of thinking through difficulties instead of rushing to action. If I had only acted on my instincts, at the primary interactive level, I would have asked for police support and this could have escalated into a major violent incident. Of course, this is not to deny that there are occasions when this would be the appropriate response. There is no desire in this example to suggest that practitioners are omnipotent – itself another form of potentially dangerous non-thinking.

Thinking at the secondary reflective level has to include considering what the practitioner does not know about a difficult mental health or child protection case. Borrowing from the psychoanalytic literature, the reflective practitioner needs to develop the capacity to bear 'negative capability' (Bion 1974), suggestive of the capacity to remain in a state of doubt without reaching after what I think of as reality-denying reassurance (see below for further elaboration). Such defensive manoeuvres can mesmerise the practitioner into a false sense of knowing and security.

The Laming Report (2009) pointed to precisely these practitioner difficulties. It drew on research that looked at child deaths and Serious Case Reviews between 2005 and 2007 and found that 'professionals have a "tendency towards justification and reassurance that all was well, rather than more objective consideration and investigation of what had occurred"' (p.23). Whatever we may think of the accuracy of this portrayal of children's social work practice as a whole, this report rightly highlighted the reality of work with families where there is a high risk. We might say that at the secondary reflective level there is the possibility that the need to 'reassure and justify' should, in itself, alert the reflective practitioner that something is being missed. The former social worker and psychoanalyst, Patrick Casement (1985) made the point that this defensive form of reassurance is 'often motivated by the helper's *own need for reassurance*' (p.135; my emphasis). This will be especially so when the practitioner's own levels of anxiety are being raised by a client's distress when suicidal, for instance, or dealing with a parent who is suspected of child abuse.

It is worth pointing out that giving or receiving reassurance is not by definition a denial of external reality. If, for example, a patient is given the all clear from a cancer scare after tests, then this can rightly be described as a form of 'reality-based reassurance'. This is not the form of reassurance Casement is referring to. His insight touches on what may be termed 'reality-denying reassurance', prompted by conscious and unconscious internal dynamics related to the practitioner's wish to deny external reality rather than giving, as suggested in the Serious Case Reviews research, 'more objective consideration and investigation of what had occurred' (Laming 2009, p.23). In brief, the key distinction lies in the drive to elucidate external reality rather than being driven internally to resort to reality-denying reassurance as a defence against inevitable anxiety.

However, even where these defensive manoeuvres are not in operation, practitioners are often dealing with families where the hoped-for 'objective consideration and investigation of what had occurred' (Laming 2009, p.23) is in itself an illusion. In reality such knowledge is beyond the social worker's reach. In such circumstances the reflective practitioner has to be guided by 'negative capability' (Bion 1974), that is, holding on to a state of doubt and uncertainty, acknowledging *not* knowing what is going on and perhaps above all remaining alert to those moments of triggered anxiety. This painful emotional stance could literally save a child's life.

The professional strength to carry this enormously high level of emotional burden has been recognised by the Social Work Task Force who have called for 'high quality professional supervision and time for reflective practice and continuing professional development'(Department for Children, Schools and Families 2009, p.9). The little research that has been done on the impact of such support makes clear that where practitioners receive supervision designed to facilitate the acquisition of relevant knowledge and skills, and not simply case management, this has a significant impact on their own sense of professional competence (Cohen and Laufer 1999). In short, they become more effective workers.

The role of research

Research does not provide solutions to practice dilemmas in a facile way; its importance to the reflective practitioner is more subtle. As Rushton (personal communication, 2002) clarified:

> what research is really useful for is demonstrating what the most likely outcomes are for groups sharing similar characteristics following a practice decision. This should play an important part in reflecting on an individual case, but it clearly can't entirely determine the action.

Evidence-based practice is not a substitute for professional judgement or for the accumulated practice wisdom of practitioners responding to the idiosyncratic complexity of any particular client or family (Webber 2008). What we are compelled to do, however, is give due weight to outcome research which can provide pointers to 'what works best' in different circumstances. This is epitomised by Case Study 1.2, presented at a case consultation by a former student on our MSc programme. All names have been changed to preserve confidentiality.

CASE STUDY 1.2 *EVIDENCE-BASED PRACTICE IN ACTION: SOLUTION-FOCUSED BRIEF THERAPY (SFBT)*

The social worker, Catherine, presented the case of David, a 75-year-old single male who has been known to psychiatric services since childhood due to depression and suicidal impulses. David had changed his name by deed poll to 'Donna' six years previously when he began to fully dress as a woman. He was originally referred to the Mental Health Older Adults Service three years ago for assessment of his mental capacity as Donna was seeking surgery for gender realignment. Despite surgery being ruled out because of his age, he was not disappointed. Catherine continued to work with him because he remained a vulnerable adult, had debts and wanted to move out of the area.

At the first audio-taped presentation Catherine asked the group to help her rethink her current non-directive, empathic and client-centred approach that had appeared to help prevent any further hospital admissions, but had also left her feeling stuck as Donna remained quite unable to take ownership of any of his problems. Hearing 15 minutes of the session confirmed Catherine's assessment. Donna presented a seemingly endless list of grievances against the warden of his sheltered accommodation who raised neighbours' complaints about his incessant swearing, to which he breathlessly opined: 'I'm never going to stop being like this. I can't. I might just as well quit before head of housing comes with the heavy boys and the police and everything else and get out. I'm not wanted here, hardly any of the tenants talk to me; they completely ignore me.'

Further complaints followed. A nurse offered him an appointment for a flu jab the following week, as there were no immediate appointments. Donna was appalled, telling her not to bother as knowing his luck he would soon die.

Struggling to find ways of helpfully responding, Catherine attempted a number of interventions including empathising with his difficult week, to which he responded with more rage and self-pity, implying he was 'always made out to be the trouble-maker'. At this point, taking a different tack, Catherine attempted to mobilise Donna's adult, more reflective self by pointing out that on other occasions he had been able to manage and she asked what was different about this week. Beginning with what appeared to be a greater self-contemplation as he acknowledged seeing 'no light at the end of the tunnel', Donna soon collapsed into a fury about the warden getting at him all the time adding ominously that one day, 'I'm going to fly.'

Having drawn breath after what felt like a torrent of verbal blows, we were able to think about Donna's immense capacity to project all the 'violence' into others. He was essentially operating in the paranoid-schizoid position (see Chapter 6 for a discussion of this concept) and there was little sense of his own agency or of him taking any responsibility for his actions. Donna lived in a thoroughly hostile environment. All that happened in his life, indeed his very experience of 'self-hood', was seen as a function of what others did to him. This analysis of what was happening in the session led the group to suggest that Catherine take a less 'free talking' approach, as she called it. It was thought that she could take a more guiding role, discouraging narrative based on endless grievances and instead focusing on what Donna actually wanted from the sessions in particular, and his future life in general.

The second presentation some months later saw a radical and somewhat unexpected shift in both Catherine's work and Donna's responses. After the first presentation, Catherine felt much more confident about the need to take a significantly different approach to her work with Donna. Having undergone in-house training in solution-focused brief therapy (SFBT), a therapy based on 'solution-building' rather than 'problem-solving' (Iveson 2002; Miller, Hubble and Duncan 1996), Catherine was feeling brave enough to try this new methodology with her recalcitrant client. A key tool used in SFBT is the 'miracle question', based on the idea that if a miracle happened and he got what he longed for, what would be different for him? Catherine put this question to Donna at the beginning of the session and his response was:

'What miracle are you talking about? [pause] Possibly that I was going to move, but it's just going to be a normal day. Or it's a Monday, Monday's a rotten day for me.'

Catherine persists: 'But this is the day where your future is different, it changes to your preferred future.'

Donna responds more positively: 'Well, well, I haven't got to wake up in this flat. I'd be somewhere else, in Devon' [laughs].

Catherine, encouraging his 'miracle' thinking, comments: 'So, so you wouldn't be in your flat, right. This is your miracle day, you've woken up…'

Donna, warming to the theme, interrupts with: 'Probably, probably in a made-up bed you know, or a hotel somewhere.'

Catherine continues: 'So a nice made-up bed. This is good, Donna. These are all the things I want you to be noticing…'

Later in the session, again therapeutically reinforcing the idea that he is exploring his preferred future, he talks of being on holiday: 'I've woken up and made myself a coffee. There'd be a coffee machine there.'

Catherine mirrors his comments and then asks: 'Yes, and what else may be happening?'

> To which, surprisingly, Donna responds: 'I would start to sing to myself because I'm happy. I'm, I'm probably going to Devon by train, something like that...'
>
> During the rest of the session Donna comes up with more plans about going on a Eurostar trip and seeing his beloved 1940s films. The depth of his emotional engagement with his preferred future is demonstrated when he is asked how he will be feeling. He responds with: 'I shall be feeling chuffed!'
>
> What is even more astonishing than hearing this transformation in Donna's way of being in this session with Catherine is that subsequent sessions of SFBT led to an enormous change. Generally, Donna had a far more positive outlook on life and did make a successful move to his beloved place of birth, somewhere he had wanted to return to for many years.

In Case Study 1.2, Catherine has effectively used an evidence-based intervention to help Donna achieve his aims. Since its origins in the mid-1980s SFBT has been found to be an effective intervention across a range of psychiatric presentations (Iveson 2002). For example, a randomised controlled trial of prisoners with psychiatric histories found that SFBT significantly lowered the treated group's level of recidivism (Lindforss and Magnusson 1997). However, a three-year follow-up study of people with mood or anxiety disorders randomly assigned to three treatment groups (long-term psychodynamic psychotherapy (LTPP) or short-term psychodynamic psychotherapy (STPP) or SFBT) found that after three years LTPP was more effective than either STPP or SFBT (Knekt *et al.* 2008). This finding raises a question about whether, given Donna's long and troubled history, he would have benefited more from a longer-term psychodynamic intervention. But we don't know. Research often provides answers to some questions, whilst at the same time giving birth to a raft of further questions. Knekt *et al.* (2008) end by suggesting that 'more research is needed to determine which patients should be given long-term psychotherapy for the treatment of mood or anxiety disorders' (p.689). It is to this issue that I now turn.

Towards the making of the advanced practitioner

If, as a profession, there is consensus that the reflective practitioner becomes the norm in social work, there is one further step: the making of the advanced practitioner. But what are we to understand by this term?

As discussed above, the development of the reflective practitioner includes being able to effectively translate the reflection-in-action into a form of practice knowledge that can be articulated and reflected upon. A further dimension is required to make an advanced practitioner. Schon (1987) puts it rather inelegantly as follows:

> It is one thing to be able to reflect-in-action and quite another to be able to reflect on our reflect-in-action so as to produce a good verbal description of it; *and it is still another to be able to reflect on the resulting description*. (p.31; my emphasis)

The Social Work Task Force's vision of social work providing a central role in delivering personalised services of the future also means developing a high-quality social work service. In the post-qualifying framework for social work, specific reference is made to the advanced practitioner being able to undertake a piece of applied research designed to address issues in the context of practice, education, applied research or management (General Social Care Council 2005). It is this that Schon (1987) is referring to when he describes going beyond the ability 'to produce a good verbal description' of our work and moving up a level in being able 'to reflect on the resulting description' (p.31).

This added dimension is put into practice in the second year of our advanced level post-qualifying MSc programme, which is wholly dedicated to conducting an original piece of research arising from the practitioner's practice.

In an early example of this kind of practitioner research, Louise Dunn was the first researcher to examine whether the introduction of home treatment for acute mental illness had any impact on the numbers and circumstances of Mental Health Act assessments (Dunn 2001). She carried out research in two districts – one offering the standard community mental health team (CMHT) service, and the other offering home treatment known as the community treatment team (CTT). Looking at the impact of these different service models Dunn made three important findings. First, the district with the CTT had an absolute and relative reduction in the number of Mental Health Act assessments. Second, there was a significant decrease in the likelihood of detention under Section 3 of the Mental Health Act 1983 (the long-term detention order) for people living in the area of the CTT. Finally, when a CTT member was involved in an assessment, the likelihood of it resulting in a Section 3 reduced by nearly half when compared with the CMHT service.

We can see that Dunn, as an evidence-based practitioner, is reflecting on more than her current 'epistemology of practice' (Schon 1992) as she is questioning the very nature of 'what works best' for service users (see Figure 1.2 for a diagrammatic representation). The arrow indicates the way in which Dunn's research looked afresh at the way social work was delivered operating different systems of innovation and which was most beneficial for clients. Advanced practitioners are capable of undertaking research that contributes to the evidence base for social work and there are an increasing number of examples in peer-reviewed journals (e.g. Dutt and Webber 2009; Furminger and Webber 2009; Kingsford and Webber 2010; Slack and Webber 2008).

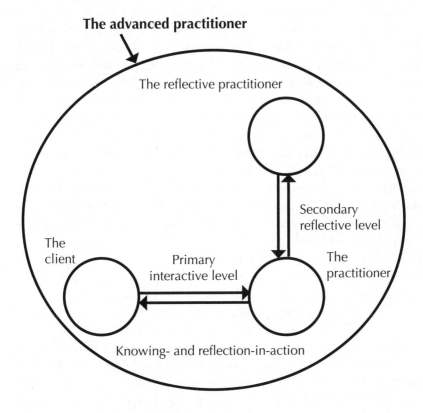

Figure 1.2 The advanced practitioner

Thus, we define an advanced practitioner as: 'A practitioner who has an explicit and articulated knowledge that is theory-driven and research-based and who can create new forms of social work knowledge that inform and shape policies and practice' (Nathan 2002, p.77).

It is important to recognise that not all research has to take place within academic portals, following the rigours of a scientific 'gold standard' that attaches itself to randomised controlled trials (see Chapter 5 for a critique of this approach). It is not our intention to imply that only fully-fledged, hard-end research is worthy of a place in the development of policy and service delivery. For the advanced practitioner, providing professional leadership can, and most often will in practice, come in the form best expressed within the workplace. It is precisely this type of action research that was carried out by another former student of our programme, Tony West (author of Chapter 12).

Working as an Approved Social Worker (ASW) in a busy London borough, West became increasingly aware through his day-to-day practice that police officers were reluctant to attend Mental Health Act assessments. He soon discovered that the Mental Health Act Commission (2005) had also noted that this was an issue in other London boroughs. At the same time a borough audit had found that over half of those detained under Section 136 of the 1983 Mental Health Act (the police detention powers) were subsequently discharged on assessment. He hypothesised that this Figure indicated inappropriate use of the police section. Following the available research evidence regarding the importance of joint working on mental health assessments, the London Development Centre for Mental Health (2005) recommended that mental health awareness training, involving both ASWs and police officers, be set up locally.

Working collaboratively with the police mental health inspector and an ASW colleague, West delivered a four-hour training programme to eight groups of 20–25 police officers. A further audit of Section 136 detentions following the training found that the number of people discharged following assessment fell to around 30 per cent. Not only was this Figure now more in line with the London average (Mental Health Act Commission 2005), there was also a steep decline in the absolute numbers of admissions under section. Finally, and just as significantly, the training and engagement process had fostered greater mutual understanding between police officers and ASWs.

Final thoughts

As I have tried to show, the making of the advanced practitioner on our MSc programme gives students the opportunity to experience and develop their use of a range of interventions without pressing practitioners to pursue a particular brand of therapy (such as cognitive behavioural therapy, psychodynamic approaches, etc.). Social workers have a much wider brief and as such have to be able to respond to the inevitable practice conflicts using an array of highly developed intellectual and communication skills. What we provide on the MSc programme is geared to encourage a capacity to reflect and work creatively with different modalities.

In a study looking at the impact of post-qualifying training on practitioners, Maitland (2001) found that social workers enjoyed a far greater professional confidence and therefore dared to experiment with different forms of interventions: something Catherine's case presentation so ably demonstrated. In addition, advanced practitioners reported feeling more able to have a key role in professional and service development, in this way raising the profile and status of social work among other service professionals: again, so successfully shown in Tony West's work with the police. This leads us once more into having to acknowledge that in the multi-disciplinary world we now live in, it is essential that this enhanced confidence also means being able to promote an evidence-based social model that can counter the hegemonic dominance of the medical model (Nathan and Webber 2010).

It is a paradox, perhaps, that at a time when social work and its practitioners are under sometimes hostile scrutiny, the Laming Report (2009) and the work of the Social Work Task Force (2009) also provide a much-needed opportunity for the coming into being of the advanced practitioner: an opportunity which will, it is hoped, transform the very nature and practice of social work itself. This Chapter is an attempt to outline a way in which this much-desired goal may be achieved. The following chapters in the first part of this book elaborate further on the context for advanced practice in social work.

References

Bion, W.R. (1974) *Brazilian Lectures.* London: Karnac.

Bollas, C. (1987) *The Shadow of the Object: Psychoanalysis of the Unthought Known.* London: Free Association.

Casement, P. (1985) *On Learning from the Patient.* London: Tavistock.

Cohen, B.-Z. and Laufer, H. (1999) 'The influence of supervision on social workers' perceptions of their professional competence.' *Clinical Supervisor 18,* 2, 39–50.

Department for Children, Schools and Families (2009) *Facing up to the Task: The Interim Report of the Social Work Task Force.* London: Department for Children, Schools and Families.

Department of Health (2009) *The Roles and Tasks of Social Work in Adult Services under 'Putting People First'. A Statement for Consultation.* London: Department of Health.

Dunn, L. (2001) 'Mental health act assessments: does a community treatment team make a difference?' *International Journal of Social Psychiatry 47,* 2, 1–19.

Dutt, K. and Webber, M. (2009) 'Access to social capital and social support amongst South East Asian women with severe mental health problems: a cross-sectional survey.' *International Journal of Social Psychiatry.* Advanced access published 4 September 2009 as doi:2010.1177/0020764009106415.

Etzioni, A. (1969) *The Semi-Professions and their Organisation: Teachers, Nurses and Social Workers.* New York: Free Press.

Furminger, E. and Webber, M. (2009) 'The effect of crisis resolution and home treatment on assessments under the Mental Health Act 1983: an increased workload for Approved Social Workers?' *British Journal of Social Work 39,* 5, 901–917.

General Social Care Council (2005) *Post-Qualifying Framework for Social Work Education and Training.* London: General Social Care Council.

House of Commons Children, Schools and Families Committee (2009) *Training of Children and Families Social Workers. Seventh Report of Session 2008-09.* London: The Stationery Office.

Iveson, C. (2002) 'Solution focused brief therapy.' *Advances in Psychiatric Treatment 8,* 149–156.

Kingsford, R. and Webber, M. (2010) 'Social deprivation and the outcomes of crisis resolution and home treatment for people with mental health problems: an historical cohort study.' *Health and Social Care in the Community.* Advanced access published 12 May 2010 as doi:2010.1111/j.1365-2524.2010.00918.x.

Knekt, P., Lindfors, O., Härkänen, T., Välikoski, M., *et al.* (2008) 'Randomized trial on the effectiveness of long- and short-term psychodynamic psychotherapy and solution-focused therapy on psychiatric symptoms during a three-year follow-up.' *Psychological Medicine 38,* 5, 689–703.

Laming, Lord (2009) *The Protection of Children in England: A Progress Report.* London: The Stationery Office.

Lindforss, L. and Magnusson, D. (1997) 'Solution-focused therapy in prison.' *Contemporary Family Therapy 19,* 89–104.

London Development Centre for Mental Health (2005) *Review of Assessments on Private Premises: Report and Recommendations.* London: London Development Centre for Mental Health.

Maitland, P. (2001) *The Impact of Achieving the Post-Qualifying and Advanced Award in Social Work on Practitioner's Professional Development.* London: GLPQ.

Mental Health Act Commission (2005) *In Place of Fear.* London: Mental Health Act Commission.

Miller, S., Hubble, M. and Duncan, B. (eds) (1996) *Handbook of Solution-Focused Brief Therapy.* San Francisco, CA: Jossey-Bass.

Nathan, J. (2002) 'The advanced practitioner: beyond reflective practice.' *Journal of Practice Teaching in Health and Social Work 4,* 2, 59–84.

Nathan, J. and Webber, M. (2010) 'Mental health social work and the bureau-medicalisation of mental health care: identity in a changing world.' *Journal of Social Work Practice 24*, 1, 15–28.

Schon, D. (1987) *Educating the Reflective Practitioner*. San Francisco: Jossey-Bass.

Schon, D. (1992) 'The crisis of professional knowledge and the pursuit of an epistemology of practice.' *Journal of Interprofessional Care 6*, 1, 49–63.

Slack, K. and Webber, M. (2008) 'Do we care? Adult mental health professionals' attitudes towards supporting service users' children.' *Child and Family Social Work 13*, 1, 72–79.

Social Work Task Force (2009) *Building a Safe, Confident Future: The Final Report of the Social Work Task Force*. London: Department for Children, Schools and Families.

Webber, M. (2008) *Evidence-Based Policy and Practice in Mental Health Social Work*. Exeter: Learning Matters.

Chapter 2

Sociology of Mental Disorder

Critical Perspectives

Paul Godin

Introduction

The academic discipline of sociology is renowned for challenging commonly held views of social reality. As Peter Berger put it in his classic book *Invitation to Sociology*, 'things are not what they seem' (1963, p.23). He explains further that through sociology we learn how: 'Social reality turns out to have many layers of meaning. The discovery of each new layer changes the perception of the whole' (Berger 1963, p.23). The medicalisation of madness that developed in the modern age of the last two hundred years has been variously criticised from a wide range of perspectives, perhaps most resoundingly in the mid to late twentieth century by such writers as Goffman, Scheff, Szasz, Rosenhan, Laing, Cooper, Foucault and Basaglia, who collectively became known as anti-psychiatrists. Many of these critics of mainstream psychiatry were sociologists or drew heavily on sociological theory. This Chapter shall concentrate particularly upon how sociology has problematised mental disorder and how, despite its challenging insights, sociology has informed the knowledge bases and practices of mental health care professionals. This Chapter also explains how sociological theory accounts for the way in which social divisions, not least between madness and sanity, are generated and sustained. The relevance of class, ethnicity, gender and age are each considered in relation to the identification of mental disorder, and how people so labelled are known and treated. Let us first turn to the social division between madness and sanity and how the distinction between the two is understood and maintained in society, with the former increasingly known in the modern era as mental illness and mental disorder.

Histories of madness

Histories commonly tell a progressive tale of how the understanding and treatment of madness overcame superstition, ignorance and brutality to create the enlightened practices of contemporary mental health care. Jones (1972) explains how concern for the plight of mad people gave rise to government policy to provide them with 'asylum', in institutions so named, for their protection from mistreatment and exploitation in society. Shorter (1997) tells how industrialising nineteenth-century society generated particular mental illnesses such as alcoholism, tertiary syphilis and schizophrenia, which the asylum-based doctors identified and treated to establish psychiatry as a legitimate branch of medical science. A number of psychiatrists offer accounts of how psychiatry developed to finally overcome diverse thinking about the aetiology and appropriate treatment of mental illness and to realise that it mainly had an organic basis which required, above all, physical methods of treatment (Hunter and MacAlpine 1982; Roth and Kroll 1986; Shorter 1997). These rather Whiggish histories, congratulating modernity's benign and enlightened achievement of psychiatry as a branch of medical science, have been challenged by a number of writers who employ social theory to offer alternative insights into the history of how and why the mad were segregated from the rest of society to become the objects of medical knowledge.

The pre-eminent social theorist, Michel Foucault (1991), argued for a more self-reflective approach to history in which the discourses of modernity (science, reason, psychiatry, etc.) do not simply tell convenient tales of the past, about how they progressively revealed the singular truth of the objects of their studies. Rather he argued that these discourses '... should be made to appear as events on the stage of historical process' (1991, p.86) in a 'history of the present' in which things (madness and psychiatry) are most definitely not what they seem.

Foucault's doctoral thesis, first published in 1961 and translated into English in 1967 as *Madness and Civilization*, led to his recognition as something of a patron saint of anti-psychiatry. For Foucault (1971), madness was not a stable reality but rather the antithesis of reason that in its changing forms had, from the Middle Ages, increasingly distanced and silenced unreason. In his presentist history of madness, Foucault endeavoured to offer a history not of psychiatry from the position of psychiatry but of madness, from the position of madness.

His history of madness commenced in the thirteenth century. Foucault (1971) argued that in a pre-Renaissance era the decline of the lazar houses (leper colonies) left a physical and moral space into which the mad would eventually enter as the new social outcasts. As reason came to dominate society, its antithesis, 'madness', was increasingly identified and separated, being expelled from the city of reason, left to wander or deported onto the *'narrenschiff'* (ship of fools), as depicted in German literature and paintings of the time. Though expelled, the mad were not totally excised from society. A certain tolerance and understanding of madness existed in the Middle Ages and Renaissance (evident in Shakespearian plays such as *King Lear* and *Hamlet*) where some dialogue existed between the sane and insane, in which the former recognised the latter to have a sort of secret knowledge about the absurdity of reason. However, in the Classical Age the mad were totally cut off from society, incarcerated by the 'great confinement' alongside criminals, paupers and other deviants. Foucault identified the opening of the Hopital General in Paris in 1656, into which one out of every hundred of the city's population found themselves only a decade later, as the landmark of this mass internment. He contended that the great confinement was driven by an economic and moral logic about production and labour that portrayed the mad as idle and animalistic. As the modern era began at the end of the eighteenth century, this generalised confinement gave way to a more differentiated treatment of deviants in prisons, hospitals and asylums.

The 'birth of the asylum' was marked by the rise of 'moral treatment', in which the mad were unchained, no longer to be seen as depraved animalistic beings beyond society but rather as people who had temporarily lost their civility. Through the disciplinary practices of surveillance and judgement, their reason could be restored. Though more benign, reason's control of the mad thus became more intrusive and insistent as it now governed not only their bodies but also their minds. The gentle confessional talking therapies that developed in the twentieth century aimed not to understand or liberate madness but rather to convert madness to reason. In his final chapter, Foucault suggested that the true voice or essence of madness can only be heard or glimpsed at through the work of mad writers and artists such as Nietzsche, Artaud, Goya and Van Gogh.

Foucault's history of madness implied that it contains an essential human quality that reason has oppressed. Dreyfus and Rabinow (1983) argue that Foucault moved beyond such hermeneutics of the identity of madness and humanity to a position of nihilism in which resistance to controlling discourses, such as psychiatry, criminology and psychology, is not born of a human essence but is rather as much a product of these discourses as is compliance to them. In short, we are nothing more than the effect of the discourses that construct and control us. However, Caputo (1992) asserted that we need not take such a nihilistic view of Foucault. Caputo argued that Foucault's work consistently pursued a hermeneutics, not of a definitive and knowable human identity but rather of difference. Thus there is no capitalised 'Truth of humanity' to be known, but rather what Foucault called the 'night truth', the truth of difference that refused to be defined by any of the discourse that attempted to define and control human identity. This is not a merely academic point, for as Caputo concluded, a willingness to listen mercifully to the 'night truth', rather than analysing and normalising it, might be more healing. The question is whether we 'enlightened' experts in the care and treatment of mental patients, concerned for 'best evidence' to direct our practices efficiently and effectively, are capable of perhaps occasionally stepping outside of our modernist mind sets of reason to listen to their night truth?

I have explained Foucault's thesis at some length as his 'anti-history of psychiatry' (as Sedgwick (1982) described it) is the most renowned challenge to conventional accounts of how and why the treatment of mental disorder developed as it did, though it should also be noted that some historians have questioned the accuracy of Foucault's history of madness (Midlefort 1980; Scull 1992). Also, with little mention of the treatment of madness in the modern age, other than of the rise of moral treatment in the eighteenth century and psychoanalysis in the early twentieth century, Foucault provided a pre-history of madness and its treatment in the modern era. Many other writers offer challenging ideas about the rise and fall of the asylum system of the modern age.

From a Marxist and Weberian perspective, Scull (1977, 1979) argued that the asylum system arose as the capitalist state's method of legitimately controlling the threat of madness to rising capitalist production in the nineteenth century. Though the growth in the asylum inmate population during the latter part of the nineteenth century was explained by asylum doctors in terms of their uncovering of unmet need, Scull argued that asylums had become: 'museums for the collection of the unwanted...a dumping ground for a heterogeneous mass of physical and mental wrecks'

(1979, pp.251–2). By the end of the nineteenth century asylum doctors served as curators and gatekeepers (and thus agents of the capitalist state) of these institutions, creating and utilising, with a great deal of discretion, diagnostic categories to recruit the disabled brought before them to become asylum lunatics. Scull (1979) posited that psychiatry's twentieth-century development of Freudian ideas enabled it to broaden its definition of mental illness yet further and so, too, its professional power. He thus asserted that beyond the asylum psychiatry had authority over a wide range of medicalised deviant activity in what had become a 'therapeutic state'.

Scull (1977) argued that the demise of the asylum system from the mid twentieth century had little to do with either the advent of psycho-active drugs or popular concerns about the therapeutic value and baneful effects of institutional care, powerfully described by Goffman (1961) in *Asylums*. Rather, Scull told us that it was the result of financial pressure upon the state to reduce spending on mental health care that led to the 'decarceration' of mental patients into society, where they could now be assured of a meagre existence by way of benefit payments and the general post-war welfare state infrastructure. Scull thus asserted that community care can be better described as 'community neglect'. However, Scull's Marxist decarceration thesis is rather too crudely economistic for, as Goodwin (1997) demonstrated in his comparative analysis, mental health policy from institutional to community care varied considerably throughout industrialised capitalist countries. Whereas Britain and the USA saw an early and rapid move towards community care, France and Germany saw a later and more gradual move in this direction, whilst Japan witnessed an increase in its psychiatric inpatient population. Furthermore, Scull's pessimism about community care is not borne out by studies of decarcerated patients, which consistently demonstrate that they prefer living in the community where they enjoy better standards of living (Tomlinson 1991). Neither is it plausible that psychiatrists and other mental health care workers simply responded to government directions to discharge patients. Histories of the asylum system by Jones (1972), Ramon (1985) and Nolan (1993) offer detailed accounts of how psychiatrists (such as the infamous anti-psychiatrist Ronald Laing), social workers and nurses initiated and led what Jones called an 'administrative revolution' within the asylums towards the rehabilitation and discharge of patients in their innovative practices of what became known as 'social psychiatry', which was then followed by government policy towards community care. Though perhaps as Warner (1994) and

Brown (1985) have both argued, it is in times of economic boom and full employment, such as the post-World War II period, that psychiatrists and other mental health care workers are inclined to develop therapeutic optimism and psychosocial methods of care, whilst in times of economic depression and high unemployment, such as the 1930s and 1980s, they are pessimistic about their patients' prognoses and accordingly restrict their practices to physical treatments and methods of containment and control.

Though developments in the capitalist economy might explain a great deal about why people enduring mental suffering were incarcerated and then decarcerated, and subjected to a variety of physical and/or psychosocial treatment regimes, the aforementioned Marxist and other economistic explanations have their limitations. Foucauldian scholars have a less economically based view of power. Castel (1983, 1988, 1991), for example, developed Foucault's ideas about the nature of 'discipline' and 'governmentality' as forms of power operating at the level of individuals and populations to explain how madness and its management developed in the modern era. Castel (1988) challenged the Marxist notion that psychiatrists gained dominion over a widely psychiatrised population as state agents of control. Castel argued that it was not so much that the normal has become psychiatrised but rather that psychiatry has been normalised, as its knowledge and practices have spread to a wide range of mental health care workers within and well beyond the psychiatric care system. Rose (1990) also made this point as he explained how the process of psychiatric/psychological knowledge has infiltrated practices of education, the army, industry and family life. Furthermore, we, the general population, are all the subjects of this knowledge, each learning and applying it to manage and shape our private self and mental health. Castel (1991) also argued that the rise and decline of the asylum system in the modern era reflected a shift from a concern with dangerousness, perceived to be within people identified as mentally disordered, to a preoccupation with the assessment and management of the risk of mental illness within the population. Accordingly, mental health care has shifted from the clinic of the subject to an epidemiological clinic. Though largely based on France and America, Castel's Foucauldian thesis of the development of mental health care has been shown to provide a highly plausible explanation of how British mental health care policy and practice has become obsessed with efficiency and the assessment and management of risk (Godin 2006; Rose 1998).

We have seen how social theory has been used to challenge conventional accounts of why and how madness came to be identified as mental disorder in the modern age and treated in a particular way. These alternative histories rather suggest that the identification of madness as mental disorder and changing methods of its treatment may have been brought about by changes in capitalism and/or changing methods of regulating individuals and populations. Let us now consider some less historically based sociological insights that help us to recognise the very social nature of mental illness.

The social nature of mental illness

There is of course an ongoing dispute amongst mental health care workers as to the degree to which mental illness should be considered to have a mainly physical or psychosocial causation, with many psychiatrists favouring the former and many social workers favouring the latter. As Strauss *et al.* (1964) demonstrated, mental health workers and groups of mental health care workers each develop their own 'psychiatric ideologies' (beliefs about what causes mental illness and how it should be treated), which are negotiated and fought over on an ongoing basis in inter-professional practice. A number of sociologists have provided compelling accounts of the social processes of being labelled and becoming a mental patient, which have been used by mental health workers to inform their socially orientated psychiatric ideologies. They will be discussed here only in brief summary form as they are probably known already to most readers.

The labelling theory of mental illness arises out of the sociological tradition of 'symbolic interactionism', and is perhaps most clearly articulated by Scheff (1966), who argued that mental illness is nothing more than a label applied to violators of social norms. Though their actions do not infringe explicitly stated laws or rules, they are known to be transgressions, what Scheff termed 'residual rule breaking'. Most deviant behaviour of this sort is largely disregarded. However, when it is persistent and/or disruptive it can become labelled by others as mental illness by those around the residual rule breaker. When s/he is then brought to the attention of medical experts, the label is usually legitimated through the application of medical terms and thereby substantially reinforced. Scheff recognised that physiological and psychological factors may cause the residual rule breaking or what he called 'primary deviance'. However, the application and validation of the label encouraged the labelled person to think and act as a mentally ill person. His/her stereotypically mad behaviour is expected and encouraged by those who have labelled the person. They will even punish the labelled person if they attempt to escape their ascribed role. Such mad behaviour, induced by this pull towards madness, is described by Scheff as 'secondary deviance'. He thus asserted that labelling is the biggest single cause of mental illness. Scheff goes on to posit that psychiatrists err towards labelling residual rule breakers as mentally ill because, as doctors, they operate according to the maxim of 'when in doubt treat'. Failure to identify and treat illness is thought to be far worse than treatment of those that are sane, for it is assumed that treatment is generally benign. However, seminal studies by labelling theorists about the processes of being and becoming a mental patient (Goffman 1961, 1995; Luske 1990; Rosenhan 1973) suggest that the label of mental illness does considerable harm as it renders people stigmatised and destined to a 'moral career' of treatment by those around them as unworthy and as 'other'. Furthermore, as Rosenhan (1973) illustrated in his infamous study of pseudo patients, mental health workers focus upon the medical diagnosis of patients to understand them as objects of psychiatry, requiring physical treatment, and thereby ignoring the possibility of understanding their actions as having interpretable subjective meaning.

The labelling theory approach does perhaps over-emphasise the pull of the label in creating secondary deviance and the social disability of living with the stigma of mental illness, whilst overlooking the importance of physiological and psychological factors that give rise to the primary deviance of residual rule breaking. For mental health workers who subscribe to physicalist psychiatric ideologies, it is the factors that cause the primary deviance which are all important as it is these, above all else, that need to be treated. To avoid labelling runs the risk of mentally ill people not receiving appropriate treatment.

Yet the stigmatisation and 'othering' of mental patients cannot be ignored. Goffman (1961, 1995), for example, poignantly described how people once labelled lose their role and status within their family, who then betray them in their admission to the asylum where they are stripped of their civil selves to then endure a progressive mortification of the self. Despite the closure programme of the old asylums in the 1980s and early 1990s, the othering of madness continued, for this decarceration/deinstitutionalisation was accompanied by a rising and disproportionate public concern about the homicidal actions of a few discharged mental patients. Furthermore, a number of studies have shown that mental patients living in the community suffer discrimination, abuse and exploitation (Kelly and McKena 1997; Read and Baker 1996). Some initiatives have attempted to address the popular stigma against mental illness. The Royal College of Psychiatrists was sponsored to conduct a 'changing minds' project, which attempted to overcome stigma (Crisp *et al.* 2005; Crisp *et al.* 2000). The project aimed to measure the prejudice and ignorance of psychiatric knowledge that was presumed to cause discrimination against mental patients, and then to launch a public education campaign. However, such an approach assumed that psychiatric diagnostic terms are objective, value neutral, and, unlike lay labels of madness, do not lead to stigma and discrimination. This point has been refuted by members of service user groups such as Mad Pride (2007), who asserted that the label of madness should be a preferred badge of honour for those who have survived the psychiatric system and its damaging diagnostic labels and discriminatory practices. Both positions attempt to repudiate the ill-informed and prejudicial ideas associated with the stigma, though the latter sees the former's knowledge base as very much part of the problem rather than the solution.

As Goffman (1970) explained, the label of mental illness operates as a 'master status' of a negative sort in the formation of self-identity to generate a moral and social division between those that bear it and those that do not. Let us now turn to see how this social division interacts with those of class, ethnicity, gender and age.

Class

Prior to the modern era, inequalities in the material and symbolic rewards between people were largely attributed to natural and divinely given differences. By contrast, the ideas of liberalism that took hold in the modern age promoted the concept of human equality, gradually leading the way to ever wider political enfranchisement of men and then women. The social inequalities that remained and developed within modernity became the subject of the emerging discipline of sociology that attempted to explain how expanding production and developing markets of industrialised capitalism generated the social divisions of class.

For Marx, capitalist class society arose out of people's relationship to the means of production. The interests of those that owned or controlled the means of production (the bourgeoisie) stood in mutual conflict against those that had to sell their labour for less than its true value in order to survive (the proletariat). Though institutions of state and its functionaries claimed impartiality, they actually operated in the interest of the ruling class (the bourgeoisie). Weber legendarily wrestled with the spectre of Marx to argue that class was not simply based upon production but also on systems of distribution (markets) and much else. Thus Weber posited that class was based on economics, party and status. Marxist and Weberian theory has been applied by a number of writers, such as the previously mentioned Scull, who brought the two together to explain how capitalist class society is played out in the identification and treatment of madness.

Generally, such accounts portray psychiatrists and mental health care workers as agents of the capitalist state, controlling the threat that madness poses to capitalism and the interest of the ruling class. Perhaps the most subtle way in which this is done is by a redefining of the poverty and other suffering caused by social class conflict as individual mental pathologies. Psychiatrists and other occupational groups seek and fulfil this role for the reward of professional status and all that goes with it. That most patients of the core psychiatric services, which often involve coercive and harsh methods of treatment, are from lower social class groupings (as defined by official statistics) is consistent with this analysis.

Yet a number of mental health care professionals have objected to playing this role and have exposed the ways in which capitalism induces sickness, such as mental illness, and sometimes attempted to institute regimes of care aimed at overcoming the ill effects of capitalism. Laing adopted somewhat vague Marxist notions (such as alienation) in his writings as he moved progressively towards his contention that it is the sane who are mad and the mad who are sane or as it was stated in the anti-psychiatry slogan of the 1960s: 'Do not adjust your mind, the fault is in reality'. Basaglia (1981), one of the main exponents of the Italian Psichiatria Democratica movement of the 1960s and 1970s, posited that psychiatry obscured class conflict in an aura of scientific objectivity to contain and isolate it within asylums. The movement led a drive towards deinstitutionalisation and community mental health care in Italy that placed patients' rights as citizens and community involvement of trade unions and other grassroots political groups at its centre.

Some sociologists have argued that social class, as conceptualised in the classical sociological theories of Marx and Weber, have little relevance today (a century later). Beck (1992), for example, argued that class society has given way to 'risk society', in which we are less divided by the 'goods' we may be able to acquire than we are by the 'bads' of the many hazards we face in an era of 'late modernity'. This change is associated with the demise of the traditional structures of families and industries, which supported class politics. By contrast, late modernity has given rise to an information age in which we can make more reflexive choices about our lives, which are far less restricted and yet far less assured. What Habermas (1981) described as 'new social movements' develop political agendas beyond class politics, more based on single issues. Crossley (2006) clearly illustrated this trend in his history of mental health service user movements that progressively moved away from an alliance with class politics towards the emerging disability politics, giving rise to organisations such as Mad Pride.

Ethnicity

From the mid 1970s a number of studies, such as that of Littlewood and Lipsedge (1982), sought to expose how the psychiatric diagnosis and treatment of mental patients from different ethnic groups and their use of mental health care services varied widely. This tradition became known as 'transcultural psychiatry'. Though the data from these studies are far from consistent, they generally show an over-representation of ethnic minority groups amongst involuntary inpatient admissions, with young black men in particular disproportionately receiving diagnoses of schizophrenia. Asians were shown to be both under- and over-represented in psychiatric care. The cause of such differences has been variously speculated on. Migration, genetic and lifestyle differences, social deprivation and racism, from both society and from within psychiatry, have all been identified as relevant factors.

Though a number of initiatives, such as the Transcultural Psychiatric Unit in Bradford (Rack 1992), were established to better serve the needs of ethnic minority groups with greater cultural sensitivity, mainstream mental health care was still subject to the criticism that it was not adequately meeting the needs of ethnic minorities or, worse, that it was racist. The latter charge was clearly made by Prins (1993) who led an enquiry into the death of three black men who were patients at Broadmoor Hospital. Prins reported that the staff at Broadmoor, who were largely white, made no attempt to understand their black patients, who they regarded as dangerous and in need of tranquillising medication. Orville Blackwood, one of the three men who died in a seclusion room after being heavily medicated, had been thought by staff to have a degree of learning difficulties, though an IQ test carried out by the hospital's psychology department revealed that he had an above average intelligence test scoring. It was thus concluded that the staff held racist stereotypes about the Afro-Caribbean men for whom they cared, who they regarded (in the words of the title of the inquiry report) as 'big, black and dangerous'.

Increasingly it was asked: 'how can racism be eliminated from mental health care practice?' This question appears naïve in the light of those that have applied sociological theory to this issue, such as Fernando (2001), who argued that ideas of racial superiority are deeply inscribed within the knowledge base of the Enlightenment, out of which modern psychiatry developed. Well before the British transcultural movement began, the Martinique psychiatrist, Fanon (1963), who was involved in the Algerian war of independence, developed a post-Marxist analysis of how colonialism induces alienation and mental distress amongst those it recklessly seeks to dominate and assimilate, and who are continually required to question their identity. Such ontological uncertainty, he argued, is at the centre of colonised people's mental suffering. However, as Samson (1999) pointed out, this dynamic is often overlooked by those attempting to develop culturally sensitive transcultural mental health care. For example, it has been asserted that Asians tend to somatise psychological distress (Leff 1986; Rack 1992; Watters 1996). Leff (1986) attributed this to an under-development of Asian culture, imputing a primitiveness about the bodily expression of distress. In keeping with Fanon, Samson argued that this 'somatisation' by Asian patients might be better understood to: 'speak more loudly as to the displacement, racism, discrimination and poverty that they have experienced in Britain than anything else [such as mental pathology]' (1999, p.277). Thus the somatisation thesis may be understood as yet another way in which psychiatry attempts to individualise, pathologise and, thereby, colonise Asian patients' suffering.

Gender

Having explored sociological theory to discover that the mental health care system stands accused of controlling and perpetuating class conflict and of being party to colonial domination, I shall now consider how sociological theory has also found it guilty of sexism.

Though women are ascribed diagnoses of mental illness more than men, some diagnoses, such as anti-social personality disorder, are overwhelmingly ascribed to men. However, women substantially outnumber men in the commonly ascribed diagnoses of depression, anxiety and dementia. It has been argued that this apparent greater incidence of mental illness amongst women, particularly for depression, is the result of the greater stress and suffering that women endure in a world dominated by men in which women's roles are more stressful (Gove and Geerken 1977; Nazroo, Edwards and Brown 1998). Furthermore, research has shown marriage to be statistically associated with better mental health for men but poorer mental health for women (Gove 1984). Possibly, when under stress, men are more likely to become angry, whilst women turn anger inwards to become depressed. It is also argued that women are more inclined to seek psychiatric help than are men, and that doctors more readily accept women as being mentally ill than they do men (Sheppard 1991). Might it be that the values of patriarchal society infiltrate the knowledge base and practices of psychiatry to accentuate the apparent greater number of women suffering from mental illness? Turner (1995) argued that psychiatry, particularly in its conceptualisation and treatment of hysteria, has acted to control and regulate female sexuality and behaviour in the interest of patriarchal social order. The history of modern psychiatry provides numerous examples of male psychiatrists (e.g. Pinel, Charcot, Freud and Laing) engaged in the exclusive study and treatment of women. Seemingly the psychiatric gaze is firmly fixed on women. However, as Chesler (1972) argued, this reflects the widely held view within society that women, by definition, are psychiatrically impaired.

Yet as Rogers and Pilgrim (2005) point out, men also suffer the effects of gender stereotyping in psychiatric care. Despite male suicides substantially outnumbering those of women, their claims to be suffering depression might be less sympathetically dealt with than are women's. Furthermore, as we have already seen in the previous section, male patients may be more readily regarded as dangerous and thus subject to harsh coercive treatments. Futhermore, Rogers and Pilgrim (2005) point out that mid-twentieth-century psychiatric treatment of homosexuality (which was then regarded as a psychiatric illness) involved far harsher technologies for men (such as electric shock aversion therapy) than were applied to women.

Age

Finally we should consider the social divisions given by age categories, which are especially apparent at either end of the life course, where people are economically less active and more likely to be subject to the care and control of others. In the last century children received particular scrutiny by psychology and psychiatry as childhood came to be understood as that which makes the type of adults we develop into. As the scope of psychiatric care expanded beyond the care of the insane to identify and attend to neuroses and mental health, childhood became particularly subject to the medical gaze (Armstrong 1995). The identification of children's deviant and disruptive behaviour as a medical phenomenon ('attention deficit hyperactivity disorder' (ADHD)), requiring medical treatment, has long been of interest to sociology (Box 1971). Timini and Radcliffe (2005) argue that the medicalisation of childhood has risen to epidemic levels in advanced industrialised countries and now threatens to become a pandemic through globalising markets, pushing western values about childrearing and pharmaceutical solutions onto other societies.

Whilst children may have suffered too much psychiatric attention, the elderly have suffered neglect in 'Cinderella' hospital services and care homes that have often been poorly regulated, where the mental suffering and abuse of older people goes unnoticed. Rogers and Pilgrim (2005) argue that, like medicine and society generally, sociology has overlooked the plight of older people. However, Kitwood (1996) provides a noticeable exception as he used social theory to challenge the commonly held belief that dementia is a degenerative illness with a purely physiological causation. He argued that biomedical science cannot firmly establish this claim, which is a myth that creates an 'Alzheimer culture' of 'malignant social psychology' in which negative expectations of relatives and health care workers condemn the person labelled as having the disease to go through the stages of ever greater loss of selfhood. Kitwood argued that the myth needs to be challenged to promote more optimistic methods of care (such as reality orientation, reminiscence, validation and resolution therapies) that could enhance and develop patients' abilities and potential.

Conclusion

Above all, I hope this Chapter has enabled the reader to recognise how sociology informs and challenges commonly held views about mental illness and its treatment. Sociology can critically inform mental health care workers to at least make them less certain of what they are doing. Better still, as in the case of anti-psychiatry, sociology has informed alternative ways of organising and practising mental health care to at least encourage more interpretative, equitable and optimistic approaches within mental health care. Yet there are those who have sought to dismiss anti-psychiatry as an unhelpful undermining influence on the eclectic good practice of mainstream psychiatry (Clare 1977).

However, it cannot be denied that the use of sociology can also support pessimism amongst mental health care workers. For example, the psychologist Oliver James (2007), from an implicitly Marxist perspective, argued that advanced, individualised and selfish capitalism has created a pandemic of affluenza in which we pursue monetary wealth to buy goods in the mistaken belief that these 'false needs' (arising out of what Marxists call 'false consciousness' and 'commodity fetishism') will secure our happiness. Happiness is thus seen as less a state of 'being' and more a state of 'having'. Though we find that our acquisitions do not make us happy, we persist in this selfish delusion at the expense of the mental health of ourselves and others, for in our selfishness we have less regard, and less charity, for those around us. Similarly, also using an implicitly Marxist analysis, the psychiatrist David Healy (2005) argued that though mainstream eclectic (but largely physicalist) psychiatrists believe they have defeated the mid to late twentieth century anti-psychiatry movement, neither were the victors. In reality capitalism changed to allow corporations to control markets to inflict what they want to sell. Thus it is now the pharmaceutical industry that controls mental health care. As Healy puts it: 'Both psychiatry and anti-psychiatry were swept away and replaced by a new corporate psychiatry' (2005, p.7).

Yet for all its undermining challenges and pessimism, sociology always enables us to realise that things are not what they seem and to thereby also imagine how they might otherwise be for the better. What we consider to be better is of course dependant upon the values and psychiatric ideologies we hold, which sociology also helps us to realise and question.

References

Armstrong, D. (1995) 'The rise of surveillance medicine.' *Sociology of Health and Illness 27*, 393–410.

Basaglia, F. (1981) 'Breaking the Circuit of Control.' In D. Ingleby (ed.) *Critical Psychiatry: The Politics of Mental Health*. Harmondsworth: Penguin Books.

Beck, U. (1992) *Risk Society: Towards a New Modernity*. London: Sage.

Berger, P. (1963) *Invitation to Sociology: A Humanistic Perspective*. Harmondsworth: Penguin Books.

Box, S. (1971) *Deviance Reality and Society*. London: Holt, Rinehart and Winston.

Brown, P. (1985) *The Transfer of Care: Psychiatric Deinstitutionalization and its Aftermath*. London: Routledge and Kegan Paul.

Caputo, J. (1992) 'On Not Knowing Who We Are: Madness, Hermeneutics, and the Night of Truth in Foucault.' In J. Caputo (ed.) *Foucault and the Critique of Institutions*. Pennsylvania State: Pennsylvania University Press.

Castel, R. (1983) 'Moral Treatment: Mental Therapy and Social Control in the Nineteenth Century.' In S. Cohen and A. Scull (eds) *Social Control and the State*. Oxford: Blackwell.

Castel, R. (1988) *The Regulation of Madness*. Cambridge: Polity Press.

Castel, R. (1991) 'From Dangerousness to Risk.' In G. Burchell, C. Gordon and P.J. Miller (eds) *The Foucault Effect: Studies in Governmentality*. London: Harvester Wheatsheaf.

Chesler, P. (1972) *Women and Madness*. New York: Doubleday.

Clare, A.W. (1977) *Psychiatry in Dissent*. London: Tavistock.

Crisp, A., Gelder, M., Rix, S. and Meltzer, H. (2000) 'Stigmatisation of people with mental illnesses.' *The British Journal of Psychiatry 177*, 4–7.

Crisp, A., Gelder, M., Goddard, E. and Meltzer, H. (2005) 'Stigmatization of people with mental illnesses: a follow-up study within the Changing Minds campaign of the Royal College of Psychiatrists.' *World Psychiatry 4*, 2, 106–113.

Crossley, N. (2006) *Contesting Psychiatry: Social Movements in Mental Health*. London: Routledge.

Dreyfus, H. and Rabinow, P. (1983) *Michel Foucault: Beyond Structuralism and Hermeneutics*. Second edition. Chicago: University of Chicago Press.

Fanon, F. (1963) *The Wretched of the Earth*. New York: Grove Press.

Fernando, S. (2001) *Mental Health, Race and Culture*. Second edition. Basingstoke: Palgrave Macmillan.

Foucault, M. (1971) *Madness and Civilization: A History in the Age of Reason*. London: Social Science Paperback, Tavistock Publications.

Foucault, M. (1991) 'Neitzsche, Genealogy, History.' In P. Rabinow (ed) *The Foucault Reader: An Introduction to Foucault's Thought*. London: Penguin.

Godin, P. (2006) 'The Rise of Risk Thinking in Mental Health Nursing.' In P. Godin (ed.) *Risk and Nursing Practice*. Basingstoke: Palgrave.

Goffman, E. (1961) *Asylums: Essays on the Social Situation of Mental Patients and Other Inmates*. Harmondsworth: Pelican Books.

Goffman, E. (1970) *Stigma: Notes on the Management of Spoiled Identity*. Harmondsworth: Penguin.

Goffman, E. (1995) 'The Insanity of Place.' In B. Davey, A. Gray and C. Seale (eds) *Health and Disease: A Reader*. Second edition. Buckingham: Open University.

Goodwin, S. (1997) *Comparative Mental Health Policy: From Institutional to Community Care*. London: Sage.

Gove, W.R. (1984) 'Gender differences in mental and physical illness: the effects of fixed roles and nurturant roles.' *Social Science and Medicine 19*, 2, 77–91.

Gove, W.R. and Geerken, M. (1977) 'Response bias in surveys of mental health: an empirical investigation.' *American Journal of Sociology 82*, 1289–1317.

Habermas, J. (1981) 'New social movements.' *Telos 49*, Fall, 33–37.

Healy, D. (2005) *Psychopharmacology and the Government of the Self*. Available at www.healyprozac.com/AcademicFreedom/lecture.pdf, accessed on 1 May 2009.

Hunter, R. and MacAlpine, I. (1982) *Three Hundred Years of Psychiatry, 1535–1860*. Carlisle: Carlisle Publishers.

James, O. (2007) *Affluenza*. London: Vermilion.

Jones, K. (1972) *A History of the Mental Health Services*. London: Routledge Kegan Paul.

Kelly, L.S. and McKena, H.P. (1997) 'Victimisation of people with enduring mental illness in the community.' *Journal of Psychiatric and Mental Health Nursing 4*, 3, 185–191.

Kitwood, T. (1996) 'Some Problematic Aspects of Dementia.' In T. Heller, J. Reynolds, R. Gomm, R. Muston and S. Pattison (eds) *Mental Health Matters: A Reader*. Basingstoke: Macmillan.

Leff, J. (1986) 'The Epidemiology of Mental Illness across Cultures.' In J. Cox (ed.) *Transcultural Psychiatry*. London: Croom Helm.

Littlewood, R. and Lipsedge, M. (1982) *Aliens and Alienists*. Harmondsworth: Penguin.

Luske, B. (1990) *Mirrors of Madness: Patrolling the Psychic Border*. New York: Aldine de Gruyter.

Mad Pride (2007) *Respectives*. Available at www.mcmaster.ca/hres/documents/hres_newsletter_20070701.pdf, accessed on 8 June 2010..

Midlefort, H.C.E. (1980) 'Madness and Civilization in Early Modern Europe: A Reappraisal of Michel Foucault.' In B.C. Malament (ed.) *After the Reformation, Essays in Honour of J H Hexter.*. Philadelphia: University of Pennsylvania Press.

Nazroo, J., Edwards, A. and Brown, G.W. (1998) 'Gender differences in the prevalence of depression: artifact, alternative disorders, biology or roles?' *Sociology of Health and Illness 20*, 3, 312–330.

Nolan, P. (1993) *A History of Mental Health Nursing*. London: Chapman and Hall.

Prins, H. (1993) *Report of the Committee of Inquiry into the Death in Broadmoor Hospital of Orville Blackwood and a Review of the Deaths of Two other Afro-Caribbean Patients: 'Big, Black and Dangerous?'*. London: Special Hospitals Service Authority.

Rack, P. (1992) *Race, Culture and Mental Disorder*. London: Tavistock.

Ramon, S. (1985) *Psychiatry in Britain: Meaning and Policy*. London: Croom Helm.

Read, J. and Baker, S. (1996) *Not Just Sticks and Stones: A Survey of the Stigma, Taboos and Discrimination Experienced by People with Mental Health Problems*. London: Mind.

Rogers, A. and Pilgrim, D. (2005) *A Sociology of Mental Health and Illness*. Third edition. Berkshire: Open University Press.

Rose, N. (1990) *Governing the Soul: The Shaping of the Private Self*. London: Routledge.

Rose, N. (1998) 'Living Dangerously: Risk-Thinking and Risk Management in Mental Health Care.' *Mental Health Care 1*, 8, 263–266.

Rosenhan, D. L. (1973) 'On being sane in insane places.' *Science 179*, 250–258.

Roth, M. and Kroll, J. (1986) *The Reality of Mental Illness*. Cambridge: Cambridge University Press.

Samson, C. (1999) 'Creating Sickness.' In C. Samson (ed.) *Health Studies*. London: Blackwell Publishers.

Scheff, T. (1966) *Being Mentally Ill: A Sociological Theory*. Chicago: Adline.

Scull, A. (1977) *Decarceration: Community Treatment and the Deviant – A Radical View*. New Jersey: Prentice-Hall.

Scull, A. (1979) *Museums of Madness: The Social Organisation of Insanity in Nineteenth-Century England*. London: Penguin.

Scull, A. (1992) 'A Failure to Communicate? On the Reception of Foucault's *Histoire de la Folie* by Anglo-American Historians.' In A. Stills and I. Velody (eds) *Rewriting the History of Madness*. London: Routledge.

Sedgwick, P. (1982) *Psychopolitics*. London: Pluto Press.

Sheppard, M. (1991) 'General practice, social work and mental health sections: the social control of women.' *British Journal of Social Work 21*, 663–683.

Shorter, E. (1997) *A History of Psychiatry*. New York: John Wiley and Sons.

Strauss, A., Schatzman, L., Burcher, R., Ehrlich, D. and Sashin, M. (1964) *Psychiatric Ideologies and Institutions*. London: The Free Press.

Timini, S. and Radcliffe, N. (2005) 'The rise and rise of attention deficit hyperactivity disorder.' *Journal of Public Health Medicine 4*, 2, 9–13.

Tomlinson, D. (1991) *Utopia, Community Care and the Retreat from the Asylums*. Milton Keynes: Open University Press.

Turner, B. (1995) *Medical Power and Social Knowledge*. Second edition. London: Sage.

Warner, R. (1994) *Recovery from Schizophrenia: Psychiatry and Political Economy*. Second edition. London: Routledge.

Watters, C. (1996) 'The Representation of Asians in British Psychiatry.' In C. Samson and N. Soth (eds) *The Social Construction of Social Policy*. London: Macmillan.

Chapter 3

A Stress-Vulnerability Model of Mental Disorder

Implications for Practice

Tirril Harris

Introduction

To hard-working practitioners in the field, academic research often appears remote and unhelpful. However, occasionally it offers a useful perspective by making certain distinctions. In this Chapter I will argue that a stress-vulnerability model can do just that because of its distinction between *stressful* experiences such as life events and a person's ongoing characteristics which may render them *vulnerable* to such stress. Such a model implies that the predicted outcome of the two interacting factors is more likely than if the stress occurs alone, but is of low probability if the vulnerability occurs in the absence of stress. I shall describe the historical development of one such model, since the manner in which its components were successively identified and tested in further samples actually serves to highlight the need to integrate a range of theoretical perspectives if practice in the mental health field is to become truly reflective.

The Brown-Harris Model of unipolar depression evolved over more than 30 years of data collection by the same team, both among psychiatric patients and among general population samples, both random and selected, both rural and urban. Starting from the perspective of investigating the origins of depressive disorder, as conventionally defined by the UK National Health Service, measures were developed to capture the meaning, within a medical sociology framework, of experiences immediately preceding onset. At this stage the focus was largely on stress, but the data nudged us into forming hypotheses about what made some more *vulnerable* to such stress than others and we pursued these ideas back in time and into other disciplines such as psychology of the self and of personal relationships. In subsequent samples ideas from psychoanalytical psychotherapy stimulated the development of yet further measures in two randomised controlled trials. Later work by colleagues focusing on other mental disorder such as anxiety, psychotic and eating disorders, confirmed and amplified the basic approach (Harris 2000).

Phase 1: the demography of stress in the basic model

The first finding of the Camberwell study initiated in 1967 was demographic. Major depressive disorder (MDD, as defined by criteria later to be ratified by the American Psychiatric Association) was more prevalent among working-class women with children at home than among other social groups (Brown and Harris 1978).

In conceptualising stress, the Life Events and Difficulties Schedule (LEDS) interview developed a contextual rating system to capture the meaning of particular experiences for individuals in the light of their personal biography and prior plans and purposes. The focus on context means that, regardless of the reported emotional reaction, not every pregnancy is considered equally stressful. Those unplanned, where the woman's career plans were likely to be affected, or even planned pregnancies where there were financial or housing restrictions, or previous health complications, would be rated as more stressful than those with none of these contextual features. 'Severe events' (Brown 1974), involving threatening or unpleasant consequences still some two weeks after first occurring, were found significantly more often in the pre-onset period among psychiatric patients than among a comparison group of women without MDD from a random sample of the community surrounding the hospital in South London (Brown and Harris 1978). Similarly, 'major difficulties' were identified as ongoing problems that preceded depressive onset. Just as with MDD, these depressogenic events and difficulties (or provoking agents) were found to be associated with lower socio-economic status and with childrearing.

In terms of implications for prevention this was by no means trivial, but without considerable political change it was difficult to see a way forward for reflective practice. However, within the same data set lay variables which showed statistical interaction with the severe events and major difficulties, thus revealing how some women were more *vulnerable* to becoming depressed after experiencing such stress. In discussing the nature and origins of these vulnerability factors it becomes possible to imagine a range of viable interventions.

Phase 2: vulnerability, the self and interpersonal support

The crucial realisation came when we examined the sub-sample with provoking agents and saw there was still a class difference, suggesting that something other than experience of provoking agents lay behind these demographic patterns. Four factors emerged as playing this interactive role. The most powerful was the presence of a current intimate confiding relationship. The second vulnerability factor identified was loss of mother before age 11, either by death or by separation of 12 months or more. The other two vulnerability factors involved current roles. Those with employment outside the home, either part-time or full-time, had lower rates of MDD-onset, while those with three or more children under 15 had higher rates (Brown and Harris 1978).

At this stage we developed hypotheses which attempted to make sense of how these four factors could link with depression (see Figure 3.1). Although this was first published many years ago the central part still conveys what we see as the essence of MDD: the generalisation of hopelessness, potentiated by lack of inner resources of self-esteem and mastery, as well as by paucity of role identities which might help withstand such generalisation. As such it can inform reflective practice even today.

Our hypotheses derived from the perspective of the founder of cognitive behavioural therapy (CBT) but added emotional and social dimensions to his then well-known cognitive triad, whereby clinical depression made the self seem worthless, the world seem pointless and the future seem hopeless (Beck 1967). We reasoned that anyone undergoing one of these provoking agents would feel somewhat hopeless about things concerning that specific role identity, but that many would be able to prevent this hopelessness generalising to the whole of their existence in the manner of MDD sufferers. Thus one woman whose son had been caught stealing might be able to persuade herself that although she had been a bad mother on this occasion, she was quite a good wife, quite an efficient receptionist, not a bad daughter and a champion darts player, and thus stave off depression with a confidence that when all was said and done she could master most situations adequately. Another woman without a job would not have that alternative role identity to fall back on, and if she had lost her mother early in life might also lack a daughterhood role. Without a confiding relationship with her marital partner she would have no confidence in herself as a 'good wife', and with three children under 15 at home her opportunity to get out of the house to build up champion skills in some leisure pursuit would be curtailed in a way that having only a couple of children might not, since they would be easier to park with neighbours. This second woman would thus be more likely to succumb to generalisation of hopelessness, thinking 'How typical! Why is it always me? Nothing I do ever turns out right' and going on to the ruminations of self-recrimination, sleeplessness, loss of interest in food and sex and even personal appearance, which form the core symptoms of MDD.

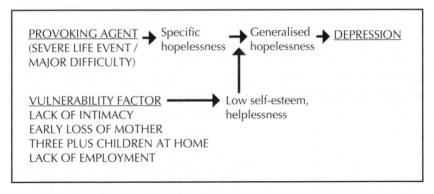

Figure 3.1 Initial theoretical model of social aetiology of depression

The words in upper case convey what the Camberwell study actually measured; those in lower case were hypothesised to be the cognitive-emotional processes linking independent and dependent variables.

We came to see that what could be protective was not only the sense of oneself as 'good' in particular role identities, but also as worthwhile in general, just as a person. The presence of a continuing relationship with a confidant who found time to listen to one's worries would act as a confirmation that one was worth listening to, thus building one's sense of self-esteem. In a parallel way the early loss of a mother, who might have acted as a similar 'looking glass' reflecting back that one was a child worth loving, would have deprived the growing self-image of its sense of worth and this might never show up with others reared without such loss.

Much later this focus on low self-worth was further emphasised when the specific emotional meaning of the typical provoking stressors was identified as involving shame, humiliation, entrapment or experiences involving self-abasement (Brown, Harris and Hepworth 1995). However, for the moment it was incumbent to push the research on by developing a measure of self-evaluation, elaborating our measures of interpersonal support and testing the postulated links. The longitudinal Islington study of women with children confirmed that negative evaluation of self (NES) at baseline rendered mothers experiencing a provoking agent in the 12-month follow-up period three times more likely than others with such stress to suffer depressive onset in that time (Brown *et al.* 1986). Moreover, as predicted, baseline NES was negatively associated with the degree of emotional support offered by partners and friends.

The elaborated scale of intimacy we used provides suggestive material for practitioners with women vulnerable to depression. We found that it was precisely at the point where a provoking agent occurred that an adequate supportive response can make all the difference and professionals could build on this. The data highlighted the doubly depressogenic effect of being 'let down' as opposed to being merely unsupported. It seemed that women who had come to expect adequate sympathy from a particular person who then for some reason did not provide it, were even more likely to become depressed than those who had been without it for some time. This has implications for the importance of a handover period when professional workers are on holiday, go on a secondment or change jobs, for example, and may be in danger of 'letting down' a client.

The study also proved a rich source of examples of how well-intentioned others sometimes fail to provide what is needed in a crisis (Harris 1992). Figure 3.2 lists some such types of failure. While type (ii) is most frequent in ordinary social relationships, with (v) a close second in close relationships, types (vii), (viii) and (xi) are danger points for professionals. Type (ix), while highlighted in professional training as strictly to be eschewed, is worth noting as a possible lurking fear in many clients that needs dispelling by frequent reminders of the confidentiality of the professional relationship, if they are to feel enough trust to utilise the help being offered.

(i)   Conflict of loyalties – O reacts disloyally, speaking up for third party (e.g. mother-in-law)
(ii) O critical of S
(iii) O minimises problem – too thick-skinned to register it
(iv) O minimises problem – and focuses on own problems (despite their triviality)
(v)   O denies there is a problem – is partly (or wholly) its source
(vi) O avoids problem as is co-victim (e.g. both spouses experienced death of child)
(vii) O is geographically too far away
(viii) O in all kindness tries to distract S, but too hurriedly
(ix) O repeats confidences to others
(x)   O is too vulnerable, gets in too much of a state herself/himself
(xi) O is in so much of a hurry to get S to take action that she doesn't leave space for the required emotional support
(xii) O is sympathetic really, but external circumstances (O's own preoccupying problems, lack of money) mean he/she cannot give time enough for S

Key:
S = Subject / client / patient
O = Other person / social worker / professional

Figure 3.2 Twelve reasons for provision of inadequate emotional support

Phase 3: the past origins of vulnerability – childhood care and attachment style

The pointers to reflective practice in the Islington study (Brown *et al.* 1986) also pushed the model back in time, again by focusing on care, abuse, supervision, parental discord and the like. This gave the vulnerability model a lifespan developmental perspective, highlighting the adequacy of parental care rather than the experience of loss itself, as best predicting depression in adulthood (Bifulco, Brown and Harris 1987, 1994). There were also highly significant associations between adequacy of childhood care and adequacy of support in current relationships. It was as if the woman had got onto a tram-line in early life which would continue unless something extraordinary could prise her out.

It seemed that exploring these historical pathways might have important implications, especially given that the related discipline of psychoanalysis had long claimed this perspective was a key tool for mental health practitioners. Although some had challenged the thought that John Bowlby's attachment theory was really psychoanalytic, its potential to integrate a number of perspectives, especially the notions of psychological defence against emotional pain (or cognitive bias) and affect regulation (or emotional stability) seemed promising. It therefore appeared the most appropriate template for further elaboration of our research team's model.

In further samples a measure of attachment style or internal working models of relating, the Attachment Style Interview (ASI), was elaborated and close associations between both childhood abuse/inadequate care and adult depression were found with insecure attachment style in adulthood (Bifulco *et al.* 2002a, 2002b), as, of course, with poor availability of current adequate emotional crisis support.

Crucial to the attachment theory perspective is the distinction between different types of insecure attachment style, with correspondingly different origins in varying types of inadequate parental caregiving. This has practical implications in that interventions to help such people overcome their insecure dispositions need to be tailored to the nature of their insecurity.

Those with an uncomplicated developmental history, and thus a *secure* approach to relating – representing about 60 per cent of most general populations researched (in Europe, USA, Israel and Japan) – do not need the defences against trusting others which constitute the various forms of insecure attachment. They manage affect regulation straightforwardly by naming the affect and seeking appropriate solutions. They have usually had early sensitive and responsive caregiving. However, affect regulation of a sort can also be achieved by building defences. Those defences built against the pain of lack of intimacy (which characterise the *insecure* attachment styles) can vary.

First, people with *anxious/ambivalent/enmeshed* attachment styles, where the mixture of clinging and un-worked-through hostility towards others can alienate any potential support figure, have usually experienced inconsistent responsiveness from early caregivers.

Second, there are a range of varying *avoidant* attachment styles where intimacy, and thus support, fails because it is avoided. This avoidance may be due to a *dismissive* style where intimacy is defensively devalued – 'I'm not getting close to anyone, as I just can't trust anyone. I'm so much better at working things out if I do it on my own' – or to a *fearful* style. The latter may be either *fearful against rejection* – 'I would love to be close to someone, but I cannot risk it in case they reject me' – or *fearful against engulfment* – 'I would like something from others but I worry that if I get too close they will take me over'. Early caregivers of all with avoidant styles have usually been consistently unresponsive. Reflective practice clearly needs to take on board the notion that clients with an enmeshed style may need a different approach from those with a dismissive one (see below).

Phase 4: modelling remission – is it a mirror image of the model of onset?

Later interviews following up the Islington sample focused on the process of remission. Two issues stood out. First, the experience of unsupportive relationships, both past and present, appeared to prolong depression. Childhood neglect or abuse, and/or a severe interpersonal difficulty at onset point, were both associated with episodes taking a chronic course.

Second, 'fresh-start experiences' tended to occur more frequently just before remission for those improving (Brown, Adler and Bifulco 1988). These involved events like starting a new job after being unemployed for a number of months, starting a course after years as a housewife or establishing a regular relationship with a new boyfriend or girlfriend after many months single. They also involved the reduction of severity level of an ongoing difficulty to non-severe, such as a teenage son ceasing drug-taking, or a landlord finally repairing the roof thus permitting the person to reoccupy the top floor of the maisonette. Particularly important are fresh-start reconciliations when a reopening of communication occurs after a long estrangement. All these experiences seem to embody the promise of new hope against a background of deprivation, the antithesis of the hopelessness featuring in the stress–vulnerability model (Figure 3.1). Clearly, helping clients to engineer such experiences for themselves should form a basic part of reflective practice.

Phase 5: research involving depression among men

It is important to acknowledge that the model was principally developed in female samples. However, three later samples investigated by the team, including men alongside women, have revealed broadly parallel findings, with certain crucial variations directly attributable to differential gender experiences (Harris 2007). All revealed the well-known two-fold higher rate of depression among women compared to men, but men showed higher rates of externalising disorders such as conduct and anti-social disorder, or substance abuse. In both sexes the links emerged between, on the one hand, depression and, on the other, severe life events, low self-esteem and childhood maltreatment. In each study there were higher rates of negative evaluation of self in the female group, even among those not depressed at the time of interview.

Phase 6: testing the model in randomised controlled trials of interventions for depression

Before drawing out the full implications of this model it is important to report on various interventions undertaken to explore it in practice. All were based on the idea that provision of good emotional support to vulnerable women would reduce rates of onset or boost remission.

(a) Volunteer befriending for women with chronic depression: a randomised controlled trial (RCT)

The research team collaborated with the Islington Family Welfare Association to set up a scheme using volunteer befrienders (who were given basic training over three weekends and minimal ongoing supervision by social worker counsellors) whereby women identified as depressed for over 12 months would be randomly allocated to the intervention or a waiting-list control group. The former were visited by a befriender for a minimum of one hour per week over one year, but contact could be more frequent if participants felt it appropriate. Volunteers were assessed by the research team in the same way as all the depressed women, at baseline and at follow-up 12 months later, using all the measures mentioned above. Remission from depression occurred significantly more often among the befriended group than among controls (Harris, Brown and Robinson 1999a, 1999b). The study specifically measured the degree of emotional support offered by the volunteers, from the perspective of both befriendee and befriender, for which there was high agreement. This was indeed identified as a mediating factor, but absence of any new severe stressor and presence of fresh-start events during follow-up, as well as baseline attachment style, also predicted remission.

(b) Volunteer befriending as a prevention for perinatal depression: the Newpin ante-natal and post-natal project

A second successful RCT involved primary prevention using the established New Parent Infant Network (Newpin), which had been offering a mixture of befriending and psycho-education about parenting to mothers for some 20 years. Identification of potential participants was based on responses to a questionnaire covering vulnerability factors handed out in ante-natal clinics and GP surgeries, along with an information sheet about Newpin. Those interested in possibly receiving the service were also asked to fill in their contact details.

Women in the intervention group were matched with a Newpin befriender and visited for baseline research assessment. The follow-up assessment occurred about a year later when the baby was approximately nine months old. Members of the control group underwent identical assessment procedures, but were told that their intake to the Newpin service would occur when their baby was nine months old (after the evaluation's follow-up assessment), rather than during pregnancy. Results showed a two-fold greater onset of depression among the control group, and again it was possible to see how this related to the emotional support provided for the mothers by the befrienders (Harris 2008).

This difference in depression between Newpin and control groups only held among those mothers who had suffered at least one humiliating stressor during follow-up. Eighty-one per cent of control group members with such an experience developed perinatal depression compared to only 30 per cent of similar Newpin group members. Among those with no such stressful experience, 29 per cent and 31 per cent suffered perinatal depression respectively. The high rate of onset overall was due to initial selection into the project only of high-risk women. Our results highlighted the way in which Newpin had prevented depressive onset by the befriender making herself available to listen to the mother's reactions to the new stress and offering her a greater sense of hope to deal with it.

(c) Time banks

A third scheme to provide social support was the building of a time bank at a South London GP surgery. A time bank is a project involving an alternative currency system, similar to bartering. When members do a job for another person, they earn time credits based on the amount of time it takes. They can then 'spend' their credits by asking another member to do something for them. In this way, the transaction is not necessarily a direct exchange between two people. People can offer various things according to their abilities or limitations – gardening, baking a cake, visiting those who are isolated, or helping filling out forms, for example.

The Rushey Green Time Bank was introduced by the doctors who hoped that members would get to know each other and build supportive bonds which would have positive effects on both emotional and physical health. A large proportion of the members were retired, or unable to work full time because of health difficulties. Some were even housebound, so the other bank members provided a valuable social lifeline. The bank also had regular social meetings.

The research team saw all time bank members, in a naturalistic longitudinal study, just before they joined and again six months later. All the usual assessments mentioned in connection with the two befriending projects were made again here, alongside some extra ones involving physical health. However, the short six-month follow-up probably did not give them enough time to realise their full potential as time bank members. While the overall results were disappointing, in those cases where another member *had* provided high emotional support alongside their practical tasks for the other person, there were noticeable improvements in mood. Such schemes have the advantage that men and others with dismissive attachment styles, who are thus reluctant to admit a need for emotional support, may be willing to participate when the relationship involves tasks like offering lifts or doing gardening, and the intimacy can then grow later almost without them having to admit it.

(d) The Cares of Life Project: an exploratory RCT

Another intervention in which the stress-vulnerability model played a substantial role was the Cares of Life Project (CoLP), so named in an effort to remove the stigma associated with mental illness and for that reason based some distance from the Maudsley Hospital, in the community. It targeted black and ethnic minority sufferers with common mental disorder (CMD) and involved Community Health Workers (CHWs) with a special training, rather than doctors or nurses (Afuwape *et al.* 2010).

Attendees were randomised to CoLP intervention or waiting-list control and given baseline and follow-up interviews which included detailed demographic questions and the LEDS, as well as recording levels of CMD and degree of trust felt for the CHW. It was not possible to include the full range of measures of confiding and emotional support throughout the social network, nor childhood experience, nor attachment style. We found that trust in the CHW was related to remission. Despite the small numbers and the short follow-up period the intervention group manifested significantly higher rates of remission. This was related to fresh-start experiences, a high proportion of which were directly due to the efforts of the CHWs.

(e) The THREAD RCT: medication and the stress-vulnerability model

Finally, it is worth mentioning the THREshold for AntiDepressant (THREAD) medication project (Brown *et al.* 2010). This compared men and women with mild to moderate depression randomised to anti-depressant medication and supportive care (intervention group) or to supportive care alone (control group). Only the LEDS, not the full battery of our research measures, was used. We found an effect for the medication intervention, but there were also clear effects for the social variables (fresh start or new provoking agent since baseline and unemployment context). This is mentioned to confirm that there is room for both pharmacological and psychosocial approaches.

Phase 7: the omission of social capital from the Brown-Harris model

There is one omission from the model which should be mentioned, that of the potentially protective role of social capital. This multi-dimensional concept has variously been used to cover a range of resources available to deal with life, both at an ecological level (e.g. community groups, levels of trust in neighbours or availability of leisure resources) and an individual level (extent of range of skills of close acquaintances or their possessions (such as large vans) which could be called on in a crisis). Although a sub-section of the LEDS interview had included questions covering such items, these had never been systematically coded and entered into the model. Recent work has suggested that social capital, when defined in the neo-capital tradition (Lin 2001), has an effect on the quality of life of depressed patients followed prospectively, but that emotional support plays a greater role in contributing to actual remission from depression (Webber 2008). This is clearly an important area where more evidence is needed to inform reflective practice.

Relevance of the model for practice

What stands out most from the above is that a particular type of social input, especially if truly emotionally supportive, can affect depression, either by helping people bear the impact of stressors with greater resilience, or by helping them produce fresh-start experiences. Whether volunteers or professionally employed, like the CHWs in the Cares of Life Project, such support figures have been found to reduce rates of depression. The key notion in all of this, however, is that of 'true' emotional support, in the sense that it really will contribute to greater security and a stronger sense of self.

Figure 3.2 listed some ways in which apparently supportive interactions (in that O was willing to be there to encourage S to disclose her worries) might turn out to have the opposite effect. Professional trainings ranging from psychodynamic social work through Rogerian counselling to psychoanalytic psychotherapy address issues of this kind, but the recommendations that emerge are usually filtered through the prism of some modality-based institutional perspective such as cognitive behavioural therapy (CBT) or dialectical behavioural therapy (DBT), where emphasis on keeping boundaries may interfere with the sense that the professional really *cares* about the client and their future. We heard over and over again in our RCT follow-up interviews from those in remission that the volunteer or the CHW had 'really seemed to care about me'. Knowing that the volunteer was unpaid appeared to reinforce this impression.

It is worth repeating that giving someone the sense that one finds them worth caring about is likely to enhance their own belief in their own worth. It is this 'looking glass effect' which professionals working in the mental health field right across the board would do well to aim for. This is where the back-up team is invaluable for the individual practitioner, whose need to protect him/herself from too many demands must be respected, but whose client's needs for access to some form of support in an emergency also need respect. In this context it may be worth reporting that in the first befriending project the social worker supervisors were strongly in favour of the volunteer befrienders withholding their home telephone numbers from the women, but the research team persuaded them to make it optional. It subsequently turned out that many volunteers were only too happy to offer them, and it was found, on checking at follow-up, that none felt the women had abused this by trespassing unnecessarily over boundaries. Certainly 24-hour availability of a *team* phone number seems to offer the best of both worlds here. But, at the risk of being repetitious, the therapeutic ingredient is not just about being available to talk by telephone in an emergency: it is also about the professional responding empathically while talking. In this context it is worth pointing out that even in CBT empathy has been found to contribute to remission over and above the manualised treatment procedures (Burns and Nolen-Hoeksema 1997).

Figure 3.2 is a reminder of the many ways a response may misfire, and documenting other ways must be a target for future work. Understanding a client's attachment style may alert practitioners to what response will be felt by the client – for example, a one-sided engineering of a fresh start may feel like a criticism by the professional for it not having happened before. One also needs to be on the look out for what will feel too hurried, confusing or even too intellectual.

One of the notable features of the reports by befriendees about those volunteer befrienders who gave the highest grade emotional support was the surprising complexity and depth of some of their conversations together. The volunteers had often been able to explain with great clarity to the befriendees complex developmental processes, linking their childhood experiences with distress in adulthood. Sometimes they would do this with reference to their own life history. One befriendee was so touched by this that she mentioned to the research interviewer that she had been very much helped by hearing something about the volunteer's own life, but she would not say what this had been because she felt she should preserve confidentiality. In her own follow-up interview that volunteer had already told the team about the same interchange, which she too thought had really helped the befriendee and had given full details to the research worker of what had happened in her own life. Thus both were conveying the degree of respect and care that each was showing for the other, the befriendee by her refusal to disclose the volunteer's private life, the volunteer by her willingness to disclose the same material to the research team as part of her wish to help.

In this connection – the ability to convey emotional intelligence to people without higher education – it is worth reporting that among the volunteers who gave this highest grade emotional support a significantly higher proportion were coded as 'earned secure' rather than merely secure. The notion of earned security (Phelps, Belsky and Crnic 1998) sub-divides those with current secure attachment style into those who did not experience neglect or abuse during childhood and those who did experience and survive such early trauma, thus somehow 'earning' a secure attachment style. There appeared to be a direct connection between this earned secure attachment style and the capacity to produce the highest rate of remission from depression among their matched befriendees (Harris, Brown and Robinson in preparation). This is reminiscent of the requirement that psychotherapy and counselling trainees should themselves go through their own therapy as a fundamental learning experience before they can be considered to have 'worked through' enough of their own past to be able to know how to formulate their insights in a way to help others. Accepted opinion suggests that psychotherapy is not suitable for those who are not already endowed with reflective skills, but this finding about volunteer befrienders indicates that such skills can be developed in many people without expensive therapies. However, the value of this personal experience of 'earning' security does not obviate the need for continuing research and evaluation. The more feedback practitioners can obtain about how they have succeeded or failed to provide the required emotional support, and the more they can relate it to assessable characteristics of clients at intake, the greater the chances of improving practice.

Although this Chapter has mainly focused on the relevance of the stress-vulnerability model for *social* interventions for mental disorder, I would maintain that the model itself also pertains to evaluations of individual psychological therapy (Harris 2006), especially given the topicality of what is called the 'common factors' debate. Space precludes a full discussion here but the central issue is whether the crucial therapeutic ingredient really is the treatment modality, such as psychoanalysis, transactional analysis, Gestalt or psychosynthesis, or, instead, some factor common to all treatment modalities, namely the relational quality between patient and therapist. This has overtones of the variable 'emotional support by the professional' as identified in the stress-vulnerability model here. But something approaching this has often been measured as the 'working alliance' in psychotherapy research and found consistently to be one of the best predictors of outcome (Horvath and Symonds 1991). This common factors debate has been fuelled by work identifying individual therapists who consistently produce better (or worse) outcomes in those attending them than do their colleagues (Okiishi *et al.* 2006; Wampold 2001) and results in the claim that this individual skill cuts across the effects of modality. The quality of recent research on both sides of this debate has been so high that, although the jury is still out on the issue itself, the proponents on each side are developing a growing respect for each other.

A second way in which this model can be of relevance to individual psychotherapy – as well as social interventions – is by reminding the practitioner of the constant interplay between outer and inner worlds, something unfortunately downplayed in many psychotherapy perspectives, though not by attachment theory. Psychotherapy can often be badly impeded by ignoring the client's social context (Harris 2006).

An emphasis on understanding how the client's prior expectations about confiding can determine how they respond to the practitioner's technique overlaps to a degree with the issue of client-treatment-preference, where prior expectations about a treatment seem able to colour its actual impact. For example in the THREAD project the client's preference for medication was found to play an independent role over and above the actual (randomly allocated) prescription of selective serotonin reuptake inhibitor (SSRI) in predicting sustained remission (Dowrick *et al.* 2010). It is important to report that uptake of volunteer befriending was low: in both RCTs only one third of those approached who were vulnerable signified an interest in having the service. So whatever its efficacy, if two thirds are never going to have access it has only a limited viability as a service in the voluntary sector. By incorporating a volunteer befriending element into one of the statutory services this shortcoming might be overcome. This would emulate the model aspired to with the CHWs in the Cares of Life Project. Later, as the practice of befriending became more widespread, the notion would seem more routine and so perhaps gain greater uptake even in the voluntary sector.

One final implication for practitioners is that at the end of the intervention the loss of their support could itself prove a severe stress, unless they have helped clients to build an alternative source of emotional support in their ordinary social network. Again this will need different discussions and strategies according to the client's attachment style and according to the reasons why this network might have proved unsupportive originally.

Conclusion

The implications of this stress-vulnerability model for reflective practice fall into two main groups: first, the need to reduce stress by helping engineer fresh-start experiences and preventing new provoking events or difficulties and, second, the need to provide true emotional support to reduce vulnerability and build the sense of self-worth and optimism. The viewpoint in this Chapter deliberately emphasises the commonalities between psychiatry, general practice, social work, community health work, counselling and the various psychotherapies, especially those based on attachment theory, in the belief that integrating theoretical perspectives can only end in cross-fertilisation of ideas and evidence that will ultimately benefit the client.

References

Afuwape, S., Craig, T.K.J., Harris, T.O., Clarke, M. *et al.* (2010) 'The Cares of Life Project: an exploratory randomised controlled trial of a community-based intervention for black people with common mental disorder.' *Journal of Affective Disorders.* Advanced access published 14 June 2010 as doi:10.1016/j.jad.2010.05.017.

Beck, A.T. (1967) *Depression: Clinical, Experimental and Theoretical Aspects.* London: Staples Press.

Bifulco, A., Brown, G.W. and Harris, T.O. (1987) 'Childhood loss of parent, lack of adequate parental care and adult depression: a replication.' *Journal of Affective Disorders 12,* 115–128.

Bifulco, A., Brown, G.W. and Harris, T.O. (1994) 'Childhood Experience of Care and Abuse (CECA): a retrospective interview measure.' *Child Psychology and Psychiatry 35,* 1419–1435.

Bifulco, A., Moran, P.M., Ball, C. and Bernazzani, O. (2002a) 'Adult attachment style. I: Its relationship to clinical depression.' *Social Psychiatry and Psychiatric Epidemiology 37,* 2, 50–59.

Bifulco, A., Moran, P.M., Ball, C. and Lillie, A. (2002b) 'Adult attachment style. II: Its relationship to psychosocial depressive-vulnerability.' *Social Psychiatry and Psychiatric Epidemiology 37,* 2, 60–67.

Brown, G.W. (1974) 'Meaning, Measurement and Stress of Life Events.' In B.S. Dohrenwend and B.P. Dohrenwend (eds.) *Stressful Life Events: Their Nature and Effects.* New York: John Wiley and Sons.

Brown, G.W. and Harris, T.O. (1978) *The Social Origins of Depression: A Study of Psychiatric Disorder in Women.* London: Tavistock Publications.

Brown, G.W., Andrews, B., Harris, T., Adler, Z. and Bridge, L. (1986) 'Social support, self-esteem and depression.' *Psychological Medicine 16,* 813–831.

Brown, G., Adler, Z. and Bifulco, A. (1988) 'Life events, difficulties and recovery from chronic depression.' *British Journal of Psychiatry 152,* 4, 487–498.

Brown, G.W., Harris, T.O. and Hepworth, C. (1995) 'Loss, humiliation and entrapment among women developing depression: a patient and non-patient comparison.' *Psychological Medicine 25,* 1, 7–21.

Brown, G.W., Harris, T.O., Kendrick, A.T., Chatwin, J., *et al.* (2010) 'Antidepressants, social adversity and outcome of depression in general practice.' *Journal of Affective Disorders 121,* 3, 239–246.

Burns, D. and Nolen-Hoeksema, S. (1997) 'Therapeutic empathy and recovery from depression in cognitive-behavioural therapy: a structural equation model.' *Journal of Consulting and Clinical Psychology 60,* 441–449.

Dowrick, C., Flach, C., Leese, M., Chatwin, J., *et al.* (2010) 'Estimating probability of sustained recovery from depression in primary care: evidence from the THREAD study.' *Psychological Medicine.* Advanced access published 29 March 2010 as doi:0.1017/S0033291710000437.

Harris, T. (1992) 'Some Reflections on the Process of Social Support and Nature of Unsupportive Behaviours.' In H.O.F. Veiel and U. Baumann (eds) *The Meaning and Measurement of Social Support.* Washington: Hemisphere Publishing Corporation.

Harris, T. (2007) 'Vulnerable to depression.' *British Journal of Psychotherapy 23,* 547–562.

Harris, T. (2008) 'Putting Newpin to the Test: A Randomised Controlled Trial of the Antenatal and Postnatal Project.' In L. Mondy and S. Mondy (eds) *Newpin: Courage to Change Together Helping Families Achieve Generational Change.* Sydney: Uniting Care Burnside.

Harris, T., Brown, G.W. and Robinson, R. (1999a) 'Befriending as an intervention for chronic depression among women in an inner city. 1: Randomised controlled trial.' *British Journal of Psychiatry 174,* 219–224.

Harris, T., Brown, G.W. and Robinson, R. (1999b) 'Befriending as an intervention for chronic depression among women in an inner city. 2: Role of fresh-start experiences and baseline psychosocial factors in remission from depression.' *British Journal of Psychiatry 174*, 225–232.

Harris, T. O. (ed.) (2000) *Where Inner and Outer Worlds Meet: Psychosocial Research in the Tradition of George W. Brown.* London: Routledge.

Harris, T. O. (2006) 'Psychotherapy Research: The Need for an Aetiological Framework.' In D. Loewenthal and D. Winter (eds) *What is Psychotherapeutic Research?* London: Karnac Books.

Harris, T.O., Brown, G.W. and Robinson, R. (in preparation) 'Befriending as an intervention for chronic depression among women in an inner city. 3: The role of support: the befriending process and characteristics of the volunteers.'

Horvath, A.O. and Symonds, B.D. (1991) 'Relation between working alliance and outcome in psychotherapy: a meta-analysis.' *Journal of Counselling Psychology 38*, 139–149.

Lin, N. (2001) *Social Capital: A Theory of Social Structure and Action.* Cambridge: Cambridge University Press.

Okiishi, J.C., Lambert, M.J., Eggett, D., Nielsen, L., Dayton, D.D. and Vermeersch, D.A. (2006) 'An analysis of therapist treatment effects: toward providing feedback to individual therapists on their clients' psychotherapy outcome.' *Journal of Clinical Psychology 62*, 9, 1157–1172.

Phelps, J.L., Belsky, J. and Crnic, K. (1998) 'Earned security, daily stress and parenting: a comparison of five alternative models.' *Development and Psychopathology 10*, 21–38.

Wampold, B.E. (2001) *The Great Psychotherapy Debate: Models, Methods, and Findings.* Mahwah, NJ: Erlbaum.

Webber, M. (2008) *Access to Social Capital and the Course of Depression: A Prospective Study.* PhD thesis, London: Institute of Psychiatry, King's College London.

Chapter 4

Mental Health Service User/Survivor Research

Pete Fleischmann

Prologue

It was sitting in an imposing committee room in central London that I first really understood just what a powerful force for change user/survivor research can be. The committee was discussing new National Institute for Clinical Excellence (NICE) guidelines about the use of Electro Convulsive Therapy (ECT). User/survivors' testimonies about ECT experiences were being traded with the dry statistics of clinical research. The committee was prepared to listen to survivors' claims of long-term memory damage due to ECT. However it was plain that it was the meta-analysis of ECT trials, which carried most weight. This sort of committee would normally dismiss survivors' personal accounts as anecdotes.

Happily that day we had a secret weapon; an innocuous looking document, photocopied and ring-bound entitled *Consumers' Perspectives of Electro Convulsive Therapy*. This user-led literature review contained analysis of user testimonies and research studies. Not only was the review focused on the perspectives of users it was also systematic and rigorous. The review showed that across all literature sources long-term memory damage was reported by at least a third of people. The review supported many of the accounts of unwanted

ECT effects made over the years by recipients of ECT. To my amazement the committee was taking us seriously. This was because we had the evidence to back up what we were saying. When the committee issued its guidance it recommended that the use of ECT be restricted and it acknowledged ECT's potential for causing long-term memory damage.

Spiralling back in time, to watch my younger self, anxiously waiting in the grim gloom of the hospital day room to be led into the ECT suite, I feel angry. If I knew what I know now, I doubt very much whether I would have so willingly agreed to have ECT. I was told the usual platitudes: it saves lives, side effects are rare. Back in those days this disinformation went unchallenged; there was no internet, no advocacy and certainly no user led research. (Fleischmann 2009, pp.177–178)

Introduction

The most exciting and challenging development in mental health services is arguably the rising influence of mental health user groups on the design and delivery of services. Of all the various activities that users and survivors are now engaged in, one of the most sophisticated and well developed is service user involvement in research.

This Chapter will explore the contribution being made to the development of mental health knowledge by people who use services. The Chapter will focus on the involvement of adult service users in mental health research. However, many of the principles and techniques discussed may have some application in children's services. The Chapter will open by describing the history and development of user/survivor research, followed by a discussion of the theory and methods of user/survivor research. Some examples of particular projects and research groups will be discussed, concluding with looking at the interests and priorities of user/survivor research.

Terminology

Mental health user activism has many things in common with other social movements such as feminism or the struggle against racism. One of these features is that the words that people choose to describe their identity, or their relationship to specific experiences, become very important. Often this is because the words that are in common usage are highly stigmatising. Labels such as 'mental patient' or 'chronic schizophrenic' are not identities that most people readily assume.

In the 1980s some people with experience of using psychiatric services began to call themselves psychiatric system survivors, or survivors for short. For some the term 'survivor' is seen as too politicised implying a complete rejection of psychiatry. Mental health service user is probably the term that is most widely used within professional discourse and also by people themselves. However, the term 'service user' has been criticised as it describes people wholly in relation to their use of services rather than acknowledging that this is only one aspect of a person's experience. To take account of this issue the Commission for Social Care Inspection (CSCI) – now merged with several other bodies to become the new Care Quality Commission (CQC) – use the terms 'people who use services' and 'experts by experience'. In mental health the term 'user/survivor' has gained currency as in most user groups there will often be a mixture of attitudes and perspectives on mental health. One of the values of the user movement is the right to self-define and the term 'user/survivor' encapsulates this well. Therefore in this Chapter the term 'user/survivor' will be used but shortened to 'user' or 'survivor' on occasion.

This Chapter uses the term 'user or survivor researcher'. This refers to people who have direct experience of using mental health services who are engaged in research. This term describes a wide range of skills and experiences; some of this group will have research qualifications and hold positions in universities whilst others may have less formal credentials.

The history and development of the user/survivor movement

The development of user/survivor research needs to be understood in the context of the user/survivor movement. User research is not just an emerging research methodology; it is part of a broader social movement. People who use mental health services and who experience mental distress are gathering together locally and nationally and demanding to be heard. Service users and survivors are imagining a very different mental health system and are campaigning for change.

The *Petition of the Poor Distracted Folk of Bedlam* (1620) is the earliest recorded evidence of patients coming together to protest against their treatment (Wallcraft and Bryant 2003). The Alleged Lunatics' Friend Society was set up by John Perceval in 1845 and was the first recognisable user group. Much later, during the 1960s and 1970s professional criticism of psychiatry developed and found expression in the writings and radical practice of anti-psychiatry. The first patient-only groups began to emerge during this period such as the Campaign Against Oppressive Psychiatry and the Union of Mental Patients. However it was the NHS and Community Care Act 1990 which really accelerated the development of user groups. It was the first piece of UK legislation to establish a requirement for user involvement in service planning. This Act was the first of a steady stream of policy and regulations, which led to the flowering of the UK user movement:

> The term 'service user/survivor movement' refers to the work of individuals who advocate for their personal and collective rights within the context of discrimination faced as a result of having experienced mental health difficulties and/or being diagnosed as having a mental illness. (Wallcraft and Bryant 2003, p.3)

Each administration since 1990 has incrementally increased the requirement for public participation in both health and social care services. The latest and most important government action in this area is arguably the personalisation agenda in adult social care services (Her Majesty's Government 2007). Personalisation is presented by the government as a major reform of the delivery of social care services, the centrepiece of which is a dramatic change to the way services are structured and funded. Social care service users will become budget holders able, via a range of brokerage and other arrangements, to have much greater choice and control over the services they access. The government promote this as a transformation of services:

> It seeks to be the first public service reform programme which is co-produced, co-developed, co-evaluated and recognises that real change will only be achieved through the participation of users and carers at every stage. It recognises that sustainable and meaningful change depends significantly on our capacity to empower people who use services. (Her Majesty's Government 2007, p.1)

From being a peripheral activity, user involvement in mental health services has become increasingly mainstream. Many funders of both research and service development now require evidence of user involvement. There is a mandatory requirement for all higher education institutions offering the new social work degree to involve users in the design and teaching of the course (Levin 2004). Consequently there are numerous user/survivor groups engaged in a wide range of activities including consultations, partnership work, self-help, social work education and research. In 2003 there were an estimated 300 user groups with 9000 people involved (Wallcraft and Bryant 2003). Many of these groups will be conducting research into local services or issues important to local service users. Nationally the Survivor Research Network is a group of user/survivor researchers whose activities have included publication of the book *This is Survivor Research* (Sweeney *et al.* 2009).

Some theory

Traditional mainstream mental health research methodologies are developed on the basis of a set of implicit values and assumptions. These are often described as positivist and biomedical, and emphasise a scientific approach of objectivity and neutrality (Tew *et al.* 2006).

Jerry Tew and colleagues summarise this approach as follows:

1. People are passive objects that are done to by the technologies and practices of expert professionals.

2. In order for research to be rigorous, it is better if people are ignorant of what is being done to them and why.

3. Questions of meaning, categorisation and significance are to be determined by the researchers and not the researched.

4. It is the individual, rather than their social/economic/political context that is problematic and needing to change.

(Tew *et al.* 2006, p.3)

This approach has been criticised by Peter Beresford in his booklet *It's Our Lives: A Short History of Knowledge, Distance and Experience* (Beresford 2003). He argued that the social sciences have attempted to apply the methods which natural scientists have used to investigate the physical world to the exploration of human behaviour. This is viewed as an error by some of the leading user researchers such as Beresford and Diana Rose (Rose 2008).

The most important values of biomedical scientific research are characterised by Beresford as follows:

- **Neutrality** – this means not being biased about something, through being involved in any way – being detached and without any vested interest.

- **Objective** – means not being influenced or affected by feelings or opinions – being able to consider something coolly and dispassionately without being emotionally involved.

- **Distance** – means not being close to the subject under consideration, being able to see the big picture and not being affected by it.

(Beresford 2003, pp.10–11)

Survivor research presents a profound challenge to all of these values. User/survivor research is not neutral; user researchers can be described as coming from a particular standpoint which is that they have experienced both mental distress and the consequent societal discrimination. David Armes draws parallels between a feminist standpoint and survivor research. He says that the idea that feminist researchers can tell 'better stories' about women's lives than male researchers can be placed in a mental health context whereby user/survivor researchers can use their experience to better explain the experiences of other people with similar histories (Armes 2009). Sometimes this is called insider knowledge or a distinctive way of knowing.

Jean Campbell uses the concept of 'voice'. She argues that more than being shorthand for a particular point of view, 'voice' is an assertion of 'individuality in the face of negative social stereotypes; an act of self-validation that can be examined as a metaphor for protest' (Campbell 2009, p.116). Similarly, Beresford argues that 'the closer the link between direct experience [of marginalisation] and knowledge the more reliable the knowledge is likely to be' (Beresford 2003, p.22).

There is emerging evidence to support the argument that user research will produce different answers when compared with traditional approaches. For example two studies have examined the responses of participants according to the status of the researcher conducting the interviews (Clark *et al.* 1999, Polwycz *et al.* 1993). The studies used randomised designs and both found that users were more critical about mental health services when the interviewer was a user rather than a professional researcher. Rather than these results being the product of professional and user researchers each getting the responses they are looking for, these findings suggest that a complex interchange of cultural mores and power differentials are at play in research interviews. Therefore, different responses may be elicited from participants depending on the status, life experience and presentation of interviewers. This is certainly an area which requires more investigation.

Consumers'Perspectives on ECT was the first national study conducted by the Service User Research Enterprise (SURE). The study was able to demonstrate that levels of satisfaction expressed by recipients of ECT varied depending on who interviewed them, the design of the interview schedule, when and where the interview took place. If a participant was interviewed by their treating psychiatrist, in a medical setting, shortly after treatment, using a short set of closed questions the results were likely to show more satisfaction with ECT (Rose *et al.* 2003). The review combined a more traditional literature review approach alongside an analysis of users' ECT experience testimonies. By using ECT recipients' testimonies to interrogate clinical research, this study was able to provide empirical evidence of user perspectives on ECT often dismissed by traditional researchers and clinicians claiming expertise in ECT.

Methods

Methodologically user/survivor research is influenced by other research models which have developed in response to critiques of positivism. Angela Sweeney cites action research, participatory research and emancipatory disability research as having a particular influence on the development of user research (Sweeney 2009). Action research was developed in the 1940s and was applied typically in organisational or agricultural arenas. Action researchers aimed to assist participants to find solutions for problems. Participatory research emerged in the developing world and aims to achieve social change through knowledge production. Participatory research seeks to de-mystify research, making it a tool which ordinary people can use to improve their lives.

Emancipatory disability research is a relatively new development and dates from 1992 when the disability researcher Mike Oliver declared that research should be emancipatory. The fundamental principle of emancipatory disability research is that it shifts control from the 'powerful' to the 'marginalised' (Sweeney 2009). Another important departure was that the researcher should be someone who is from the same community as the research participants. In emancipatory research, rather than focusing on each individual study, the emphasis is on a project to develop a new body of knowledge which addresses and challenges the exclusion of disabled people.

Alison Faulkner (2004) echoes many of the concerns of emancipatory research. She emphasises that at the core of survivor research is the goal of the empowerment of users. There should also be a commitment to changing and improving the lives of survivors. In addition she argues that an underlying theoretical approach which challenges medical model issues, such as the incontestability of diagnosis, should be at the heart of survivor research.

The majority of user research has been qualitative. This flows quite naturally from the strong interest of user researchers in 'voice' and testimony. It is also in epistemological opposition to randomised controlled trials (RCTs), which are considered the gold standard of medical research. Essentially, RCTs have this status because two of their features are seen as guarantors of objectivity. First, allocation of participants to the treatment and control arms of the study is randomised. Second, in its ideal type, both the investigators and research subjects do not know which arm of the study participants are in, known as 'blinding'.

A full discussion of the strengths and limitations of RCTs follows in the next chapter, but it is important to note additionally that survivor researchers tend to be highly critical of RCTs. It is argued that blinding is often compromised because both investigators and research subjects can work out which arm of the trial they are in. For statistical reasons RCTs use a single primary outcome measure. As mental health interventions are often extremely complex and need to be understood in context, using one outcome measure such as 'bed-days' may not capture the richness of people's responses. (The term 'bed-days' refers to the number of days a patient spends in hospital.) Currently, funding for user researchers to undertake large-scale multi-centre research is not forthcoming and also the capacity to undertake such work is not fully developed. These factors have led to a scepticism and suspicion of quantitative methods among many user researchers. However user researcher capacity and interest in quantitative work or mixed methods is growing.

The approach and practice of user research is not without its critics. Often quoted, as representative of comments whispered in the corridors of research departments, is Peter Tyrer's warning: 'There is a real danger that the engine of user initiatives in mental health services, although positive in principle, will accelerate out of control and drive mental health research into the sand' (Tyrer 2002, p.406).

The criticisms that user research lacks rigour, is anecdotal, biased and that the researchers are over-involved will continue to be made for some time, especially as user research becomes more commonplace. Diana Rose defends user research from such accusations by stating that: 'All research comes from a particular standpoint that infuses its

epistemology, its methodology and the knowledge produced as a result'
(Rose 2008, p.447).

Jo Frankham mounts one of the most sophisticated critiques of user
research. She acknowledges that her critique treads a delicate line and
is not made from a position of hostility to user research. One of her key
arguments is around representativeness:

> In suggesting that one person 'knows' what it means to live
> with a learning disability, for example, that individual is taken
> to be representative of a group who share that characteristic.
> These accounts, then, can act as a new form of ventriloquism –
> one person speaking for others – and to the homogenisation of
> groups of people, as accepted accounts of what this experience
> means are repeated and reified. (Frankham 2009, p.16)

Her analysis over-estimates how far the pendulum has swung toward
user involvement in research becoming part of the mainstream. It is,
however, an indication of how far the field has developed that both
Frankham and Tyrer feel the need to voice their reservations.

User activists' and researchers' representativeness are routinely placed
under a level of scrutiny that would be both unthinkable and intolerable
if applied to mental health professionals or academics:

> If a user is articulate enough to participate in change
> management activities then they are not 'representative' of
> ordinary users. Ordinary users are not articulate (but they are
> satisfied). Activists cannot speak on behalf of ordinary users
> and ordinary users cannot speak for themselves. In such a
> discourse, no service user can have a voice. (Rose, Fleischmann
> and Schofield 2010)

Little or no empirical work has been done to explore the closely allied
issues of representativeness of user activists or researchers. There has
also been little serious theoretical discussion of this issue. However, the
'Catch 22' challenge to the credibility of user/survivors who seek to play
an active role in the design and development of services is often couched
in terms of their representativeness. Interestingly a recent pilot study
demonstrated no demographic variation, including length of use of
mental health service and diagnosis, between two groups of local mental
health service users categorised as either active or not active in user
groups. The study also found evidence that there were few differences
between the way activists and non-activists perceived local mental

health services and their support for user involvement as a vehicle for improvements (Rose *et al.* 2010).

Levels and models of user involvement in research

User research is an emerging and extremely diverse field. The term is used to describe a range of quite different activities. This section will explore how these various and sometimes disparate activities can be categorised. This is important, as at its heart user/survivor involvement in research is a project aiming to equalise power differentials in knowledge production between a marginalised group – mental health service users – and academic researchers – who in the domain of public policy have high status. Therefore, clarity in the description of power relations in this field is extremely important. The following discussion applies equally well to descriptions of user involvement in research and service delivery more generally.

Sherry Arnstein's (1969) ladder of citizen participation (Figure 4.1) is probably the most frequently cited model of user involvement. Since its first publication in 1969 it has been frequently cited and quoted. An internet search of 'Arnstein's ladder of participation' in June 2009 yielded 17,000 results including over 500 different visual representations of the famous ladder, for example. Arnstein defined citizen participation as the redistribution of power that enables citizens who are excluded from the political and economic processes to become involved. The ladder was originally devised for use in urban community regeneration. It is obviously an over-simplification and Arnstein herself said that it was designed to be provocative. However, it does offer a very helpful typology through which to understand the distribution of power in research and other involvement activity. Arguably this is why the ladder has gained such extraordinary currency.

In her introduction to the ladder Arnstein referred to a poster painted by a student from the Sorbonne University during the unrest in Paris in 1968:

> I participate
>
> You participate
>
> He she or it participates
>
> We participate
>
> They profit.

> (Arnstein 1977, p.41)

It is fairly easy to locate most mental health research projects somewhere on the ladder. User/survivor controlled research, for example, will be located on the top two levels of the ladder of citizen control or delegated power.

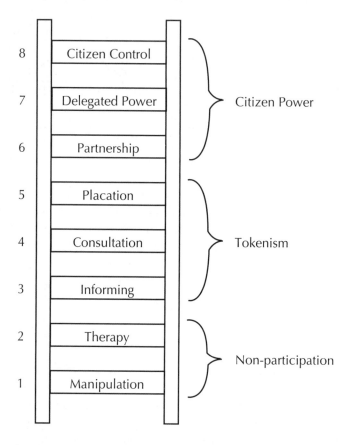

Figure 4.1 Eight rungs on the ladder of citizen participation

Source: Arnstein, S.R. (1969) 'A ladder of citizen participation.' *Journal of the American Institute of Planners 35*, 4, 216–244. Reprinted with permission from Taylor & Francis.

Angela Sweeney and Louise Morgan (2009) have used Arnstein's ladder and the continuum developed for INVOLVE[1] by Hanley and colleagues (2004) to develop a continuum of user involvement in research:

---

1   INVOLVE is a national advisory group funded by the National Institute for Health Research (NIHR). Its role is to support and promote active public involvements in NHS, public health and social care research (www.invo.org.uk/index.asp).

Consultation

'During consultations service user/survivors are invited to comment on research, but crucially the power to act on those comments resides with traditional researchers' (Sweeney and Morgan 2009, p.28).

Contribution

'Research where service users/survivors make a significant and meaningful contribution to the research but with power and decision making still residing with traditional researchers' (Sweeney and Morgan 2009, p.29).

Collaboration

'The crucial defining feature of collaborative research is that power is genuinely shared between service users/survivors and traditional researchers, with decisions taken jointly' (Sweeney and Morgan 2009, p.29).

Control

'Service users controlling all stages of the research process; design, recruitment, ethics, data collection, data analysis, writing up and dissemination' (Rose cited in Sweeney and Morgan 2009, p.29).

Both Arnstein's ladder and the Sweeney and Morgan continuum are linear models which tend to imply that there is more merit if a project can be described as sitting on a higher level or rung. However, real partnerships in Arnstein's terms, or, in Sweeney and Morgan's terms, collaborations between users and professional researchers, can be extremely powerful. The Sweeney and Morgan category of 'contribution', which sits between 'consultation' and 'collaboration' is certainly not without the capacity to exert a powerful influence on studies. In some circumstances consultation is the only viable option. User involvement has to be proportionate to the task otherwise there is a danger of wasting time, energy and good will.

The Social Care Institute for Excellence (SCIE) has identified five sources of knowledge in social care (Pawson *et al.* 2003), which should be included in work it commissions. User knowledge, described as knowledge gained from experience of and reflection on service use, is one of the five sources. Sweeney and Morgan (2009) emphasise that it is important for researchers to be honest and open about the level of user involvement in a particular project. This will not only facilitate better relations between users and traditional researchers but also makes it possible to evaluate the impact of user involvement.

A further model of user involvement in research that is very helpful in understanding the tensions within the field is Beresford's (2002) distinction between the consumerist and democratic model (Table 4.1). This model is not so focused on the degree or level of involvement but is more concerned with the values and ideology. Consumerist research, Beresford (2002) argued, will not challenge the fundamentals of service provision and will not have an overtly political agenda whereas research in the democratic model will do so explicitly and openly.

	Consumerist model	Democratic model
Focus	Policies and systems	People's lives and aspirations
Change	Consumers are asked for their input but managers decide whether to make changes	People are encouraged and enabled to give their own input
Power	'Managerialist': managers retain power	'Liberatory': aims to empower groups and individuals
Services	Services are provider-led	There is an interest in user-led and controlled services
Ideology	Treated as unrelated to any overt ideology	Overtly political

Table 4.1 A comparison of the major features of consumerist and democratic models

Source: adapted from Beresford 2002

Examples of user research methods and research centres

The most widely used and established user research methodology is user-focused monitoring (UFM) developed by Diana Rose at the Sainsbury Centre for Mental Health in the 1990s. The method involves training a group of users of a specific service or from a particular locality in research skills. As part of the training research instruments such as questionnaires are developed. The trained group of service users then proceed to use the questionnaire to conduct interviews with a wider group of service users sampled from their locality. The data is analysed and a report is produced which is shared with local managers and commissioners with a view to making improvements to services. It is interesting to note that the choice was made to describe this work as monitoring rather than research only in order to avoid the need to seek ethical approval which, certainly during this period, would not have been given to research which proposed using survivor interviewers. In its purest form UFM is an example of user-controlled research in which users decide the topic for research, design the instruments, administer the research, analyse and disseminate the results with a view to affecting changes in local services. The initial user-focused monitoring study User Voices (Rose 2001) looked at acute and community services in north-west London. Since this publication the method has been widely used in a wide range of settings and locations.

Another important user-led research initiative was Strategies for Living, a National Lottery funded project run by the Mental Health Foundation which ran from 1995 to 2000. It was led by Alison Faulkner, a user researcher, and steered by an advisory group of service users. The project supported several large-scale user-led studies including Knowing Our Own Minds (Faulkner 1997), which surveyed 400 people questioning them in particular about their strategies for self-help. Strategies for Living also funded and supported a wide range of small pieces of user research. Methodologically, Strategies for Living was mainly qualitative and illustrates the interest of user researchers in narratives and recovery testimony.

In 2000 the Service User Research Enterprise (SURE) was established at the Institute of Psychiatry (IoP), co-directed by Dr Diana Rose, a user researcher, and Til Wykes, a Professor of Psychology. The centre was established to promote collaboration between clinical, academic and user researchers. SURE has undertaken both user-led and collaborative studies, as well as several ground-breaking initiatives including establishing a user-led methodology for literature reviews and pioneering a method for generating user-defined outcome measures (Rose *et al.* 2009). Being based at the IoP has the advantage of giving SURE the capacity to offer fellowships to user researchers and opportunities to collaborate in large-scale studies. However, being based in such a large, mainstream psychiatric research centre is not without its challenges for both the user researchers involved and the host institution. The success of SURE relies on the abilities of the user researchers and clinical academics involved to negotiate their ideological and cultural differences. SURE exists to present a different perspective on the research that takes place at the

IoP. To ensure that this is meaningful rather than tokenistic, takes place within a context of mutual respect and provides opportunities for shared learning, is demanding.

User/survivor priorities for research

Whilst it can be argued that there is a clear agenda for user research, there has in fact been surprisingly little empirical examination of this issue. Daniel Fisher, Executive Director of the National Empowerment Centre in the USA, a system survivor and psychiatrist, asked consumer/ survivor leaders in the USA to list their recommendations to improve mental health research. This expert group's top three recommendations were:

1. More emphasis on recovery narratives and lived experience of recovery.

2. Studies of the way psychosocial philosophy of causation and treatment enable the person to become an expert in their recovery.

3. Consumer/survivor involvement in all aspects of research.

(Fisher 2009, p.238)

What Are Mental Health Service Users' Priorities for Research in the UK? (Rose, Fleischman and Wykes 2008) is a user-led study which sits between 'control' and 'collaboration' on the Sweeney and Morgan (2009) continuum. The two lead researchers, Diana Rose and Pete Fleischmann, both have experience of using mental health services. Central to the study was the input of the Consumers Research Advisory Group (CRAG), a group of local users supported by SURE, though Til Wykes contributed to the writing up of the study making it more of a collaboration than a user-controlled study. This study built on the other published piece of research on this issue (Thornicroft *et al.* 2002), which also investigated the priorities for research of service users in the South London and Maudsley NHS Foundation Trust. The combination of qualitative and quantitative data in Rose *et al.*'s (2008) study provides a list of research priorities for research and a short explanation. The top three priorities were:

1. Users' roles in the research process: there should be more user involvement in research and personal narratives or testimonies should be incorporated into research.

2. Social issues: how is mental health affected by social and economic circumstances?

3. Medication: how people's lives are affected by taking medication and reducing or coming off medication.

The authors observe that these priorities are very similar to those of the previous study (Thornicroft *et al.* 2002). The top three priorities in that study were:

1. User involvement in all stages of the research process.

2. Discrimination and abuse.

3. Social and welfare issues.

Rose *et al.* (2008) speculated that the reason for the emergence of medication as a high priority in their user-led study, in contrast to Thornicroft *et al.* (2002), may have been because users were inhibited by the presence of professionals from raising concerns about medication. This would chime with the evidence from Clark *et al.* (1999) and Polwycz *et al.* (1993) discussed above (p.87).

From the three investigations into user/survivor priorities, a clear research agenda begins to emerge. This is likely to include much greater emphasis on user involvement in research, testimony and recovery narrative approaches, investigation of social perspectives and a more sceptical view of the role of medication.

Conclusion

The emerging user/survivor research agenda has many parallels with the interests of mental health researchers with a psychosocial perspective: for example an interest in the social causes of mental health problems and the effectiveness of psychosocial interventions. However, the methodologies which user researchers advocate particularly emphasise empowerment, user involvement and emancipation. User researchers such as Rose, Beresford and Faulkner argue that knowledge is less valid if it excludes the meaningful involvement of service users. Survivor research places particular value on the integrity and importance of personal accounts of people's experience of mental health problems. One of the most interesting aspects of survivor research is how an emphasis on the value of individual experience can be reconciled with the need to create generalisable knowledge that can be used to improve services. The way in which user testimonies were used alongside a more traditional literature review methodology in the Consumers' Perspectives on ECT study, or the inclusion of user knowledge as one of SCIE's five sources of knowledge, offer some possible ways forward. Increasingly it seems difficult to justify the exclusion of users and survivors from the production of mental health knowledge. There is a great need to build the research capacity of both individual survivors and their user groups in order that more user-led research is produced. It is hoped that this Chapter provides a rationale to help readers to argue for user involvement in research.

References

Armes, D. (2009) '"Getting Better – in Theory": Creating, Then Using a Foucauldian Mental Health Service User/Survivor Theoretical Standpoint in my own Journey of "Recovery".' In A. Sweeney, P. Beresford, A. Faulkner, M. Nettle and D. Rose (eds) *This is Survivor Research*. Ross-on-Wye: PCCS.

Arnstein, S.R. (1969) 'A ladder of citizen participation.' *Journal of the American Institute of Planners 35*, 4, 216–224.

Arnstein, S.R. (1977) 'A Ladder Of Citizen Participation.' In P. Marshall (ed.) *Citizen Participation Certification for Community Development: A Reader on the Citizen Participation Process*. Washington: National Association of Housing and Redevelopment Officials.

Beresford, P. (2002) 'User involvement in research and evaluation: liberation or regulation?' *Social Policy and Society 1*, 2, 95–105.

Beresford, P. (2003) *It's Our Lives: A Short History of Knowledge, Distance and Experience*. London: OSP for Citizen Press in association with Shaping Our Lives.

Campbell, J. (2009) 'We are the Evidence: An Examination of Service User Research Involvement as Voice.' In J. Wallcraft, B. Schrank and M. Amering (eds) *Handbook of Service User Involvement in Mental Health Research*. Chichester: John Wiley.

Clark, C.C., Scott, E.A., Boydell, K.M. and Goering, P. (1999) 'Effects of client interviews on client reported satisfaction with mental health services.' *International Journal of Social Psychiatry 45*, 1, 1–6.

Faulkner, A. (1997) *Knowing Our Own Minds*. London: Mental Health Foundation.

Faulkner, A. (2004) *The Ethics of Survivor Research: Guidelines for the Ethical Conduct of Research Carried Out by Users and Survivors*. Bristol: Policy Press.

Fisher, D. (2009) 'Politics of Research in Mental Health.' In J. Wallcraft, B. Schrank and M. Amering (eds) *Handbook of Service User Involvement in Mental Health Research*. Chichester: John Wiley.

Fleischmann, P. (2009) 'Shocking Memories.' In A. Sweeney, P. Beresford, A. Faulkner, M. Nettle and D. Rose (eds) *This is Survivor Research*. Ross-on-Wye: PCCS.

Frankham, J. (2009) *Partnership Research: A Review of Approaches and Challenges in Conducting Research in Partnership with Service Users*. ESRC National Centre for Research Methods Working Paper. London: ESRC.

Hanley, B., Bradburn, J., Barnes, M., Evans, C. *et al.* (2004) *Involving the Public in NHS Public Health and Social Care Research: Briefing Notes for Researchers*. Second edition. Eastleigh: INVOLVE.

Her Majesty's Government (2007) *Putting People First: A Shared Vision and Commitment to the Transformation of Adult Social Care*. London: Department of Health.

Levin, E. (2004) *Guide 4: Involving Service Users and Carers in Social Work Education*. London: SCIE.

Pawson, R., Boaz, A., Grayson, L., Long, A. and Barnes, C. (2003) *Knowledge Review 3: Types and Quality of Knowledge in Social Care*. London: Social Care Institute for Excellence/Policy Press.

Polwycz, D., Brutas, M., Orvietto, B. S., Vidal, J. and Cipriana, D. (1993) 'Comparison of patient and staff surveys of consumer satisfaction.' *Hospital and Community Psychiatry 44*, 6, 589–691.

Rose, D. (2001) *User Voices: The Perspectives of Mental Health Service Users on Community and Hospital Care*. London: Sainsbury Centre for Mental Health.

Rose, D. (2003) 'Collaborative research between users and professionals: peaks and pitfalls.' *Psychiatric Bulletin 27*, 11, 404–406.

Rose, D. (2008) 'Service user produced knowledge.' *Journal of Mental Health 17*, 5, 447–451.

Rose, D., Fleischmann, P. and Wykes, T. (2008) 'What are mental health service users' priorities for research in the UK?' *Journal of Mental Health 17*, 5, 520–530.

Rose, D., Fleischmann, P. and Schofield, P. (2010) 'Perceptions of user involvement: a user-led study.' *International Journal of Social Psychiatry 56*, 4, 389–401.

Rose, D., Fleischmann, P., Wykes, T., Leese, M. and Bindman, J. (2003) 'Patients' perspectives on electroconvulsive therapy: systematic review.' *British Medical Journal 326*, 7403, 1363–1365.

Rose, D., Sweeney, A., Leese, M., Clement, S. *et al.* (2009) 'Developing a user-generated measure of continuity of care: brief report.' *Acta Psychiatrica Scandinavica 119*, 4, 320–324.

Sweeney, A. (2009) 'So What Is Survivor Research?' In A. Sweeney, P. Beresford, A. Faulkner, M. Nettle and D. Rose (eds) *This is Survivor Research*. Ross-On-Wye: PCCS.

Sweeney, A. and Morgan, L. (2009) 'The Levels and Stages of Service User/Survivor Involvement in Research.' In J. Wallcraft, B. Schrank and M. Amering (eds) *Handbook of Service User Involvement in Mental Health Research*. Chichester: John Wiley.

Sweeney, A., Beresford, P., Faulkner, A., Nettle, M. and Rose, D. (eds) (2009) *This is Survivor Research*. Ross-on-Wye: PCCS.

Tew, J., Gould, N., Abankwa, D., Barnes, H., *et al.* (2006) *Values and Methodologies for Social Research in Mental Health*. Bristol: Policy Press.

Thornicroft, G., Rose, D., Huxley, P., Dale, G. and Wykes, T. (2002) 'What are the research priorities of mental health service users?' *Journal of Mental Health 11*, 1, 1–5.

Tyrer, P. (2002) 'Commentary: research into health services needs a new approach.' *Psychiatric Bulletin 26*, 406–407.

Wallcraft, J. and Bryant, M. (2003) *The Mental Health Service User Movement in England*. London: The Sainsbury Centre for Mental Health.

Chapter 5

The Evidence Base for Psychosocial Mental Health Practice

Martin Webber

Introduction

Research evidence of effectiveness is increasingly influential in the practice of social workers and other psychosocial mental health practitioners. Originating in the health disciplines, the paradigm of evidence-based practice has encroached into the world view of psychosocial practitioners. In UK mental health services where employers prefer to recruit practitioners trained in evidence-based interventions recommended in National Institute for Health and Clinical Excellence (NICE) guidelines, it is particularly important for practitioners to be aware of underpinning research evidence and its contested nature.

In the previous chapter, Pete Fleischmann provides a critique of traditional research methodology from a user/survivor perspective. We take a similarly critical approach to the nature of research evidence in this Chapter with the argument that clinical guidelines are biased in favour of medical and psychological interventions which can be more readily defined, delivered and evaluated in a way that satisfies the evidential hierarchy (Webber 2008a). Psychosocial interventions are devalued within the traditional hierarchy of evidence as they are less amenable to testing using a randomised controlled trial (RCT) methodology (Wolff 2000). However, the evidence base for psychosocial mental health practice is developing in size and methodological rigour and provides the context for the reflective practice discussed within this book. Although it is not possible to meaningfully review the entire evidence base in one chapter, I discuss here some of its key features and invite the reader to explore it further with open and enquiring minds.

Randomised controlled trials

The combined efforts of the *National Service Framework for Mental Health* (Department of Health 1999) and NICE guidelines (e.g. National Collaborating Centre for Mental Health 2004, 2009) have brought research evidence of effectiveness to the forefront of mental health practice in the first decade of the twenty-first century. Individual or service level interventions with good evidence of their effectiveness have been promoted by the government at the expense of practice that does not have a supporting evidence base. The judgement about what constitutes 'good' evidence relies on scientific peer review and the location of the evidence within a hierarchy of study designs. It is often assumed that the RCT, located towards the top of the hierarchy of evidence (see Figure 5.1), has the potential to produce the most unbiased estimates of the effectiveness of an intervention. However, its limitations in providing evidence for psychosocial practice in mental health are manifold and one must consider these in order to understand the current state of the evidence base.

Type 1 evidence – at least one good systematic review, including at least one randomised controlled trial

Type 2 evidence – at least one good randomised controlled trial

Type 3 evidence – at least one well-designed intervention study without randomisation

Type 4 evidence – at least one well-designed observational study

Type 5 evidence – expert opinion, including the opinion of service users and carers

---

Figure 5.1 Hierarchy of evidence used in *National Service Framework for Mental Health*

Source: Department of Health 1999, p.6

Widely viewed as the 'gold standard' method of intervention evaluation, RCTs are used in medicine to evaluate drug treatments and in psychological therapy in the evaluation of talking therapies. This research method minimises selection bias through the random allocation of a study population to two groups. One group receives the intervention being evaluated, known as the 'intervention group', whilst the other receives a benign intervention, known as the 'control group'. The random allocation helps to ensure that variables associated with individuals which may impact on the effectiveness of the intervention – such as age, gender, ethnicity, socio-economic status, for example – are equally distributed between the two groups. The only difference between the two groups, if the randomisation is successful, is the intervention under evaluation.

Critics of the epistemology of positivist science argue that RCTs are contrary to the value base of modern mental health services which aim to promote recovery, partnership and social inclusion. The process of randomisation in an RCT reinforces that 'people are passive objects that are *done to* by the technologies and practices of expert professionals' (Tew *et al.* 2006, p.3). The disempowerment of mental health service users remains intact within the design of the RCT and, unsurprisingly, deters many people from volunteering to participate. As a result of this many trials in mental health services face difficulties in recruiting participants. Despite the facilitation role provided by the Mental Health Research Network, there is still a potential for trials to under-represent the population (Slade and Priebe 2001).

RCT samples may be biased towards enthusiastic volunteers who do not have a strong preference for which intervention they receive, leading to biased estimates of the effectiveness of the intervention. One response to this has been the development of patient preference trials to overcome potential confounding factors such as the perceptions, preferences and experiences of potential participants (Howard and Thornicroft 2006). Participants in patient preference trials are allowed to choose which intervention they would like. Those with no preference are randomised as usual to either the intervention or the control group. If the randomised participants are otherwise similar to those who express a strong preference, this will boost the external validity and representativeness of the randomised sample, as demonstrated by Ward *et al.* (2000) in their trial of non-directive counselling, cognitive behavioural therapy and GP care for depression. There have been very few patient preference trials of psychosocial interventions in mental health, but they may feature more prominently in the evidence base in the future.

RCTs can only be sanctioned if there is genuine uncertainty about the effectiveness of an intervention. This state of critical equipoise is reached when a novel intervention shows some evidence of positive outcomes but clinicians are genuinely uncertain as to whether or not it is more or less effective than an existing intervention (or none at all, if the problem it is addressing is new). This poses both opportunities and challenges for researchers using an RCT methodology to evaluate the effectiveness of psychosocial interventions. On the one hand, if researchers attempt to evaluate a novel psychosocial intervention in comparison with a traditional intervention that already has extensive evidence of its effectiveness, they need to demonstrate its potential for producing better outcomes through high quality non-randomised studies before an RCT could be justified. As the quality threshold for research in mental health is gradually being raised, researchers are required to conduct extensive additional studies prior to seeking funding and approval for an RCT. This rigorous process ensures that effective interventions are not being denied to study participants through the process of randomisation. However, it diminishes the possibility of generating high-quality evidence of the effectiveness of psychosocial interventions through an RCT because of the attendant difficulties in securing funding and ethical approval.

On the other hand, there is generally less evidence available about the effect of interventions on social outcomes such as quality of life, social inclusion and access to social capital. Researchers are more likely to be able to demonstrate critical equipoise for interventions with social outcomes because traditional interventions have primarily focused on improving psychopathology. However, as the majority of mental health research funding in the UK is from health sources, researchers have to make a special case for using social outcomes instead of traditional symptom-based measures.

RCTs can only effectively evaluate interventions which can be consistently and reliably delivered to all recipients. It would not be possible to reliably ascertain the effect of an intervention if it was delivered differently by different practitioners. Whether it is a new drug, psychological therapy or a complex psychosocial intervention, it is important to ensure that participants in the trial are receiving the same *bona fide* intervention. To achieve this, practice is prescribed within intervention manuals or protocols and intervention fidelity is tested within trials to minimise deviations. Intervention manuals permit replication of the trial in different locations and settings to help develop an evidence base. However, not all complex social interventions are reducible to an intervention manual or are replicable elsewhere. For example, the emerging evidence base on supporting housing for people with mental health problems has limited generalisability because of the variety of housing models that have been evaluated (Leff *et al.* 2009; Rog 2004). The lack of a homogenous evidence base leads some reviewers (e.g. Chilvers, Macdonald and Hayes 2006) to conclude that there is insufficient evidence of its effectiveness to recommend it as an intervention, despite observational evidence to the contrary (e.g. Brunt and Hansson 2004; Nelson *et al.* 2007; Siegel *et al.* 2006). This is an important reason why complex social interventions rarely feature in clinical guidelines.

A further difficulty with employing randomised experiments in determining the effectiveness of complex social interventions is in finding a suitable comparison. The choice of intervention for the control group is important in demonstrating the relative effectiveness of the new intervention. If there is no established intervention for the particular health or social problem, the control group will receive a neutral intervention designed to mimic the effect of the intervention but containing no 'active ingredient'. In pharmacological trials the control group may receive a placebo, an inert drug such as a sugar pill. In the evaluation of complex psychosocial interventions, researchers are faced with a more complex task in mimicking the effect of the intervention. One solution is to provide information sessions to the control group which provides equivalent contact with a mental health professional but not the intervention under evaluation (e.g. Henderson *et al.* 2004). If there is already an established intervention for the health or social problem, it would be unethical to withhold this. In these cases the trial will test a new intervention against the standard treatment. For example, in trials of new mental health services such as crisis resolution and home treatment teams the control group receives treatment as usual from the community mental health team (e.g. Johnson *et al.* 2005). A further alternative is to give the intervention group an existing intervention supplemented with a new one, with the control group having just the standard treatment (e.g. Kuipers *et al.* 1997). Finally, where there are typically long waiting lists for interventions, it may be ethical to use a waiting-list design whereby participants are randomly allocated to a group receiving the intervention or to a waiting list control group which receives it at a later point (e.g. Harris, Brown and Robinson 1999).

Some mental health social work practice cannot be evaluated using a trial methodology. For example, statutory interventions undertaken by

Approved Mental Health Professionals are not amenable to randomised evaluation, as randomised experiments of the effectiveness of compulsory detention under mental health law are unethical and could not be sanctioned. However, this does not prevent practitioners from being evidence-informed and there is a growing literature from which they can inform their practice.

The Social Care Institute for Excellence synthesises this literature and disseminates it to practitioners according to types of knowledge rather than a hierarchy of knowledge (Pawson *et al.* 2003). An inclusive approach validates knowledge drawn from a range of other research methods such as qualitative approaches (Gould 2006). It provides practitioners with a wide variety of sources of knowledge to inform their practice, but it potentially makes it more difficult for practitioners to ascertain how effective certain interventions may be. For example, Quirk *et al.*'s (2000) ethnographic study of Mental Health Act assessments provided a revealing insight into their organisation and process, but it was not able to evaluate the effectiveness of detention in hospital on improving mental health. Although RCTs are certainly not 'the only gold that glitters' (Slade and Priebe 2001), their importance in shaping social work practice through clinical guidelines cannot be under-estimated. Advanced practitioners in social work need to be critically aware of the research evidence supporting their practice and this is emphasised throughout consultation group seminars on the MSc in Mental Health Social Work with Children and Adults programme (see Chapter 1). We will review some of this evidence now, starting with the teams in which mental health social workers practice.

Contexts for mental health social work practice

Most mental health social workers in statutory settings are employed in community mental health teams (CMHTs) which form the bedrock of community mental health care but have been surprisingly under-evaluated. The Cochrane systematic review of CMHTs (Malone *et al.* 2007) included only three RCTs, all conducted in the UK. The only consistent difference it found in comparison with non-team standard care was lower hospital admission rates for people in receipt of CMHT care. Many of the presumed benefits of CMHTs such as lower cost, improved social functioning, and greater user and carer satisfaction were not found in these RCTs.

Case management has long been the *modus operandi* of CMHTs, but this too has not fared too well in RCTs. The Cochrane review of case management for people with severe mental health problems (Marshall *et al.* 1998) found that it increased the numbers of people maintaining contact with services but almost doubled the numbers admitted to hospital in comparison to standard community care. The US model of assertive community treatment (ACT), however, appears much more effective.

The Cochrane review of randomised controlled trials of ACT, which showed its effectiveness in reducing hospital admissions and time spent in hospital, and increasing engagement with services in contrast to community care (Marshall and Lockwood 1998), was highly influential in the development of assertive outreach in the UK. However, the majority of studies included in this review were conducted in the US.

UK studies have provided less convincing evidence. The largest trial of intensive case management (the UK700 study) found no significant decline in overall hospital use among those who received intensive case management or any significant gains in clinical or social functioning (Burns *et al.* 1999). A more recent trial (Killaspy *et al.* 2006) found similar findings and concluded that CMHTs were as effective as ACT teams, but that ACT may be better at engaging people and may lead to greater satisfaction with services.

The social outcomes of UK assertive outreach teams are also equivocal. The UK700 study found that standard community mental health team care improved the quality of life of people with psychosis to the same extent as intensive case management (Huxley *et al.* 2001). The social functioning of the participants in the REACT trial in London also did not differ between the intervention or control group (Killaspy *et al.* 2006). Similar findings were found in an observation study of assertive outreach users in north Birmingham (Commander *et al.* 2005).

The relative ineffectiveness of assertive outreach in the UK can be explained in part by the findings of a recent systematic review (Burns *et al.* 2007). This found that assertive outreach works best in trials in which participants make more use of hospital. In areas which have lower hospital admission rates, possibly as a result of better community care, assertive outreach should therefore be a lower priority. The review also highlighted that trials with less fidelity to the ACT model had poorer outcomes (Burns *et al.* 2007). The lack of convincing evidence in support of assertive outreach has led to a call for the end of 'treatment as usual' studies and recognition that CMHTs are the most cost-effective and evidence-based approach to the provision of community care (Burns 2009).

Systematic reviews of trials of crisis resolution and home treatment (CRHT) teams have not produced definitive results. The Cochrane review of crisis intervention teams found that it may help to avoid repeat hospital admissions and it appears more satisfactory than inpatient care (Joy, Adams and Rice 1998). A later systematic review of home treatment (Burns *et al.* 2001) found similar results. Home treatment was successful at reducing length of hospital stays in comparison to inpatient services. However, when home treatment was compared to usual community services, there was no difference.

The introduction of CRHT teams in the UK has led to a reduction in the rate of inpatient admissions (Glover, Arts and Babu 2006). This finding corresponded with the results of an RCT of a crisis resolution team in north London which reduced hospital admissions at the time of a crisis in comparison to community mental health team care (Johnson *et al.* 2005). However, CRHT teams do not appear to reduce compulsory admissions. Two observational studies undertaken by practitioners on our programme found that the use of Section 2 of the Mental Health Act 1983 (assessment orders) increased after the introduction of CRHT teams whilst the use of Section 3 (treatment orders) decreased over time (Dunn 2001; Furminger and Webber 2009). Social workers report that by assessing people for home treatment prior to a mental health act assessment, CRHT teams may increase the likelihood of a compulsory admission because the individual's mental health has deteriorated further and an informal admission can be difficult to negotiate following a reduction in the number of beds (Furminger and Webber 2009).

More research is needed on which interventions within CRHT teams produce the best outcomes, and a wider range of outcomes need to be studied. There is an important role for social workers in these teams, particularly as there is evidence that people referred to CRHT teams from CMHTs – who live in more deprived areas – have poorer outcomes (Kingsford and Webber 2010). Therapeutic relationships with the CRHT professionals are highly valued by service users (Hopkins and Niemiec 2007), but there are many social interventions, such as social network enhancements, which remain untested in CRHT contexts (Johnson 2007).

A further context of mental health social work practice is early intervention in psychosis teams. The idea of early intervention in psychosis is not new, but the rigorous evaluation of specialist early intervention in psychosis services is still in its infancy (Singh and Fisher 2007). Two RCTs of early intervention in psychosis services have shown promising results. The Lambeth Early Onset service in London has provided some evidence that early intervention can reduce and maintain engagement over longer periods of time than community mental health team care (Craig *et al.* 2004). Eighteen months later, those receiving support from this service were more likely to regain or establish new social relationships, spend longer in vocational activity, have better social functioning, have a better quality of life and be more satisfied with their service than the comparison group, but there was no improvement in their psychotic symptoms (Garety *et al.* 2006). A trial in Denmark produced similar results (Petersen *et al.* 2005). Other trials, however, have found that early intervention teams are no more effective than CMHTs (e.g. Kuipers *et al.* 2004).

There is some evidence to suggest that working closely with young people and focusing on their needs helps in a number of life domains such as education, employment, housing, income, leisure, religion and social relationships. For example, the Antenna Outreach Team in Haringey, London, provides a culturally sensitive service to young people from the African and Caribbean communities and helps to engage them in a range of community services (Greatley and Ford 2002). As there are fewer opportunities for social workers in these teams, it is perhaps not unsurprising that the social outcomes of these services have not received a higher profile in the research conducted to date.

Mental health social work practice

There have been no recent RCTs of the effectiveness of social work practice in community mental health services. However, older trials have indicated that social work is at least as effective as psychological or pharmacological approaches to mental health problems.

A trial of a home-based social work family intervention for children who deliberately poisoned themselves in the late 1990s found that the intervention reduced suicidal ideation in the children without major depression at no extra cost to mental health services (Byford *et al.* 1999; Harrington *et al.* 1998). Although the trial did not show the efficacy of the intervention for children with severe depression, it does indicate that social workers can provide effective services within child and adolescent mental health settings. Further, a trial of task-centred social work with adults who had deliberately poisoned themselves found that it did not reduce the risk of future self-poisoning, but it did help people with their social problems and they were more satisfied with it than standard care (Gibbons *et al.* 1978).

Two trials of social work with people with depression in primary care found that it was just as effective as GP care in terms of clinical and social outcomes (Corney and Clare 1983; Scott and Freeman 1992). In one trial the social work intervention cost twice as much as GP care but it was the most positively evaluated by the patients (Scott and Freeman 1992). In the other trial social work was most effective for women with both major difficulties with their partner and enduring depression (Corney and Clare 1983).

Statutory mental health social work practice

In the absence of experimental research there is a wealth of evidence from observation studies to inform statutory mental health social work practice. First, compulsory detention is patterned by socio-demographic variables. Studies have consistently indicated that people who are assessed under the Mental Health Act are predominantly socially disadvantaged and rates of detention are highest in areas of social deprivation (Bindman *et al.* 2002; Hatfield 2008). Those who have low social support are particularly at risk of being admitted under an emergency compulsory order (Webber and Huxley 2004). People of African and Caribbean origin are over four times more likely to be detained than those of white British origin (Bhui *et al.* 2003; Harrison 2002; Morgan *et al.* 2005). Women aged over 65 are more likely to be detained than men in this age group, whereas the converse is true for younger men (Audini and Lelliott 2002). People aged over 65 are more likely to be detained because of self-neglect and their risk of suicide is lower than younger people (McPherson and Jones 2003). Detention rates increased in the 1990s, particularly for young men, but have since levelled off (Lelliott and Audini 2003; Wall *et al.* 1999). Both older and younger people with a full understanding of their rights are more likely to appeal against their detention (Rimmer, O'Connor and Anderson 2002). However, success rates of appeals are low, ranging from 2 per cent (Nilforooshan, Amin and Warner 2009) to 12 per cent (Aziz 2009, Singh and Moncrieff 2009).

The low success rate of appeals may be a result of Approved Mental Health Professionals appropriately diverting away from compulsory care those people who do not meet the criteria for it. It is likely that over the last two decades Approved Social Workers have helped the 'least restrictive alternative' principle, which underpinned the Mental

Health Act 1983 Code of Practice, to permeate community mental health practice as data indicates that very few Mental Health Act assessments result in alternatives to hospital care. Only 7 per cent were diverted from hospital during Mental Health Act assessments in a large study in north-west England (Hatfield 2008), for example, suggesting that clinicians have applied 'least restrictive alternative' principles prior to referral for a Mental Health Act assessment. A systematic review of residential alternatives to acute hospital admission found little evidence of the effectiveness of the former, although it did suggest that community-based residential crisis services may provide a feasible and acceptable alternative to hospital admission for some people with acute mental health problems (Lloyd-Evans *et al.* 2009). As we have argued elsewhere (Nathan and Webber 2010), social workers undertaking statutory functions should perhaps be more concerned about the 'best interests' of the person they are assessing rather than the 'least restrictive alternative' which may already have been considered or simply not be available.

Supervised discharge, the precursor to supervised community treatment under the Mental Health Act 2007 in England and Wales, was used for people who were more likely to be non-compliant with treatment plans and had problems of substance misuse (Hatfield *et al.* 2001). A higher proportion of people of African Caribbean origin were subject to supervised discharge (Hatfield *et al.* 2001), but the majority of people subject to supervised discharge were compliant with their orders (Hatfield, Bindman and Pinfold 2004; Pinfold *et al.* 2001), but mental health professionals did not rate it very highly (Pinfold *et al.* 2002). Service users appeared to simultaneously resist and accept the orders (Canvin, Bartlett and Pinfold 2005). A comprehensive analysis of 72 empirical studies of community treatment orders across the world found that there was no robust evidence for either their positive or negative effects (Churchill 2007). However, as there is evidence to suggest that compulsory detention may decrease the risk of suicide on discharge from hospital (in comparison with informal patients) (Hunt *et al.* 2009), the use of compulsion, however unpalatable, can be justified.

The role of the nearest relative has been an important one in mental health law (Rapaport and Manthorpe 2008). However, there is evidence to suggest that they have been generally under-informed of their rights (Marriott *et al.* 2001). In spite of this, one study found that people discharged by their relative had no worse clinical outcomes than those who were not (Shaw, Hotopf and Davies 2003).

Only one intervention that has been evaluated in a randomised controlled trial has been found to reduce the risk of compulsory detention. Joint crisis plans have reduced the likelihood of a compulsory detention under the Mental Health Act 1983 (Henderson *et al.* 2004), unlike advance directives which have not been found to have this effect (Papageorgiou *et al.* 2002).

Social interventions

As previously discussed, the evidence base for social interventions that are at the disposal of mental health social workers is small, incomplete and disproportionate in size to that available to psychologists or psychiatrists. Clinical guidelines in mental health are dominated by psychological or pharmacological interventions. However, there are some rigorously evaluated interventions which social workers can deliver or refer people to. For example, as Tirril Harris discusses in Chapter 3, there is RCT evidence that volunteer befriending helps people to recover from depression (Harris, Brown and Robinson 1999). As a result of this trial, befriending appeared in the NICE depression guidelines (National Collaborating Centre for Mental Health 2004) as a recommended intervention for clinicians. It was the only social intervention to feature in these guidelines, highlighting the importance of RCT evidence of the effectiveness of social interventions. It also highlights the dearth of effectiveness studies conducted on social interventions.

Social support is associated with better outcomes for people with depression (see Chapter 3) and bipolar disorder (Johnson *et al.* 2003). Whilst there is good evidence that emotional support is important for mental health, there is also emerging evidence that social capital – resources embedded within social networks (Lin 2001) – is associated with mental health. Cross-sectional studies have found that social capital is negatively correlated with depression, independent of socio-economic status (Song 2007; Song and Lin 2009; Webber and Huxley 2007). Further, longitudinal studies have found that access to social capital increases for people with depression as symptoms of depression decrease (Webber 2008b); and for people with severe and enduring mental health problems involved in volunteering (Murray, Easter and Bellringer 2007). As mental well-being is associated with better social and economic outcomes (Friedli 2009), enhancing the access of people with mental health problems to social resources may make a modest contribution to narrowing existing inequalities (Webber 2008b).

Social networks are important resources for people with mental health problems, impacting upon both physical and mental health (Berkman 1995), providing 'opportunity structures' for people with disability to manage relationships and social supports (Forrester-Jones *et al.* 2006). There is evidence to suggest that day service users have larger social networks than day hospital users (Catty *et al.* 2005). However, the drive towards social inclusion has meant the closure of many traditional day services which may mean the loss of these valuable social contacts, potentially leading to social isolation for those previously dependent upon these services. Further work is needed to develop and evaluate interventions which may be effective in enhancing the quality of social networks and increasing access to social capital.

Fresh-start events such as gaining employment after a long period of unemployment are also important for recovery from mental health problems (Harris 2001). There is good evidence that paid employment encourages recovery and promotes social inclusion (Leff and Warner 2006; Warner 2000). Mental health services have invested in supported employment programmes to assist people to regain employment as there is robust evidence that supported employment is the most effective way of helping people with severe mental health problems to gain, and stay in, competitive employment (Crowther *et al.* 2001). Although most trials have used specialist employment workers, social workers can play an important role in supporting employment and education (Shankar, Martin and McDonald 2009).

A number of psychosocial interventions for people with schizophrenia have now been evaluated using RCTs and feature in clinical guidelines. For example, arts therapies – music, movement or art – are effective in reducing negative symptoms of schizophrenia (e.g. Green 1987; Ulrich 2007). Further, it has long been established that family interventions which reduce expressed emotion within households reduces the likelihood of relapse or hospital admission for people with psychosis (Pharoah, Mari and Streiner 2003).

Conclusion

Evidence-based practice has the potential to deliver more effective and efficient services to recipients of health and social care. The lack of high-quality evidence about the effectiveness of social interventions – and their subsequent absence from clinical guidelines – should not prevent practitioners from working towards goals such as social inclusion, enhanced social networks, increased access to social capital and improved quality of life. These outcomes are key priority areas for social research (Gould, Huxley and Tew 2007) and government policy (Her Majesty's Government 2007).

There are encouraging signs that the evidence base for social care and social work practice will expand with the establishment of a new National Institute for Health Research School of Social Care Research. Even without funding for large studies, practitioners are contributing original empirical research to the evidence base (e.g. Dunn 2001; Dutt and Webber 2009; Furminger and Webber 2009; Slack and Webber 2008). Further, in the absence of RCT evidence, practitioner research is influencing clinical guidelines (e.g. Webber and Huxley 2004 cited in National Collaborating Centre for Mental Health 2006), highlighting its relative importance in the evidence base for mental health practice.

Through the use of case studies, the next part of this book will explore how psychosocial theories and intervention models, frequently informed by research, can help to produce positive changes in the lives of people with mental health problems. These case studies will also provide practitioners with the opportunity to reflect upon their practice and increase their knowledge about different intervention models.

References

Audini, B. and Lelliott, P. (2002) 'Age, gender and ethnicity of those detained under Part II of the Mental Health Act 1983.' *British Journal of Psychiatry 180*, 3, 222–226.

Aziz, V.M. (2009) 'Trends in the Mental Health Act Review Tribunals: A Welsh experience 2004–2008.' *Journal of Forensic and Legal Medicine 16*, 7, 375–377.

Berkman, L.F. (1995) 'The role of social relations in health promotion.' *Psychosomatic Medicine 57*, 3, 245–254.

Bhui, K., Stansfeld, S., Hull, S., Priebe, S., Mole, F. and Feder, G. (2003) 'Ethnic variations in pathways to and use of specialist mental health services in the UK: systematic review.' *British Journal of Psychiatry 182*, 2, 105–116.

Bindman, J., Tighe, J., Thornicroft, G. and Leese, M. (2002) 'Poverty, poor services, and compulsory psychiatric admission in England.' *Social Psychiatry and Psychiatric Epidemiology 37*, 7, 341–345.

Brunt, D. and Hansson, L. (2004) 'The quality of life of persons with severe mental illness across housing settings.' *Nordic Journal of Psychiatry 58*, 4, 293–298.

Burns, T. (2009) 'End of the road for treatment-as-usual studies?' *British Journal of Psychiatry 195*, 1, 5–6.

Burns, T., Creed, F., Fahy, T., Thompson, S., Tyrer, P. and White, I. (1999) 'Intensive versus standard case management for severe psychotic illness: a randomised trial.' *The Lancet 353*, 9171, 2185–2189.

Burns, T., Knapp, M., Catty, J., Healey, A. *et al.* (2001) 'Home treatment for mental health problems: a systematic review.' *Health Technology Assessment 5*, 15.

Burns, T., Catty, J., Dash, M., Roberts, C., Lockwood, A. and Marshall, M. (2007) 'Use of intensive case management to reduce time in hospital in people with severe mental illness: systematic review and meta-regression.' *British Medical Journal 335*, 7615, 336–340.

Byford, S., Harrington, R., Torgerson, D., Kerfoot, M., Dyer, E., Harrington, V., Woodham, A., Gill, J. and McNiven, F. (1999) 'Cost-effectiveness analysis of a home-based social work intervention for children and adolescents who have deliberately poisoned themselves. Results of a randomised controlled trial.' *British Journal of Psychiatry 174*, 56–62.

Canvin, K., Bartlett, A. and Pinfold, V. (2005) 'Acceptability of compulsory powers in the community: the ethical considerations of mental health service users on Supervised Discharge and Guardianship.' *Journal of Medical Ethics 31*, 8, 457–462.

Catty, J., Goddard, K., White, S. and Burns, T. (2005) 'Social networks among users of mental health day care.' *Social Psychiatry and Psychiatric Epidemiology 40*, 6, 467–474.

Chilvers, R., Macdonald, G.M. and Hayes, A.A. (2006) 'Supported housing for people with severe mental disorders.' *Cochrane Database of Systematic Reviews 2006 Issue 4*. Art. No.: CD000453. DOI: 10.1002/14651858. CD000453.pub2.

Churchill, R. (2007) *International Experiences of Using Community Treatment Orders.* London: Institute of Psychiatry, King's College London.

Commander, M., Sashidharan, S., Rana, T. and Ratnayake, T. (2005) 'North Birmingham assertive outreach evaluation: patient characteristics and clinical outcomes.' *Social Psychiatry and Psychiatric Epidemiology 40*, 12, 988–993.

Corney, R.H. and Clare, A.W. (1983) 'The effectiveness of attached social workers in the management of depressed women in general practice.' *British Journal of Social Work 13*, 1, 57–74.

Craig, T.K.J., Garety, P., Power, P., Rahaman, N., *et al.* (2004) 'The Lambeth Early Onset (LEO) Team: randomised controlled trial of the effectiveness of specialised care for early psychosis.' *British Medical Journal 329*, 7474, 1067–1070.

Crowther, R.E., Marshall, M., Bond, G.R. and Huxley, P. (2001) 'Helping people with severe mental illness to obtain work: systematic review.' *British Medical Journal 322*, 7280, 204–208.

Department of Health (1999) *National Service Framework for Mental Health: Modern Standards and Service Models.* London: Department of Health.

Dunn, L. (2001) 'Mental health act assessments: does a community treatment team make a difference?' *International Journal of Social Psychiatry 47*, 2, 1–19.

Dutt, K. and Webber, M. (2009) 'Access to social capital and social support amongst South East Asian women with severe mental health problems: a cross-sectional survey.' *International Journal of Social Psychiatry*. Advanced access published 4 September 2009 as doi:2010.1177/0020764009106415.

Forrester-Jones, R., Carpenter, J., Coolen-Schrijner, P., Cambridge, P. *et al.* (2006) 'The social networks of people with intellectual disability living in the community 12 years after resettlement from long-stay hospitals.' *Journal of Applied Research in Intellectual Disabilities 19*, 4, 285–295.

Friedli, L. (2009) *Mental Health, Resilience and Inequalities.* Copenhagen: WHO.

Furminger, E. and Webber, M. (2009) 'The effect of crisis resolution and home treatment on assessments under the Mental Health Act 1983: an increased workload for Approved Social Workers?' *British Journal of Social Work 39*, 5, 901–917.

Garety, P.A., Craig, T.K.J., Dunn, G., Fornells-Ambrojo, M. *et al.* (2006) 'Specialised care for early psychosis: symptoms, social functioning and patient satisfaction: randomised controlled trial.' *The British Journal of Psychiatry 188*, 1, 37–45.

Gibbons, J.S., Butler, J., Urwin, P. and Gibbons, J.L. (1978) 'Evaluation of a social work service for self-poisoning patients.' *British Journal of Psychiatry 133*, 2, 111–118.

Glover, G., Arts, G. and Babu, K.S. (2006) 'Crisis resolution/home treatment teams and psychiatric admission rates in England.' *British Journal of Psychiatry 189*, 5, 441–445.

Gould, N. (2006) 'An inclusive approach to knowledge for mental health social work practice and policy.' *British Journal of Social Work 36*, 1, 109–125.

Gould, N., Huxley, P. and Tew, J. (2007) 'Finding a direction for social research in mental health: establishing priorities and developing capacity.' *Journal of Social Work 7*, 2, 179–196.

Greatley, A. and Ford, R. (2002) *Out of the Maze. Reaching and Supporting Londoners with Severe Mental Health Problems.* London: The Sainsbury Centre for Mental Health.

Green, B. (1987) 'Group art therapy as an adjunct to treatment for chronic outpatients.' *Hospital and Community Psychiatry 38*, 9, 988–991.

Harrington, R., Kerfoot, M., Dyer, E., McNiven, F., Gill, J., Harrington, V., Woodham, A. and Byford, S. (1998) 'Randomized trial of a home-based family intervention for children who have deliberately poisoned themselves.' *Journal of the American Acadamy of Child and Adolescent Psychiatry 37*, 512–518.

Harris, T. (2001) 'Recent developments in understanding the psychosocial aspects of depression.' *British Medical Bulletin 57*, 1, 17–32.

Harris, T., Brown, G.W. and Robinson, R. (1999) 'Befriending as an intervention for chronic depression among women in an inner city. 1: Randomised controlled trial.' *British Journal of Psychiatry 174*, 219–224.

Harrison, G. (2002) 'Ethnic minority and the Mental Health Act.' *British Journal of Psychiatry 180*, 3, 198–199.

Hatfield, B. (2008) 'Powers to detain under mental health legislation in England and the role of the Approved Social Worker: an analysis of patterns and trends under the 1983 Mental Health Act in six local authorities.' *British Journal of Social Work 38*, 8, 1553–1571.

Hatfield, B., Bindman, J. and Pinfold, V. (2004) 'Evaluating the use of Supervised Discharge and Guardianship in cases of severe mental illness: a follow-up study.' *Journal of Mental Health 13*, 2, 197–209.

Hatfield, B., Shaw, J., Pinfold, V., Bindman, J. *et al.* (2001) 'Managing severe mental illness in the community using the Mental Health Act 1983: a comparison of Supervised Discharge and Guardianship in England.' *Social Psychiatry and Psychiatric Epidemiology 36*, 10, 508–515.

Henderson, C., Flood, C., Leese, M., Thornicroft, G., Sutherby, K. and Szmukler, G. (2004) 'Effect of joint crisis plans on use of compulsory treatment in psychiatry: single blind randomised controlled trial.' *British Medical Journal 329*, 7458, 136.

Her Majesty's Government (2007) *Putting People First: A Shared Vision and Commitment to the Transformation of Adult Social Care.* London: Department of Health.

Hopkins, C. and Niemiec, S. (2007) 'Mental health crisis at home: service user perspectives on what helps and what hinders.' *Journal of Psychiatric and Mental Health Nursing 14*, 3, 310–318.

Howard, L. and Thornicroft, G. (2006) 'Patient preference randomised controlled trials in mental health research.' *British Journal of Psychiatry 188*, 4, 303–304.

Hunt, I.M., Kapur, N., Webb, R., Robinson, J. *et al.* (2009) 'Suicide in recently discharged psychiatric patients: a case-control study.' *Psychological Medicine 39*, 3, 443–449.

Huxley, P., Evans, S., Burns, T., Fahy, T. and Green, J. (2001) 'Quality of life outcome in a randomized controlled trial of case management.' *Social Psychiatry and Psychiatric Epidemiology 36*, 249–255.

Johnson, L., Lundstrom, O., Aberg-Wistedt, A. and Mathé, A. A. (2003) 'Social support in bipolar disorder: its relevance to remission and relapse.' *Bipolar Disorders 5*, 2, 129–137.

Johnson, S. (2007) 'Crisis resolution and intensive home treatment teams.' *Psychiatry 6*, 8, 339–342.

Johnson, S., Nolan, F., Pilling, S., Sandor, A. *et al.* (2005) 'Randomised controlled trial of acute mental health care by a crisis resolution team: the north Islington crisis study.' *British Medical Journal 331*, 599–603.

Joy, C.B., Adams, C.E. and Rice, K. (1998) 'Crisis intervention for people with severe mental illnesses.' *The Cochrane Library, Issue 4*. Oxford: Update Software.

Killaspy, H., Bebbington, P., Blizard, R., Johnson, S. *et al.* (2006) 'The REACT study: randomised evaluation of assertive community treatment in north London.' *British Medical Journal 332*, 815–819.

Kingsford, R. and Webber, M. (2010) 'Social deprivation and the outcomes of crisis resolution and home treatment for people with mental health problems: an historical cohort study.' *Health and Social Care in the Community*. Advanced access published 12 May 2010 as doi:2010.1111/j.1365-2524.2010.00918.x.

Kuipers, E., Garety, P., Fowler, D., Dunn, G. *et al.* (1997) 'London-East Anglia randomised controlled trial of cognitive-behavioural therapy for psychosis. I: effects of the treatment phase.' *British Journal of Psychiatry 171*, 4, 319–327.

Kuipers, E., Holloway, F., Rabe-Hesketh, S. and Tennakoon, L. (2004) 'An RCT of early intervention in psychosis: Croydon Outreach and Assertive Support Team (COAST).' *Social Psychiatry and Psychiatric Epidemiology 39*, 5, 358–363.

Leff, H.S., Chow, C.M., Pepin, R., Conley, J., Allen, I.E. and Seaman, C. A. (2009) 'Does one size fit all? What we can and can't learn from a meta-analysis of housing models for persons with mental illness.' *Psychiatric Services 60*, 4, 473–482.

Leff, J. and Warner, R. (2006) *Social Inclusion of People with Mental Illness*. Cambridge: Cambridge University Press.

Lelliott, P. and Audini, B. (2003) 'Trends in the use of Part II of the Mental Health Act 1983 in seven English local authority areas.' *British Journal of Psychiatry 182*, 68–70.

Lin, N. (2001) *Social Capital: A Theory of Social Structure and Action*. Cambridge: Cambridge University Press.

Lloyd-Evans, B., Slade, M., Jagielska, D. and Johnson, S. (2009) 'Residential alternatives to acute psychiatric hospital admission: systematic review.' *The British Journal of Psychiatry 195*, 2, 109–117.

Malone, D., Marriott, S., Newton-Howes, G., Simmonds, S. and Tyrer, P. (2007) 'Community mental health teams (CMHTs) for people with severe mental illnesses and disordered personality.' *Cochrane Database of Systematic Reviews Issue 3*. Chichester: John Wiley and Sons.

Marriott, S., Audini, B., Lelliott, P., Webb, Y. and Duffett, R. (2001) 'Research into the Mental Health Act: a qualitative study of the views of those using or affected by it.' *Journal of Mental Health 10*, 1, 33–39.

Marshall, M. and Lockwood, A. (1998) 'Assertive community treatment for people with severe mental disorders.' *The Cochrane Library, Issue 2*. Oxford: Update Software.

Marshall, M., Gray, A., Lockwood, A. and Green, R. (1998) 'Case management for people with severe mental disorders.' *Cochrane Database of Systematic Reviews, Issue 2*. Art. No.: CD000050. DOI: 10.1002/14651858.

McPherson, A. and Jones, R.G. (2003) 'The use of sections 2 and 3 of the Mental Health Act (1983) with older people: a prospective study.' *Aging and Mental Health 7*, 2, 153–157.

Morgan, C., Mallett, R., Hutchinson, G., Bagalkote, H. *et al.* (2005) 'Pathways to care and ethnicity. 1: Sample characteristics and compulsory admission: report from the AeSOP study.' *British Journal of Psychiatry 186*, 4, 281–289.

Murray, J., Easter, A. and Bellringer, S. (2007) *Evaluation of Capital Volunteering. Third interim report: outcomes and experiences at six months*. London: Health Service and Population Research Department, Institute of Psychiatry, King's College London.

Nathan, J. and Webber, M. (2010) 'Mental health social work and the bureau-medicalisation of mental health care: identity in a changing world.' *Journal of Social Work Practice 24*, 1, 15–28.

National Collaborating Centre for Mental Health (2004) *Depression: Management of Depression in Primary and Secondary Care. National Clinical Practice Guideline Number 23.* London: British Psychological Society and Royal College of Psychiatrists.

National Collaborating Centre for Mental Health (2006) *Bipolar Disorder. The Management of Bipolar Disorder in Adults, Children and Adolescents, in Primary and Secondary Care. National Clinical Practice Guideline Number 38.* London: British Psychological Society and Gaskell.

National Collaborating Centre for Mental Health (2009) *Schizophrenia. Core Interventions in the Treatment and Management of Schizophrenia in Primary and Secondary Care (Update). National Clinical Practice Guideline Number 82.* London: National Institute for Health and Clinical Excellence.

Nelson, G., Sylvestre, J., Aubry, T., George, L. and Trainor, J. (2007) 'Housing choice and control, housing quality, and control over professional support as contributors to the subjective quality of life and community adaptation of people with severe mental illness.' *Administration and Policy in Mental Health and Mental Health Services Research 34*, 2, 89–100.

Nilforooshan, R., Amin, R. and Warner, J. (2009) 'Ethnicity and outcome of appeal after detention under the Mental Health Act 1983.' *Psychiatric Bulletin 33*, 8, 288–290.

Papageorgiou, A., King, M., Janmohamed, A., Davidson, O. and Dawson, J. (2002) 'Advance directives for patients compulsorily admitted to hospital with serious mental illness: randomised controlled trial.' *British Journal of Psychiatry 181*, 513–519.

Pawson, R., Boaz, A., Grayson, L., Long, A. and Barnes, C. (2003) *Knowledge Review 3: Types and Quality of Knowledge in Social Care.* London: Social Care Institute for Excellence/Policy Press.

Petersen, L., Jeppesen, P., Thorup, A., Abel, M.-B. *et al.* (2005) 'A randomised multicentre trial of integrated versus standard treatment for patients with a first episode of psychotic illness.' *British Medical Journal 331*, 7517, 602–605.

Pharoah, F.M., Mari, J.J. and Streiner, D. (2003) 'Family intervention for schizophrenia.' *The Cochrane Library, Issue 1.* Oxford: Update Software.

Pinfold, V., Bindman, J., Thornicroft, G., Franklin, D. and Hatfield, B. (2001) 'Persuading the persuadable: evaluating compulsory treatment in England using Supervised Discharge Orders.' *Social Psychiatry and Psychiatric Epidemiology 36*, 5, 260–266.

Pinfold, V., Rowe, A., Hatfield, B., Bindman, J. *et al.* (2002) 'Lines of resistance: exploring professionals' views of compulsory community supervision.' *Journal of Mental Health 11*, 2, 177–190.

Quirk, A., Lelliott, P., Audini, B. and Buston, K. (2000) *Performing the Act: A Qualitative Study of the Process of Mental Health Act Assessments. Final report to the Department of Health.* London: Royal College of Psychiatrists' Research Unit.

Rapaport, J. and Manthorpe, J. (2008) 'Family matters: developments concerning the role of the nearest relative and social worker under mental health law in England and Wales.' *British Journal of Social Work 38*, 6, 1115–1131.

Rimmer, M.A., O'Connor, S. and Anderson, D. (2002) 'Appeal against detention under the Mental Health Act 1983: relationship to age and incapacity.' *International Journal of Geriatric Psychiatry 17*, 9, 884–885.

Rog, D.J. (2004) 'The evidence on supported housing.' *Psychiatric Rehabilitation Journal 27*, 4, 334–344.

Scott, A. and Freeman, C. (1992) 'Edinburgh primary care depression study: treatment outcome, patient satisfaction, and cost after 16 weeks.' *British Medical Journal 304*, 6831, 883–887.

Shankar, J., Martin, J. and McDonald, C. (2009) 'Emerging areas of practice for mental health social workers: education and employment.' *Australian Social Work 62*, 1, 28–44.

Shaw, P., Hotopf, M. and Davies, A. (2003) 'In relative danger? The outcome of patients discharged by their nearest relative from sections 2 and 3 of the Mental Health Act.' *Psychiatric Bulletin 27*, 2, 50–54.

Siegel, C.E., Samuels, J., Tang, D.-I., Berg, I., Jones, K. and Hopper, K. (2006) 'Tenant outcomes in supported housing and community residences in New York City.' *Psychiatric Services 57*, 7, 982–991.

Singh, D.K. and Moncrieff, J. (2009) 'Trends in mental health review tribunal and hospital managers' hearings in north-east London 1997–2007.' *Psychiatric Bulletin 33*, 1, 15–17.

Singh, S.P. and Fisher, H.L. (2007) 'Early intervention services.' *Psychiatry 6*, 8, 333–338.

Slack, K. and Webber, M. (2008) 'Do we care? Adult mental health professionals' attitudes towards supporting service users' children.' *Child and Family Social Work 13*, 1, 72–79.

Slade, M. and Priebe, S. (2001) 'Are randomised controlled trials the only gold that glitters?' *British Journal of Psychiatry 179*, 4, 286–287.

Song, L. (2007) *Your body knows who you know: social capital and depressive symptoms in the United States*, Annual Meeting of American Sociological Association, New York.

Song, L. and Lin, N. (2009) 'Social capital and health inequality: evidence from Taiwan.' *Journal of Health and Social Behavior 50*, 2, 149–163.

Tew, J., Gould, N., Abankwa, D., Barnes, H. *et al.* (2006) *Values and Methodologies for Social Research in Mental Health*. Bristol: Policy Press.

Ulrich, G. (2007) 'The additional therapeutic effect of group music therapy for schizophrenic patients: a randomized study.' *Acta Psychiatrica Scandinavica 166*, 5, 362–370.

Wall, S., Churchill, R., Hotopf, M., Buchanan, A. and Wessely, S. (1999) *A Systematic Review of Research Relating to the Mental Health Act (1983)*. London: Department of Health.

Ward, E., King, M., Lloyd, M., Bower, P. *et al.* (2000) 'Randomised controlled trial of non-directive counselling, cognitive-behaviour therapy, and usual general practitioner care for patients with depression. I: Clinical effectiveness.' *British Medical Journal 321*, 7273, 1383–1388.

Warner, R. (2000) *The Environment of Schizophrenia: Innovations in Practice, Policy and Communications*. London: Routledge.

Webber, M. (2008a) *Evidence-Based Policy and Practice in Mental Health Social Work*. Exeter: Learning Matters.

Webber, M. (2008b) *Access to Social Capital and the Course of Depression: A Prospective Study*. PhD thesis, London: Institute of Psychiatry, King's College London.

Webber, M. and Huxley, P. (2004) 'Social exclusion and risk of emergency compulsory admission: a case-control study.' *Social Psychiatry and Psychiatric Epidemiology 39*, 12, 1000–1009.

Webber, M. and Huxley, P. (2007) 'Measuring access to social capital: the validity and reliability of the Resource Generator-UK and its association with common mental disorder.' *Social Science and Medicine 65*, 3, 481–492.

Wolff, N. (2000) 'Using randomized controlled trials to evaluate socially complex services: problems, challenges and recommendations.' *Journal of Mental Health Policy and Economics 3*, 2, 97–109.

Part II

Theoretical Perspectives

Chapter 6

The Place of Psychoanalytic Theory and Research in Reflective Social Work Practice

Jack Nathan

Introduction

In this Chapter I will outline a range of different psychoanalytic concepts and will demonstrate their relevance in direct work with social work clients. I will also refer to the burgeoning evidence base that the psychoanalytic community has begun to develop in recent years. This research has added weight to the uniquely rich ways of thinking that psychoanalysis offers. We are no longer in the position reported nearly 40 years ago by Rachman (1971) at the Institute of Psychiatry who boldly concluded that there was no 'satisfactory evidence to support the claim that psychotherapy is effective' (p.162). Likewise, we are beyond the situation in the late 1990s where psychoanalysis was seen as being in a state of terminable decline (Nathan 2002a) and casework skills, which were considered irrelevant for social work practice (Lyons 1997), had all but disappeared (Martindale *et al.* 2000).

In many ways the psychoanalytic account I will give, whatever its theoretical complexities, is one that is bred in the bones of most social work practitioners who understand the key role of relationship-building in any therapeutic endeavour. It is no surprise to learn that as long ago as 1962 a book called *The Caseworker's Use of Relationships* (Ferard and Hunnybun 1962) was published, making precisely this point. Its contemporary incarnation is found in the importance placed on 'working in partnership'. The research base for this methodology has been summarised by Cheetham *et al.* (1996) who discuss how service users appreciate the practitioner's ability to listen, negotiate and enter into partnership to deal with their problems. It is the psychoanalytic understanding of the dynamics that such work involves that I will discuss in this chapter. Communication, psychoanalytically speaking, is conceptualised in terms of some key concepts that I will elaborate using examples taken from social work practice that has been presented in the consultation group I facilitate on the MSc in Mental Health Social Work with Children and Adults programme (see Nathan 2002b for more details).

Key psychoanalytic concepts 1: the transference relationship

I will begin with a case study to underline the fact that the transference is not merely an interesting abstraction for psychoanalytic practitioners, but is a construct for use in everyday practice. In all the examples used in this Chapter names have been changed to preserve confidentiality.

CASE STUDY 6.1 THE DISTURBED PRACTITIONER

A male mental health social worker reported on a disturbing encounter with Barbara, a client he was seeing for the first time. Barbara accused the worker of being nasty and cruel as his only interest was in seeing her back in hospital.

At one level, it is easy to understand that Barbara could be extremely anxious about seeing a new practitioner whose intentions are unclear. On further discussion in the consultation group it emerged that Barbara had been severely abused in childhood by her father. Barbara came to the encounter having had the experience of a father who polluted his relationship with her through abuse. But you may well ask: what has this to do with Barbara's response to her new worker?

It was Freud (1896) who originally discovered both the nature of this experience and its consequences. He called it 'the transference'. It is a term that encapsulates the relationship dynamic that inevitably arises in engaging with our clients and so, equally inevitably, fundamentally affects the work we do with them. Freud (1905) described the nature of the transference relationship as 'a whole series of psychological experiences that are revived, *not as belonging to the past*, but as applying to the person of the physician *at the present moment*' (my emphases) (p.157). It seems that the old joke claiming 'that the problem with history is that it has no future' turns out to be untrue. The traumatic past usually casts a long shadow over the disturbingly ruminative present.

It is in this psychological climate that we could begin to see that Barbara was carrying an historical burden that corrupted so many of her interactions. But more than this, we could see that she 'understood' that those in authority, and especially male figures, were not to be trusted. The practitioner met both requirements for distrust – he was an authority Figure and male, just like her father. The difficulty for Barbara, let alone the practitioner, was that this meant her automatic experience of male authority figures remained essentially hostile. Clearly, this has hugely detrimental and limiting consequences in terms of her experience of her psychosocial world in which emotional arousal mostly revolves around disturbance and panic.

It is striking that some of the work pioneered by Freud over one hundred years ago has, over the last two to three decades, begun to be underpinned by research on the brain. Advances in the neurobiological study of the brain show the role played by regulatory hard-wired structures and functions. These psychobiological mechanisms located in the right hemisphere of the brain process social and emotional information at non-conscious levels regulating feelings, motivation and even bodily states (Schore 1997).

It adds another layer to our understanding of Barbara's 'instinctual' response to the male practitioner. Her reaction is a product of both her instinctive genetic endowment and her psychosocial developmental environment, that is, how she was treated as a child. It is for this reason that the neuroscientist Schore (2000) has pointed to the need to integrate the psychological and the biological as it is now clear that the biological system, in what is termed 'the *emotional* brain' (Schore 2000; my emphasis), is profoundly implicated in regulating affectively driven instinctive behaviour. It is through the seminal work of Bowlby that we have come to understand these processes (see Chapter 9). What we now understand is that Barbara comes into the encounter with the new worker with a pre-existing 'internal working model' (Bowlby 1988), or what I call 'the relationship template' (Nathan 2006).

Key psychoanalytic concepts 2: projection

If the transference operates as the structurally hard-wired way in which Barbara engages in organising her experiences of self and the world around her, what are the operational mechanisms for creating these experiences over and over again? Let us consider another case study.

CASE STUDY 6.2 *THE FRIGHTENED CLIENT*

Carole encountered considerable suffering through her experience that people were often hostile towards her in the street. Of course, at times, they were. More often they weren't. On one occasion Carole was on a bus and thought she was being kicked by the passengers sitting behind her. She was so incensed that when the pair got off the bus she followed them and kicked them from behind, just as she had been, with a triumphant sense of 'see how you like it'. As soon as they turned round, without needing to say anything, Carole was horrified to see that she had attacked two elderly women who looked terrified and uncomprehending. What happened to produce this experience, so devoid of any externally validated reality?

Once more it is Freud (1896) who began to provide the answer when he drew attention to a mechanism of defence, or what is more accurately described as a mechanism of survival, which he termed 'projection'. He defined this as a defence in which the individual unconsciously engages in two psychological activities. The first involves splitting off unwanted, usually hated, parts of their personality and experience; followed, secondly, by attributing these characteristics onto 'bad' others. Homophobic attacks by young men can be understood as attempts to get rid of their dread of homosexuality at a time when, unconsciously, their sexual identity may be fragile. In a violent act of public machismo, there is a wish to kill off any association with this possibility within. Freud (1925) puts it starkly when he suggests that in its earliest oral form, it is as if the infant is saying '"I should like to eat this" (the Good) or, "I should like to spit it out" (the Bad)' (p.439). Psychologically, what is 'bad' is projected, perceived as external (i.e. not within oneself), and finally expelled.

Melanie Klein took up Freud's ideas agreeing that the 'bad' attributes an individual expels are *consciously identified* with the person or group onto whom they are projected. However, Klein (1946) added that the attributes which have been got rid of – 'spat out' – remain *unconsciously identified* with the unwanted and hated part of the self. She termed this process 'projective identification', suggestive of the fact that whatever is projected is also internally identified with. Klein is making clear that there can be no ultimate evacuation onto others (e.g. marginalised groups such as bisexuals, lesbian and gay men, Jews or Eastern Europeans) of all that we find unpalatable in ourselves. In short, it is still a part of our (unconscious) self. Coming to terms with our own complex contradictions is a lifelong task we all share and succeed in to a greater or lesser extent.

This has profound and significant implications in our work. In Carole's case (Case Study 6.2) for many years she was able to unselfconsciously perpetuate what Feldman (2008) called a sense of grievance, in which her explanations for so much that was wrong lay in the external environment, based on the reality of a childhood mired in abuse. This meant that Carole looked, and often justifiably found, an object world that was hostile and abusive exactly in the way she viscerally experienced the attack on her that fateful day on the bus. Crucial to Carole's understanding was her unquestioned conviction that once more she had to suffer the indignity of yet more abuse. In this state of mind there was no other possible explanation for her experience or for what the women were actually doing: the violence was in them, she was again its victim.

Witnessing the women's reactions brought her, in this case, literally face to face with her own hostility; she had to confront her own violent self. Carole was no longer in the all too familiar position of being a victim with a grievance. On this occasion Carole understood at a deep emotional level that it was she who was the perpetrator. In theoretical terms this meant that Carole had to take back and own the hostility that was usually projected into the environment. It was a turning point in her development as, despite continuing problems, Carole was never again able to take such a casually non-reflective view of herself as vulnerable to others' violence. Put simply, she was no longer paranoid. I use this term advisedly as it leads directly to what this concept means developmentally from a Kleinian psychoanalytic perspective.

Key psychoanalytic concepts 3: the paranoid-schizoid and the depressive positions

If there is a developmental model within the Kleinian tradition, then it is represented by Melanie Klein's formulation of the paranoid-schizoid and depressive positions. The hesitation implied by the word 'if' centres on the fact that it is not ultimately a developmental model in any chronological sense. Klein is essentially giving descriptive backbone to what she understands to be the nature of human experience. It is an existential account about the struggle every human subject has to manage throughout life. There is therefore never a once-and-for-all resolution, a maturing from the paranoid-schizoid to the depressive position, or what Winnicott (1963) called 'the capacity for concern'. At times of crisis, for example, we are all prone to paranoid-schizoid functioning.

Klein conceptualised the human infant as struggling with enormous anxieties stirred up by an innate conflict, from birth, between life and death instincts. Although current research suggests that the ego exists practically from birth (Stern 1985), the neonate begins life in an extremely fragile state that cannot be managed internally. In Klein's view this is not just because of the environment provided by the caregivers, but also because of the innate destructive instinct that is directed against the self. As a way of dealing with this internal existential threat, the infant resorts to using schizoid mechanisms by splitting the self into two psychic states, either 'good' and 'bad', and projecting ('spitting out') into a 'maternal object' thereby mitigating the dangers posed by self-directed attacks on the nascent self. As a consequence of taking these 'psychic actions', we might say that the infant now has a relationship with two entirely segregated mothers; one with an idealised loving mother and another with a bad hating mother. It is the relationship with the idealised all-giving object that produces the Buddha-like serenity associated with infants who feel comforted. However, because of the projection of the 'bad' self, a second terrifyingly cruel bad mother also confronts the infant who is now assailed by what Klein calls persecutory anxiety, as the destructive self that originated *within*, is viscerally experienced as a fear of annihilation coming from *without*. It is precisely because of these survivalist defensive manoeuvres that the infant in the paranoid-schizoid position is left feeling paranoid. The infant has now 'created' an externally attacking 'bad' mother that is terrifying and hated. For example, infants can exhibit intense states of dread and rage when frustrated by a 'witholding' mother who does not cater immediately to their needs.

According to Klein it is at around four to six months that the baby begins to negotiate the depressive position. This means coming to recognise 'that the loving, good arms, face and breast that fulfil his needs, and the hateful, depriving ones are all part of one whole person' (Hargreaves 1998, p.2). The two mothers, the totally bad and the idealised, are one and the same. This is a pivotal moment for the developing child, as it must face a number of dawning realisations in order to work through the depressive position. First, that the mother is separate, not under their control and that they could lose her. Second, their hateful (full of hate) attacks on the 'bad' mother have meant that the idealised mother has also been under attack. As a result the baby now fears the destructive damage their hostility has wreaked against the loving and loved mother. Thus, they have to deal with the pain they have caused to the now 'whole' mother. Third, a process of mourning begins that includes 'pining' (Hinshelwood 1989) for the loss of the idealised object. And finally, the infant has to come to terms with a relationship world which is not just made up of 'good' and 'bad', but carries the emotional burden of ambivalence, hating as well as loving the object of the baby's profoundest desires and needs.

In working through the depressive position the child is engaged in an experience that is transformatory. This is because, according to the Kleinian paradigm, human experience is mediated through anxiety. In the paranoid-schizoid position it is persecutory, the human subject is under attack. In the depressive position the nature of this experience fundamentally changes as the human subject comes to emotionally understand that they too are active 'agents', with justified (and sometimes unjustified) feelings of hate and envy, and has to deal with these in their most intimate relationships. Maturity in psychoanalytic terms entails the capacity to manage ambivalence; namely, being able to hold both hating as well as loving feelings towards the same person.

What helps the infant combat these massively complex and painful processes are the repeated experiences of what Winnicott (1960) called 'the good enough mother' who can be comforting and is not destroyed by the baby's sometimes hateful demands. Where the external object provides a generally loving 'secure base' (Bowlby 1988) the baby can internalise a good maternal object from which they can develop and grow.

Even if this theoretical journey through the intra- and inter-psychic experiences of the infant seems fanciful or too abstract, what research has now established through observations of mother–infant interactions is that the mother's actions are meaningful to the infant and that the infant responds to these meaning-generating engagements with the mother. In other words, human relationships are primary and 'foundational' to the infant's meaning systems and very subjectivity (Boston Change Process Study Group 2007).

Returning to Carole (Case Study 6.2), we can now see that her childhood abuse experiences meant that she had not been able to, or helped to, successfully negotiate the depressive position. Instead, she remained stuck in the paranoid-schizoid position. Meaning could only be understood in terms of her own disturbing, and thereby distorting, perceptions. The women on the bus were not separate, but had become incorporated into an internal drama, all too familiar to Carole, where they did her damage. By occupying the paranoid-schizoid position the women's 'kicks' retriggered Carole's narrative of lifelong abuse and suffering. It was only on seeing the projected pain in the women's faces that Carole had the insight to recognise that she, not they, was the abuser. She had so successfully projected her internal world that they were now the abused. As stated above, Carole was able to make use of this experience to move to depressive position functioning. This meant she was now able to consider others' actions and motivations as separate from herself, not always in self-referential terms. And of course, most importantly, Carole no longer felt as persecuted by people, something that over the years had got her into some highly distressing anti-social, and sometimes serious, incidents.

Recent research helps us to understand more about childhood development and its impact on later adult life for those who suffer like Carole. It is in the relatively new psychoanalytic field of mentalisation-based treatment (MBT), that Bateman and Fonagy (2004) have undertaken research based on the child's capacity to mentalise. By this is meant the child's evolving development in the first five years of life to make sense of their own, as well as others', mental states. Fonagy (2003) has shown that being able to mentalise is a developmental achievement that enables the child to know about and interpret their own experiences as well as what others are thinking and feeling. Crucially, this capacity emerges through interpersonal experience with their primary carers. It is not a genetic given 'as it critically depends on interaction with more mature minds, assuming these are benign, reflective and sufficiently attuned (to the child's needs)' (Fonagy 2008, p.4). Sadly for Carole, as well as those like her often diagnosed with a borderline personality disorder (BPD), this is not a picture of the environment in which they were brought up in. Rather, theirs is usually an experience of childhood maltreatment in a terrifying and insecure emotional environment. Indeed, there is now considerable research evidence pointing to the fact that abused children have deficits in their ability to accurately mentalise and that those with BPD are poor at mentalisation following experiences of severe abuse (Fonagy *et al.* 1996).

Key psychoanalytic concepts 4: the use of environment-centred and patient-centred interpretations

In this section I address how to work with people in the paranoid-schizoid position where someone is either ready *to feel persecuted by* us and/or *leaves us feeling controlled and impotent.*

In a book called *Psychic Retreats,* the psychoanalyst John Steiner (1993) devotes a highly instructive Chapter to psychoanalytic technique. He begins by giving an account of the kind of client who leaves us feeling stuck and impotent. Steiner makes the seemingly paradoxical point that this state of affairs exists alongside the client's sometimes urgent need for contact, typically saying things like 'I don't know what I'd do without your visits to see me'.

In outline, these dynamics were present with a client brought by a student to the consultation group (Case Study 6.3).

CASE STUDY 6.3 THE STUCK PRACTITIONER

Yvonne's children aged eight and four were referred to children's services as staff at school had seen her struggling to manage their unruly behaviour. She was depressed and exhibiting features associated with borderline personality disorder. Her social worker conveyed, with some frustration, the sense that no amount of support seemed to help bring about any change. Yvonne continued to express her long-standing grievance against her estranged husband due to his lack of support in looking after their two young children. What are we to make of this impasse?

The first difficulty was the practitioner's, not the client's. What became clear in the group discussion was that Yvonne did not share the worker's unconscious assumption that she wanted to use the space to think about the seemingly parlous nature of her marital relationship. This was all the more surprising as Yvonne was well able to articulate her understanding of the detrimental effect it was having on her children as well as on herself. Yet this is to miss the point. Here we see an example of what Steiner considers a client longing to *be understood* (note the passive grammatical form), not looking to *acquire understanding.* Yvonne could be more properly described as a woman tormented by her life situation, desperate to have someone on her side, giving her space to evacuate her difficulties into the worker; in psychoanalytic terms, 'a toilet mother'.

The worker's interventions revolved around understanding how it was hard for Yvonne to cope given her husband's verbal attacks and lack of support. She would say things like 'It sounds like you really tried hard over the years', but 'he was not able to show you love' and 'something about his behaviour made you start doubting yourself'. Finally, the worker acknowledged Yvonne's experience by saying 'It sounds like you have all been affected, you and the children', to which Yvonne responded by complaining that it had affected her behaviour and her 'ability to deal with stress, to deal with feelings of resentment and anger'.

Adapting the psychoanalytic constructs Steiner (1993) has developed, to make them more pertinent to social work practice, I have coined the phrase 'environment-centred' interpretations or interventions to describe this dynamic. The practitioner was 'attuning' (Stern 1985) or 'validating' (Linehan 1993) the client's experience in a way she had not been attuned to or validated as a child. There is research evidence suggesting that strategies like validation and acceptance interventions may play an important role in bringing about change (Koerner and Linehan 2000). The practitioner was certainly providing this kind of support but it appeared to have the opposite effect.

These environment-centred interventions also had a paralysing quality since the worker was, by implication, providing a form of legitimacy to Yvonne's narrative as this account made plain that the children's problems were due to her husband. There was no sense of ownership of her state of mind. She was a victim just like the children and could not therefore be expected to shoulder any adult agency. In short, our formulation was of a client functioning with many of the characteristics associated with the paranoid-schizoid position and whose aim was to *be understood*, not to *gain understanding* of what she was projecting into her husband (including what Yvonne correctly perceived), her part in maintaining the familial dynamics and, above all, her responsibility for what was going on.

Steiner (1993) agrees that validating the client's experience is crucial. Certainly, Yvonne was relieved to have someone in authority, a good transference object, giving her an experience of being heard. This aspect cannot be over-estimated. Demonstrating that the client has been understood is perhaps *the* cornerstone of any therapeutic work. However, if it is a necessary condition for good work, it is not always sufficient to facilitate change. Worse than this it may even be counter-productive, as what is being enacted over and over again is a message that legitimised Yvonne's passivity. Steiner (1993) daringly suggests that as a way of tackling these potentially interminable threats to progress we sometimes have to take risks and give what he calls 'patient-centred interpretations even if this may lead to a persecuted patient' (p.144). In patient-centred interpretations Steiner is shifting the focus of the work and challenging the client to look at their role in what is happening. This means having to face that we are all participants and, more than this, active agents, however much there is a wish to deny this 'fact' of life. It is a form of communication that implies personal responsibility, one that cannot entirely be lodged in the other, the bad object. Yvonne's husband could not be a repository of all that was wrong in her life.

Taking courage from the consultation group the social worker was encouraged to make more patient-centred interpretations, in particular to challenge statements that put all blame on her husband. During the next case presentation it was evident that the worker had taken up Yvonne's acknowledgement of her 'stress' and asked how it affected *her* parenting, thereby shifting the emphasis to her behaviour as agent not a victim. In an honest response that testified to her trust in the worker, Yvonne divulged that she was sometimes, 'the most terrifying mother in the world'. Perhaps not surprisingly Yvonne was soon blaming her husband once more. But on this occasion, because the worker was able to maintain the patient-centred stance concentrating on Yvonne's agency, she rather gently but firmly came back with: 'You have said quite a lot about your struggle to manage. Can you tell me a bit more about what you are doing when you are being the terrifying mother?' Yvonne then gave a harrowing account of shouting at the children, which the worker then linked to Yvonne's own experience as a child. Yvonne began to cry as she recognised that she did not want 'to put the kids through what I went through' and she could also identify with her 'mother's massive struggles'. Although no 'solution' magically emerged, the worker felt she was working with a client who was no longer stuck but one who was now able to think about her role in what was going on with the children.

It is worth noting that it was the shift *in the worker* from interventions which were predominantly environment-centred to interventions which were patient-centred that brought about change. In a schematic way we can say that whilst environment-centred interventions can validate the client's emotional world, as they feel *understood*, they can also reinforce paranoid-schizoid functioning. By contrast, patient-centred interventions can help the client develop an adult self as agent through negotiating the depressive position. Despite the profound pain, so clearly expressed by Yvonne, associated with *understanding* her projections, there was now hope. There was a chance she would not be stuck in her life nor, as she was all too aware, would she shape her children's futures with a similar sense of grievance and victimhood.

These case studies highlight that reflective practice confronts the practitioner with hugely complex dilemmas many of which we are not conscious of. The psychoanalyst Bion (1974) goes so far as to say that in 'every consulting room there ought to be two rather frightened people; the patient and the psychoanalyst' (p.13). I will now turn to look at the powerful emotions inevitably stirred up in working with our clients, referred to, in psychoanalytic terms, as the practitioner's counter-transference.

Key psychoanalytic concepts 5: the counter-transference
(a) Counter-transference: idiosyncratic and indicative forms

The current view of counter-transference is that it refers to the totality of the practitioner's emotional responses to their client. It was Freud (1910) who coined the term, specifically emphasising its disruptive connotation, observing that as practitioners we are limited by 'our own complexes and internal resistances' (p.289), that is, the personal issues we bring to our work. He was right. However, the view that counter-transference is simply a manifestation of the worker's 'neurosis' and can therefore stifle therapeutic work began to be questioned in the early 1950s. A seminal paper by Paula Heimann (1950) led the way by suggesting that the counter-transference (the feelings aroused in the practitioner) could also be understood as an 'instrument of research', giving us insight into the client's state of mind. Whilst our emotional reactions in the counter-transference are always our own personal responses, in order to distinguish the two views, I term Freud's version, the *idiosyncratic* form of counter-transference and Heimann's the *indicative* form of counter-transference (see Figure 6.1).

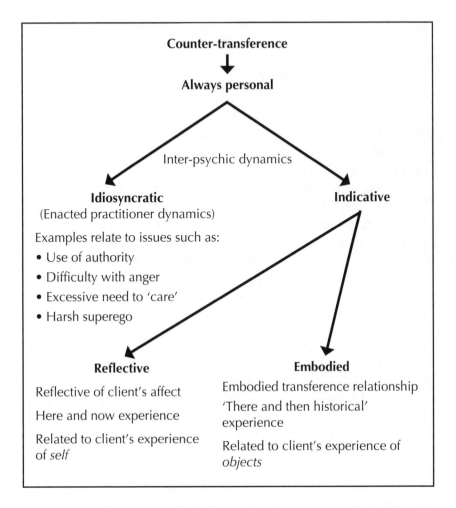

Figure 6.1 The counter-transference

Before moving on to give examples of this special kind of indicative communication, it is important to reaffirm Freud's point. The counter-transference can be misused if we project our problems onto the client along the lines of 'my feelings of upset are really his (the client's) feelings'. To reiterate, our experiences are never anything other than our personal responses. More than this, sometimes our work can touch on areas where we are susceptible, triggering powerful responses due to our own vulnerabilities. A child care social worker I knew had to consider leaving the profession as she found herself feeling unbearably upset seeing mothers being neglectful or abusive to their children at a time when she was unable to have her own. In this example of idiosyncratic counter-transference, the worker understood the distress she felt was primarily her own.

(b) Indicative counter-transference: reflective and embodied forms

As Heimann (1950), Winnicottt (1949) and others showed we can also learn something about the client. It is this form of counter-transference I call indicative. This takes two different forms: *reflective* or *embodied* counter-transference (Samuels 1985) (originally termed concordant or complementary (Racker 1968)).

We shall first consider an example of reflective counter-transference. When the child care social worker first presented Yvonne to the consultation group, her uncensored experience of Yvonne left us in no doubt that here was a practitioner who was endeavouring to do her best, but was mostly left feeling stuck, frustrated and controlled. When considering these counter-transference reactions after we had heard the session, the practitioner's response could be seen in a new light. We reflected on the possibility that Yvonne was projecting an internal experience that she was communicating by emotional impact. This had the effect of arousing an emotional response in the worker that was mirroring, and therefore reflective of, Yvonne's own current life experiences. After all, the worker also felt, however hard she tried, that she was stuck, frustrated and controlled. Being able to capture this form of reflective counter-transference can help the practitioner more easily attune, from inside one's own experience, the nature and intensity of a client's state of mind.

The importance of trying to reflect on our counter-transferences in everyday casework practice cannot be over-estimated (see Chapter 1 for a discussion on advanced reflective practice). Otherwise, the client is in danger of coming up against dynamics of which we are not conscious, in particular those related to what Winnicott (1949) called 'hate in the counter-transference'. This can result in a social work practice that, paraphrasing Winnicott (1949), is adapted to the needs of the practitioner rather than to the needs of the client. We are in particular difficulty when working with clients who are given a personality disorder diagnosis or have personality disordered traits. Research indicates that they are a patient group who are most vulnerable to being disliked as they tend to be 'regarded as manipulative, attention-seeking, annoying' (Lewis and Appleby 1988, p.44).

To complicate matters further, a client can arouse both forms of counter-transference experience. This was the case with Yvonne as the practitioner became more and more frustrated by her. It was a tribute to the worker's capacity that she could contain her frustration towards Yvonne and did not end up giving vent to her feelings and 'spitting them out'. But had she done so, it is likely that we would have seen an enactment of Yvonne's internal drama in which once more she had fashioned an abusive, hostile relationship, emanating from her childhood experiences, replayed once more in her relationship with her husband and now re-evoked in the transference relationship with her worker. It is as if the worker will have been 'lassoed' (Symington 1983) into acting out the part of being a persecuting bad object. It is this quality of 'role responsiveness' (Sandler 1976) which is the preset relationship template that is referred to as embodied (Samuels 1985) or complementary (Racker 1968) counter-transference.

In summary, reflective counter-transference relates to the client's disowned and projected emotional experience of *self*, such as distress or anger in the session that the practitioner is made to bear. Embodied counter-transference, on the other hand, relates to the client's experience of hostile bad *objects* re-evoked and viscerally embodied and played out by the practitioner, usually as a persecuting Figure reminiscent of the internal representation of the client's inner world of objects.

Psychoanalysis and evidence-based practice

I want to end where I began by saying something about the current status of research in psychodynamic work. First, the evidence base is expanding. As with many aspects of psychosocial mental health practice more evidence of effectiveness is required, particularly using randomised controlled trials (see Chapter 5). However, there is increasing evidence of its effectiveness across a range of psychiatric diagnoses. A Cochrane review of short-term psychodynamic psychotherapy for common mental disorders such as anxiety and depression found that benefits from the therapy were generally maintained in medium- and long-term follow-up (Abbass *et al.* 2006). Another meta-analysis of long-term work lasting at least one year concluded that psychodynamic psychotherapy is also an effective intervention for more complex mental disorders (Leichsenring and Rabung 2008). This leads on to the work over the last 20 years on people diagnosed with borderline personality disorder (BPD). The research message is clear: they are a group of people who can be helped to deal with their sometimes harrowing lives. We have come a long way from the time they were considered 'untreatable', as they were in the 1980s when I first became a social worker.

As to the type of treatment, the evidence is, first, that clients with BPD respond positively to structured treatments in outpatient settings. A recent study of two psychoanalytically based therapies, transference-focused psychotherapy (TFP) and supportive psychotherapy (SP), and one cognitive behavioural therapy (CBT)-based treatment, dialectical behavioural therapy (DBT) found that after one year of treatment, when compared with those who received treatment as usual, clients made significant improvements in depression, anxiety, global functioning, and social adjustment, and particular improvements in reduced suicidal behaviour, in the TFP and the DBT arms (Clarkin *et al.* 2007). As discussed above, another psychoanalytically based therapy, mentalisation-based treatment (MBT), pioneered by Bateman and Fonagy (2004) has also shown positive results. In a follow-up to the original study (Bateman and Fonagy 1999), the authors found that as well as having made improvements as a result of the original interventions these clients continued to make positive gains (Bateman and Fonagy 2008). What is particularly striking about these findings is that they suggest that these clients have not only directly benefited from the MBT but, over and beyond this, have internalised something of the good object the worker represented and were able to draw on the now internal good self to continue their own healing process. In this light two findings are particularly of note: that the treated group were more than three times less likely to have attempted suicide post-treatment when compared with the group who received standard care, and that only 13 per cent of them now met the diagnostic criteria for BPD compared with 87 per cent of those in receipt of standard care (Bateman and Fonagy 2008).

One message begins to come through from these research findings. The form of intervention used is less important than the relational quality developed between practitioner and client. In a highly cited review of service user experience it was found that by far the largest predictor of outcome was the nature of the relationship with their worker (Lambert and Barley 2001). It is therefore no surprise to learn that a study on the use of CBT with people with depression discovered that the chances of getting better were enhanced when the practitioner was seen as empathic (Burns and Nolen-Hoeksema 1997).

More studies need to be undertaken that are geared towards 'what works for whom' to help us to tailor our interventions to fit individuals, thereby avoiding a 'one model fits all' approach. This is especially relevant as there is now a growing body of research providing evidence for an increasing range of treatment options for service users.

Concluding thoughts

In this Chapter I have argued that psychoanalytic ideas can play a direct, pertinent and key role in social work practice. This is not to suggest that practitioners have to become therapists, following a particular 'brand' of therapy. Rather, I have tried to show that psychoanalytic ideas can form a centrepiece of practice. These concepts do not have to remain available only to those professionals fully trained in the rarefied and mystifying idiom of psychoanalysis, nor exclusively accessible to a white, middle-class constituency that can afford such treatment. With the rise and rise of CBT, practitioners have been increasingly denied the benefits of exploring the richness and complexity of meaning that their clients bring to the casework encounter. As we have argued in Chapter 1, this knowledge base, amongst others, needs to be more explicitly articulated through an expanded understanding of a range of theoretical models as well an enhanced research literacy. Finally, as in the whole of this volume, there is an understanding now recognised by government (Laming 2009) that practitioners are in daily contact with massively complex, highly charged psychosocial human environments, for which I have attempted to give a psychoanalytic understanding. It is this level of understanding that is now the challenge facing social work. I suggest that this requires practitioners to hold a 'double stance' towards their clients. One that is respectful of their experience and another of curiosity and confrontation where necessary, so that the reality of these sometimes life-and-death situations are faced and we are not drawn to collusion with all the inherent danger this poses, especially in child protection cases or in work with suicidal people.

References

Abbass, A.A., Hancock, J.T., Henderson, J. and Kisely, S.R. (2006) *Short-Term Psychodynamic Psychotherapies for Common Mental Disorders*. Cochrane Database of Systematic Reviews. Issue 4. Art. No.: CD004687. DOI: 10.1002/14651858.CD004687.pub3.

Bateman, A. and Fonagy, P. (1999) 'Effectiveness of partial hospitalization in the treatment of borderline personality disorder: a randomized controlled trial.' *American Journal of Psychiatry 156*, 10, 1563–1569.

Bateman, A.W. and Fonagy, P. (2004) *Psychotherapy for Borderline Personality Disorder: Mentalisation-Based Treatment*. Oxford: Oxford University Press.

Bateman, A.W. and Fonagy, P. (2008) '8-year follow-up of patients treated for borderline personality: mentalisation-based treatment versus treatment as usual.' *American Journal of Psychiatry 165*, 631–638.

Bion, W.R. (1974) *Brazilian Lectures.* London: Karnac.

Boston Change Process Study Group (2007) 'The foundational level of psychodynamic meaning: implicit process in relation to conflict, defense and the dynamic unconscious.' *International Journal of Psychoanalysis 88*, 843–860.

Bowlby, J. (1988) *A Secure Base: Clinical Applications of Attachment Theory.* London: Routledge.

Burns, D. and Nolen-Hoeksema, S. (1997) 'Therapeutic empathy and recovery from depression in cognitive-behavioural therapy: a structural equation model.' *Journal of Consulting and Clinical Psychology 60*, 441–449.

Cheetham, J., Fuller, R., McIvor, G. and Petch, A. (1996) *Evaluating Social Work Effectiveness.* Buckingham: Open University Press.

Clarkin, J.F., Levy, K.N., Lenzenweger, M.F. and Kernberg, O.F. (2007) 'Evaluating three treatments for borderline personality disorder: a multiwave study.' *American Journal of Psychiatry 164*, 922–928.

Feldman, M. (2008) *Doubt, Conviction and the Analytic Process.* London: Routledge.

Ferard, M.L. and Hunnybun, N.K. (1962) *The Caseworker's Use of Relationships.* London: Tavistock.

Fonagy, P. (2003) 'The development of psychopathology from infancy to childhood: the mysterious unfolding of disturbance of time.' *Infant Mental Health Journal 24*, 212–239.

Fonagy, P. (2008) 'The Mentalization-Focused Approach to Social Development.' In F.N. Busch (ed.) *Mentalization: Theoretical Considerations, Research Findings and Clinical Implications.* New York: Analytic Press.

Fonagy, P., Steele, M., Steele, H., Moran, G. and Higgitt, A. (1996) 'Associations among attachment classifications of mothers, fathers and their infants: evidence for a relationship-specific perspective.' *Journal of Consulting and Clinical Psychology 64*, 22–31.

Freud, S. (1896) 'Further Remarks on the Neuro-Psychoses of Defence.' *The Standard Edition of the Complete Psychological Works of Sigmund Freud, Vol 3.* London: Hogarth Press.

Freud, S. (1905) 'Fragment of an Analysis of a Case of Hysteria.' *The Standard Edition of the Complete Psychological Works of Sigmund Freud, Vol 7.* London: Hogarth Press.

Freud, S. (1910) 'The Future Prospects of Psychoanalytic Therapy.' *The Standard Edition of the Complete Psychological Works of Sigmund Freud, Vol 11.* London: Hogarth Press.

Freud, S. (1925) 'Negation.' *The Pelican Freud Library, Vol 11.* Harmondsworth: Penguin Books.

Hargreaves, E. (1998) *The Depressive Position and Defences Against It.* External lecture at the Institute of Psychoanalysis, London, 25 November.

Heimann, P. (1950) 'On counter-transference.' *International Journal of Psychoanalysis 31*, 81–84.

Hinshelwood, R.D. (1989) *A Dictionary of Kleinian Thought.* London: Free Association Books.

Klein, M. (1946) 'Notes on some schizoid mechanisms.' *International Journal of Psychoanalysis 27*, 99–110.

Koerner, K. and Linehan, M. (2000) 'Research in dialectical behavioural therapy for patients with borderline personality disorder.' *Psychiatric Clinics in North America 23*, 151–167.

Lambert, M.J. and Barley, D.E. (2001) 'Research summary on the therapeutic relationship and psychotherapy outcome.' *Psychotherapy 38*, 357–361.

Laming, Lord (2009) *The Protection of Children in England: A Progress Report.* London: The Stationery Office.

Leichsenring, F. and Rabung, S. (2008) 'Effectiveness of long-term psychodynamic psychotherapy: a meta-analysis.' *Journal of the American Medical Association 300*, 13, 1551–1565.

Lewis, G. and Appleby, L. (1988) 'Personality disorder: the patients psychiatrists dislike.' *British Journal of Psychiatry 153*, 44–49.

Linehan, M.M. (1993) *Cognitive-Behavioural Treatment of Borderline Personality Disorder.* New York: Guilford Press.

Lyons, K. (1997) *Social Work in Higher Education: Demise or Development?* Basingstoke: Ashgate.

Martindale, B., Bateman, A., Crowe, M. and Margison, F. (2000) *Psychosis: Psychological Approaches and their Effectiveness.* London: Gaskell.

Nathan, J. (2002a) 'Psychoanalytic Theory.' In M. Davies (ed.) *The Blackwell Companion of Social Work.* Second edition. Oxford: Blackwell.

Nathan, J. (2002b) 'The advanced practitioner: beyond reflective practice.' *Journal of Practice Teaching in Health and Social Work 4*, 2, 59–84.

Nathan, J. (2006) 'Self-harm: a strategy for survival and nodal point of change.' *Advances in Psychiatric Treatment 12*, 5, 329–337.

Rachman, S. (1971) *The Effects of Psychotherapy.* Oxford: Pergamon.

Racker, H. (1968) *Transference and Counter-Transference.* London: Hogarth Press.

Samuels, A. (1985) *Jung and the Post-Jungians.* London: Routledge.

Sandler, J. (1976) 'Counter-transference and role-responsiveness.' *International Review of Psychoanalysis 3*, 43–47.

Schore, A.N. (1997) 'A century after Freud's project: is a rapprochement between psychoanalysis and neurobiology at hand?' *Journal of the American Psychoanalytic Association 45*, 3, 807–840.

Schore, A.N. (2000) 'Attachment and the regulation of the right brain.' *Attachment and Human Development 2*, 1, 23–47.

Steiner, J. (1993) *Psychic Retreats.* London: Routledge.

Stern, D.N. (1985) *The Interpersonal World of the Infant.* New York: Basic Books.

Symington, N. (1983) 'The analyst's act of freedom as agent of therapeutic change.' *International Review of Psychoanalysis 10*, 283–291.

Winnicott, D.W.W. (1949) 'Hate in the counter-transference.' *International Journal of Psychoanalysis 30*, 66–79.

Winnicott, D.W.W. (1960) 'Ego Distortion in Terms of True and False Self.' *The Maturational Process and the Facilitating Environment: Studies in the Theory of Emotional Development.* London: Hogarth Press.

Winnicott, D.W.W. (1963) 'The Development of the Capacity for Concern.' *The Maturational Process and the Facilitating Environment: Studies in the Theory of Emotional Development.* London: Hogarth Press.

Chapter 7

Reflective Practice Using Cognitive Behavioural Therapy

Its Uses in Social Work

Florian Ruths

Introduction

The International Federation of Social Workers (2000) states:

> Social work bases its methodology on a systematic body of
> evidence-based knowledge derived from research and practice
> evaluation... It recognizes the complexity of interactions
> between human beings and their environment, and the
> capacity of people both to be affected by and to alter the
> multiple influences upon them including bio-psychosocial
> factors. The social work profession draws on theories of human
> development and behaviour and social systems to analyse
> complex situations and to facilitate individual, organizational,
> social and cultural changes.

The theoretical frameworks of cognitive behavioural therapy (CBT) and
social work could not be closer: CBT is an empirically validated form
of talking therapy that uses evidence-based knowledge, derived from
randomised controlled trials and practice evaluation. CBT recognises the
complexity of the interaction between environmental situational triggers,
and the emotional, cognitive, physiological and behavioural responses
of an individual. CBT aims to broaden the individual's awareness of

their responses and open the possibility of change in order to reduce emotional suffering. While social theory targets both suffering among groups and individuals, CBT is largely directed towards individuals. It makes perfect sense to promote CBT as a practical tool in social work to bring evidence-based interventions to clients and groups of clients.

Mental health 2010: a reflection and an outlook

Something interesting has happened when we look at the guidance on every single mental health disorder that has been published by the National Institute for Health and Clinical Excellence (NICE). Cognitive behavioural therapies feature in most of the guidance as an essential intervention, often as a first-line treatment for mental disorders. Psychological interventions, including CBT, are now recognised as the treatment of choice as the initial step to deal with mental illness. This is a revolution in psychiatric thinking and care, and whoever wants to learn about mental health should be interested in the success story that is CBT.

This Chapter will take a slightly different look at why CBT has become a key element in the treatment of mental disorders in all age groups. It will start from seeking to define mental disorders beyond the *Diagnostic and Statistical Manual of Mental Disorders* (American Psychiatric Association 1994). We will go into the past and look at how our emotional life had an adaptive function in order to survive in our environment. We will then understand how emotions are going wrong in a rather different environment and causing us suffering, disabilities and sometimes death through mental illness.

The good news is that CBT is a way to help our emotions get back into balance again by the power of using our reasoning capacity and creating new experiences and putting our emotions into perspective. We will learn the basic principles of how CBT works. CBT is a collection of sophisticated techniques that have been developed over the last 30 years. You will not be able to practise CBT after you have read this chapter, but you may find that you can experiment with talking to your clients in a slightly different way. Even though CBT is mainly developed for individuals and small groups of specifically ill clients, for social workers interested in mental health there will be scope to look at the role and the benefit of CBT skills like collaborative empiricism and meta-emotional awareness for society as a whole.

The target of CBT: emotions

What are emotions? When we talk about mental well-being, we are in fact talking about emotional well-being. Emotions are ultimately the targets of most psychological interventions. When a client suffering from panic disorder no longer experiences episodes of catastrophic anxiety, an emotion, we would assume that our intervention has worked.

Cognitive behavioural therapy should really be called Cognitive behavioural *emotional* therapy, as the primary target of our intervention is the emotional state of our client. Or in other words, we are using the client's thoughts, beliefs and assumptions (the cognitions), and their behaviour to alter our client's emotional state.

Emotions can therefore be described as a state of mind that serves as a pre-set programme for the reactions of the body, the processes of the mind and a set of standardised actions and behaviours (Cosmides and Tooby 2000).

Emotions are triggered by certain specific cues and mediate the relationship between the internal universe, that is, our body and mind, and the external universe, our environment. It is crucial to understand that all emotions such as positive ones like happiness, love, trust, admiration, calmness, are as important and useful for our survival as anxiety, sadness, disgust, mistrust, shame and anger. Each emotion serves as a conductor to the orchestra of different musical instruments: hormonal responses of different parts of the body, the interplay of processes of the mind like reasoning and behavioural responses of the body, each carefully conducted in response to an external cue, so that their interplay becomes harmonious and co-ordinated. For each emotion a standardised song unfolds, as if this orchestra, called the human being, is sitting in a juke box, always playing the same song when the right button is pressed.

The evolutionary perspective

Looking at the development of our emotions over hundreds of thousands of years, evolutionary psychology argues that all emotions have been given to us for one specific reason: to ensure our survival, and more specifically, the continuation of our genetic heritage, giving us a better chance of adapting and surviving to a constantly changing environment (LeDoux 1994). This environment can be our physical environment, the varying landscapes, climates and seasons, as well as our social environment, our family, tribe, village, city and country.

By way of example: the situation (or external universe) 15,000 years ago. Francois, the ancestral caveman from the Cosquet Grottes in Southern France is happily walking along the local river. He is singing and rubbing his arm, which still causes him some discomfort after an attack by a wolf six months earlier. Suddenly he hears a noise in the bush a few metres away. This is the cue for the conductor to play the orchestral classic 'Existential Threat Song': the mind, relying on programmed memories, reasons: 'Is this a predator? Am I going to be attacked?' The emotional mind experiences intense catastrophic anxiety, with the adrenal gland instruments secreting adrenaline, and within a few heartbeats the body is flooded with danger hormones. The heart instrument is pumping fast, the breathing instrument is increasing, the muscle instruments are tensing, blood is being diverted from the bowels towards the muscles and blood sugar levels are increasing to provide energy. With the body, the mind modes also change: the attention instrument is focused on the bush, forgetting about his discomfort. Within milliseconds, the mind instrument has figured out escape routes, analysed the odds of escaping alive versus using his long stick as a weapon to fight. With regards to body movement and visible behaviour the leg muscles have initiated steps backwards covering his back by leaning against a rock, arm muscles and nerves have lifted his stick to cover his abdomen, chest and face, turned his head carefully to check the distance to the river. All this has happened in less than two seconds (see Figure 7.1). In this scenario, the ability to feel anxiety has saved Francois' life. Anxiety has been useful and healthy.

The Origins of CBT

CBT was developed in the late 1960s and early 1970s in the USA. The leading figures are Aaron T. Beck and Albert Ellis. CBT was a response to the behavioural theorists who postulated that belief and thoughts did not carry importance when looking at emotional problems. Beck *et al.*'s (1979) seminal book on CBT for depression postulated that thoughts and beliefs were crucial in the development of depression, and that facilitating a change in the meaning attached to an event would facilitate emotional change.

CBT is firmly based in empiricism and pragmatism, the guiding principles of most scientific research conducted throughout the world. From a philosophical point of view, CBT is associated with the thinking of radical constructivism (von Glasersfeld 1995).

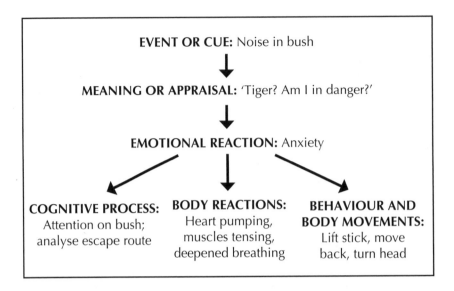

Figure 7.1 Human reaction to existential threats

CBT principles and aims

The basic principle of CBT is deceptively simple: it is based on the understanding of emotional and cognitive reactions. This principle determines that our emotional reaction to any event in our life is mediated by the meaning that we give to the situation (Beck *et al.* 1979). To repeat, almost all mental health problems are emotional problems, where the emotions have become dys-regulated and are no longer serving the individual to achieve their goals. If we have a client who has emotional problems, emotional change requires changing the information processing of the client. For this to happen, we need to look at the meaning being attached to an event that is causing an unhelpful emotional state.

CBT aims to teach the client how our emotions work. This does not mean we tell them. CBT is designed to help the client find this out for themselves. It is as if the client discovers the principles for the first time in human history. The client is a scientist and we as practitioners set up the experiments to prove the hypothesis, as illustrated in Figure 7.2.

Figure 7.2 CBT therapeutic process

How we do CBT: the skill base of communication and learning

1. Collaborative empiricism and guided discovery

Did your mother ever tell you that friendship could include cruelty? Did you believe her? At what stage did you *know* that she was right? Was it the moment when you found out for yourself? It was when you *felt it within your own skin*! It is that moment of 'feeling it for ourselves' that we *know* that something is probably true. We ultimately need to discover our truths for ourselves; it is not enough that somebody tells us. This is what we mean by guided discovery (see Case Study 7.1). How do we do this? We do it by collaborative empiricism.

CASE STUDY 7.1 *GUIDED DISCOVERY*

First, an example of non-guided discovery:

> *Practitioner:* 'Your mother made you feel so anxious that however hard you tried, you always felt and now continue to feel a failure.'

It is not enough to give the client your interpretation of what is happening. This ultimately represents your reality, not the client's. Now for an example of guided discovery:

> *Practitioner:* 'So you say you had the thought "I felt like a failure". Do you remember any situation in your childhood when you felt this way for the first time?'

> *Client:* 'Yeah, I remember a sports event where I came last when I was seven years old.'

> *Practitioner:* 'OK, tell me what happened.'

> *Client:* 'Mum came up to me and said "You could have done better, you should have done better. Next time I won't let you watch TV before any sports events".'

> *Practitioner:* 'Do you remember what went through your mind then?'

> *Client:* 'I thought, I must always do my best, but even that will never be
> good enough to please her!'
>
> *Practitioner:* 'How does this compare to what is happening today?'
>
> *Client:* 'It seems I am still thinking as if I am seven years old.'

Case Study 7.1 is an example of how the client has discovered that his thinking process has become stuck. The client becomes aware about how thinking as an adult is intimately linked to a thinking process when we were children. The client has found this fact out by himself, being guided by the practitioner.

Collaborative empiricism is like going on a journey with our clients. The first step is to make the decision to go on the journey to the unknown to find out what this better place might look like. We do this leap of faith with the client. If we can let go of needing to achieve change for our client, and rather be guided by what unfolds as we get to know our client better in each session, we relieve the pressure that we put on ourselves as practitioners. Paradoxically, this often makes CBT therapy easier.

We begin from the client's perspective, using our capacity to empathise. We cannot possibly know the precise meaning that a client attributes to a situation without exploring and finding out. Letting go of our habitual way of thinking that we know what a client must be going through, is crucial in engaging in this journey.

2. Empathic conversation

Empathy is not that easy to put into words. It is as much a behaviour as it is the ability to feel what another being may be feeling. One of the many verbal and non-verbal clues that we use is based on repeating and summarising what has been said by the client in her own words. The importance is not to paraphrase or interpret what has been said.

CASE STUDY 7.2 EMPATHIC ENGAGEMENT

First, an example of non-empathic engagement:

> *Client:* 'I always feel that I should do more to please others, like I always
> wanted to please my mum as a child.'
>
> *Practitioner:* 'You have got it, you are clearly just re-enacting your
> pathological relationship with your mother.'

Now, for a response exemplifying empathic engagement:

Practitioner: 'That is really interesting. Tell me if I have understood that correctly. What you are saying is that you always feel like pleasing others, like you tried to please your mother?'

It is often not necessary to interpret or rectify a thought or a feeling. Making the client feel understood can already be the first step to engage in a therapeutic working relationship to change the belief and thought system that is driving the client's emotional distress (see Case Study 7.2).

What we do in CBT: the CBT vehicle, providing a structure when confusion reigns

We take our metaphorical journey in a nice CBT vehicle, with wheels, doors, engine and so on. Metaphorically speaking, we are picking a client up in a desert of confusion. The client is torn between a range of confusing emotions arising from his mind and frightening experiences in his own body, and his relationships are affected by unhelpful reactions to situations. Our client is often in a mess and chaos. The first thing we offer is a framework where we put the chaos into a manageable structure and build scaffolding around a crumbling mess. This structure is inherent in each CBT session, which is highly structured, with an agenda being set at the beginning and followed through to the end. Each session has got five elements that are followed rigorously.

1. Mood check

Checking how the client is feeling at the moment through completing a questionnaire. This mood check will normally throw up events that have caused the client to feel upset, anxious or elated. This should be put on the agenda (see Case Study 7.3).

CASE STUDY 7.3 *THE OPENING OF A CLIENT SESSION*

Client: 'This week was awful, I had a massive row with my husband over money again on Monday, and after that he did not talk to me for four days. It was hell.'

Practitioner: 'That sounds like your week was awful. Shall we put the Monday row on the agenda?'

2. The bridge

The next step is to get feedback from your client from the previous session. CBT encourages feedback. This is an opportunity to find out if your therapeutic relationship is strong. For example we may say: 'Obviously we have a lot to talk about today. Before we set an agenda for our meeting, would you like to tell me if there is anything that you found useful about our last meeting? What did you find difficult about our last meeting?'

3. Agenda setting

The most important structural element of a CBT session is the agenda. An agenda does not have to be too detailed, but make it clear that both the social worker's ideas and the client's ideas for the session will be addressed. From the agenda, you can have an idea about how much time you can spend on each point and make a note for yourself on your session record (see Case Study 7.4).

CASE STUDY 7.4 COLLABORATIVE AGENDA SETTING

Practitioner: 'I am glad you made your way here today. How do you think we could best make use of the rest of the session? What are the most pressing issues that you would like to deal with today?'

Client: 'I still have not received my benefits and my daughter is still not wanting to talk to me because of my mood swings recently…'

Practitioner: 'That sounds worrying. Shall we put "benefits chaos" and "row with my daughter" on the agenda?'

Although in social work the agenda cannot always just be set by the client, it is crucial to find out what they want to discuss at the beginning of each session.

4. Review of homework

Homework is an important aspect of how CBT works. We are empowering and giving responsibility to our client to take things they have learnt in the session back home and use them. Change in CBT is largely achieved through inviting the client to move from *thinking about issues* to *doing things by putting into practice what they have learnt in the session*. Homework should follow SMART principles (see Case Study 7.5).

5. Symptom-orientated cognitive and behavioural reattribution

The main content of a CBT session revolves around the items on the agenda: often discussion of the nature of unpleasant thoughts and feelings in particular situations, using concrete examples. Through analysing examples of our client's distress, we learn about the client's patterns of thinking and reacting and their bodily response to strong emotions. Depending on which thought or feeling is being identified to be most distressing for the client, we enter a dialogue about testing the client's thoughts. 'Is this thought really fair? Does this thought help you to cope better in life? Is this thought reflective of a more objective truth, or does it just mirror or even perpetuate the distress that you are feeling?' Cognitive restructuring and the planning of behavioural experiments to test alternative or fairer beliefs are at the core of the change that is being promoted by CBT.

(A) IDENTIFY DYSFUNCTIONAL BELIEF/BEHAVIOUR

Once we have the target emotion, it is important to identify the thought that was going through the client's mind in that moment. For example: 'As you felt anger rising, what was going through your mind?'

We may want to identify the 'hot' thought, the thought that has got the strongest emotional impact. In the case of the househusband who will be described in Case Study 7.6 he may think 'Why does she always do this to me?' This is not the hot thought if it does not cause that much anger. We may need to look for a deeper, more upsetting thought: 'She just hates me, I am useless anyway!' Only then may we find an emotionally more powerful thought, the 'hot' thought.

(B) RATE BELIEF STRENGTH

Once we identify the 'hot' belief, we need to check how much our client considers the content to be reality at the time that we see him: 'On a scale from nought to ten, how much do you believe that the thought "She hates me, I am useless" is the truth?' We are trying to identify the distortion in the client's thinking, a pattern of focusing excessively on negative or unfair information.

(C) FORMULATE ALTERNATIVE FAIRER BELIEF/ADAPTIVE BEHAVIOUR

Once we have identified the hot thought, and we have reassured ourselves that this thought or belief has got the impact on the emotion that we are trying to remediate, we attempt to restructure the belief or behaviour.

Here CBT gets more complex. We need to spend time and effort to guide the client towards a fairer way of thinking about a situation or themselves. For the purpose of this synopsis, a simple and effective way of restructuring or suggesting a fairer thought process is to encourage the client to identify his own thinking process by recording thoughts in a diary. With time, patterns of thoughts arise that are unfair and distorted. We can encourage the client to identify some of the following thinking errors:

- *All or nothing thinking:* 'If I am not a total success, I am a failure.'

- *Catastrophising:* 'I'll fail the exam and my career will be over.'

- *Discounting the positive:* 'I was just lucky to pass all other exams.'

- *Emotional reasoning:* 'I know that I know my stuff, but I just feel that my head is completely empty.'

- *Labelling:* 'I'm a loser.'

- *Magnification/minimisation:* 'My mistakes are unforgiveable, my achievements don't count.'

- *Mental filter:* 'Because I could not do one of the questions in the critical appraisal, I have done badly in the exam.'

- *Mind-reading:* 'He's thinking that I am useless.'

- *Over-generalisation:* 'All men are bastards.'

- *Personalisation:* 'The receptionist was rude to me, so I must have done something wrong.'

- *'Should' or 'must':* 'I should always do my best.'

- *Tunnel vision:* only seeing the negative aspects of a situation.

6. Setting homework for the next session

The session is concluded with setting specific homework for the following week. The client is trained to become her own practitioner by making use of some of the techniques that have been discussed in therapy. This use should be practical, and in line with any goal that a client is setting for themselves. In other words, any homework set in session should be based on SMART principles: Specific, Measurable, Achievable, Realistic and Time scaled. It should be specific and its completion easily measureable. The homework should be agreed collaboratively in order for it not to overwhelm or feel imposed. It should also be time scaled, so that the client has a precise idea when he is going to do the various tasks until your next contact.

CASE STUDY 7.5 *SMART HOMEWORK TASKS*

First, an example of a non-SMART homework task:

> *Practitioner:* 'How about applying for benefits as a task for the next week?'

> *Client:* 'Maybe, when I find time over all the other stresses in my life...'

Now for an example of a SMART homework task:

> *Practitioner:* 'Any suggestions how you could make a slight difference to your serious financial situation over the next week?'

> *Client:* 'How about if I went to the DSS office in Fleet Street on Monday at 9.30am after dropping my daughter off. I could fill in Form 11a to apply for Incapacity Benefit at the advice desk with Margaret. How long do you think they normally take to process the form?'

---

7. Feedback from the session

Asking for genuine feedback about your interaction or session can be a good way of finding out if you are on the right track with your client and eliciting obstacles to your client making use of your session. For example: 'This is a chance for you to feed back if I got it right. Please let me know if I have answered your questions, and if you feel that there is anything that you would like me to clarify. It really helps me to know if I did understand correctly all you said...'

The structure of a course of CBT

A CBT course has six general phases or treatment stages.

1. Sessions 1–3: case formulation and goal setting

The formulation is the compass for the journey through the desert. In CBT terms, it is making sense of the client's experiences and developing a plan to change the client's way of feeling emotions via changing her way of thinking (or processing information), her way of reacting or behaving, and her way of relating to her experience of the body. It is an essential tool in cognitive therapy. The formulation or the map is an ongoing project. The formulation will evolve as we learn more about our client. The journey makes the map more precise.

In cognitive therapy we distinguish between a cross-sectional formulation and a longitudinal formulation. The longitudinal formulation helps us to make sense of how the client came to be the person that she is and points the way to change. The cross-sectional formulation helps us to understand what is happening to our client in the few moments that lead to significant distress.

CASE STUDY 7.6 EXAMPLE OF A BIO-PSYCHOSOCIAL CASE FORMULATION

A 33-year-old unemployed gas engineer and father to a two-year-old daughter and a six-month-old son presents with low mood, thoughts of hopelessness, tearfulness and perceived inability to cope with the care of his children. His partner works full time in order to support the family. The couple have got six months rent arrears, no further savings and have been threatened with eviction. When he speaks to you he states that he feels that he is a bad father. He says things like: 'I cannot cope with my children, I know I am useless.' His wife describes him as a loving husband, but has noticed deterioration in his mood over the last six months. This was in the context of her husband losing his job after an accident at work, which has left him in chronic pain and difficulty getting around.

In discussion with the couple, you develop the following formulation:

1. Psychological issues: the husband suffers from probable depression, complicated by low self-esteem and self-perceived inability to cope with his children. He has had negative thoughts like 'I'm useless' and 'I'm a bad father'.

2. Social issues: there are rent arrears and the family is faced with eviction and possible rehousing.

3. Biological issues: your client suffers from a chronic pain condition and mobility problems.

In Case Study 7.6 we have arrived at a bio-psychosocial formulation of the client's problems. It may be useful to understand his current mood problems specifically in a cognitive way. For that purpose, it would be useful to identify a particular situation when the client noted a significant shift in his mood. We call this a cross-sectional formulation. In this particular example, the client describes a situation when he had an argument with his wife over her ridiculing his ironing capacities. A useful question to ask about this is: 'In that situation when you were ironing and your wife criticised you, how did that feel inside?' Figure 7.3 represents this process of cognitive formulation graphically.

In combination with our goals, the formulation is the road marker of how to change the client's way of feeling in difficult situations. Every contact with our clients should include us revisiting the formulation.

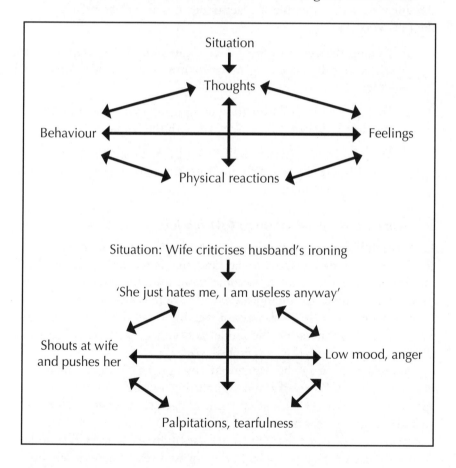

Figure 7.3 A cognitive formulation

Goal-setting helps us find answers to the following important questions: what is it we are trying to achieve? How do we actually know that we have achieved what we wanted to achieve? Are the ambitions and hopes that we have for our client realistic? Or are we following an ideal that will set us, and our client, up for failure and subsequent increased misery? How long do we want to continue trying our intervention and at what stage do we have to rethink and consider another intervention other than our own? In other words, we are trying to make our goals SMART.

For example, in reference to the client in Case Study 7.6, to improve the client's overall situation a practitioner might collaboratively agree the following three goals:

1. To help the client to feel better about himself and improve his self-esteem by becoming more comfortable with his skills as a father.

2. To improve the social situation by agreeing to negotiate a realistic schedule to pay off his rent arrears with the landlord.

3. To improve his physical well-being by making an appointment with his GP in order to improve his pain management and physical rehabilitation.

2. Sessions 1–4: socialisation to CBT model

CBT is a different way of thinking about oneself as, at its core, emphasis is placed on thinking about today and making a better future. We are encouraging the client to become more mindful about his way of processing reality today and now. We will have to ask the client to really become an expert at his own ways of reacting to all the challenges that life gives us. So reiterating the model and engaging the client in this different way of doing things is crucial.

Socialisation may be enhanced by giving reading material, recommending CBT books and signposting towards computer-based material. Recording of the session is encouraged for the client to be able to listen again to what has been said.

In order to engage the client from Case Study 7.6 in the CBT model it may be useful to consider bibliotherapy and recommend a self-help guide such as Paul Gilbert's (2000) *Overcoming Depression* or to visit a CBT website such as www.livinglifetothefull.com.

3. Sessions 2–11: symptom-orientated cognitive and behavioural reattribution

If we have identified the patterns among our client's thinking distortion, we may think together what would be a fairer assessment of oneself and others' behaviour:

CASE STUDY 7.6 *(CONTINUED)*

Practitioner: 'Rather than labelling yourself (*thinking distortion*) 'I am useless' and mind-reading (*thinking error*) 'She must hate me', what would be a fairer way of looking at the situation?'

Client: 'Well, I know that my wife is having a tough time at work and sees that I am depressed, so to be fair to me, I think "She has probably had a rough day, that is why she is so critical".'

We then rate the strength of the new belief or frequency of alternative behaviour:

CASE STUDY 7.6 *(CONTINUED)*

Practitioner: 'How strongly do you believe that this is truer than the other thoughts?'

Client: 'Well, she told me exactly that a few days after the incident, so it is probably fairer, although at the time I did not believe it at all.'

Practitioner: 'How does that make you feel right now seeing it this way?'

Client: 'Interesting, I don't feel angry with her at all seeing it this way.'

We take this alternative way of looking at things into daily life by encouraging the client to observe himself closely and rate emotional peaks over time while keeping a thought diary. This is the homework which incorporates a behavioural change that needs to be tied in with in-session discoveries. We then start again with other target emotions.

4. Sessions 2–5: behavioural monitoring, activation and scheduling

Behavioural activation, the use of increased physical activity to fight depression, has been shown to be as effective as cognitive therapy in reducing depressive symptoms in several multi-centre trials (Jacobson *et al.* 1996). For a social work practitioner without training in CBT, behavioural activation is an alternative way of treating depression and anxiety successfully.

We can observe that not only do our emotions influence our actions, but also the other way round: what we do influences the way we feel (see Figure 7.3). We are trying to highlight that some activities make us happier than others. But this is not only about pleasure. It is also about achievement and mastery. Even if a client is not able to feel pleasure, he can still use the sense of achievement to become more active.

We can make use of this fact to improve a client's emotional well-being by asking him to take three steps:

1. Monitoring daily activity on an hourly basis by recording activity.

2. Rating the pleasure and achievement derived from each activity on a scale from nought to ten.

3. Making an effort to schedule activities that have a higher score in pleasure or mastery into daily life and reducing idle and unhelpful activities.

CASE STUDY 7.6 *(CONTINUED)*

Practitioner: 'When we look at your chart on the Sunday, we can see that when you went to the gym between 10.00am and 11.00am, you scored your pleasure at '4' and your mastery at '5'. Also, here, mowing the lawn gave you a '5' in mastery and a '2' in pleasure. What do you make of this exercise?'

Client: 'Well, the first thing I noticed is that I am actually doing more during the day then it felt like. That was surprising. And the second thing is that even though I don't get a lot of pleasure out of certain chores, it is still worth doing them, it moves things forward.'

Practitioner: 'So how could you use this knowledge in the future?'

Client: 'Well, I just have to make a more detailed plan of how I am spending my time and force myself more to do things, even chores, rather than to just sit about.'

5. Sessions 8–11: schema-focused work

We all develop rules and regulations about the functioning of ourselves, other people and the world during childhood. As we get older our environment, both the emotional landscapes and the people around us, may change. But our rules may not change with the rapidly changing world around us. So the rule that made perfect sense when we were children (e.g. 'I should always give my best, otherwise my achievement counts nothing to Daddy') may no longer be very useful once Daddy has stopped being such an important Figure in our life. The external environment changes, but our internal world seems to get stuck in childhood and adolescent patterns. In the case of unhelpful parenting, the mental scars left in the form of unhelpful schemas may follow us to fuel unhelpful patterns of relating to others and dealing with stress in our life.

The change in beliefs at the core of our personality (core beliefs or schemas) requires skills in identifying and modifying those over many weeks or months. In general terms, we are encouraged to leave unhelpful beliefs as 'seeds in our soul' and untouched. Instead, we use CBT to try to create more helpful seeds, 'watering' them with old and new positive experiences ('positive data log'), and drying the others out by not feeding them unnecessarily.

So, in practical terms, the core belief 'Deep down I do not deserve to be loved, I am useless' is replaced by collecting real life evidence from past, present and future. The alternative belief 'I am a lovable and a caring father' is made much fairer and more realistic by 'watering' this belief with a written log of the little and big bits of information that confirm this new alternative belief.

6. Sessions 9–12: relapse prevention work

Relapse of mental health distress is a common event. In the case of people with chronic depression, their relapse risk is up to 80 per cent over 18 months (Keller *et al.* 1983), for example. Relapse prevention happens through various avenues. We are trying to stop our client falling into the old habits of interpreting the world within them and around them by asking some important questions:

- What situations have upset me in the past?

- Can I prepare myself for similar situations in the future?

- What can I do to deal with them in a different way, using the knowledge from my therapy?

- Who could help me to identify when things are going wrong for me?

- What can I do on a daily basis to look after my well-being and honour myself as much as others around me?

All the above can be done in writing with the practitioner reviewing this plan towards the end of the course of therapy.

CASE STUDY 7.6 *(CONTINUED)*

Practitioner: 'What have been the triggers of your depression in the past?'

Client: 'In the past, it was increased workload often at the same time I had bad colds and felt run down physically.'

Practitioner: 'What could you do differently when the triggers arise again?'

Client: 'Well, in the first instance, I need to monitor my workload more closely and watch out for peaks. When I notice increased stress, I will have to look after myself better by sticking to the things that keep me well: seeing my mates on Friday night, and going to the gym on Mondays and Thursdays. And when I get a cold, I should really take a day out and recover properly.'

Practitioner: 'Sounds good, would be great to have this somewhere in writing so you can look at it again...'

Summary and conclusions

This Chapter has tried to highlight four important aspects that make CBT skills useful in the daily work of social workers and other psychosocial practitioners.

The first involves a more cognitive way of looking at human development and embracing the concept of welcoming our ability to experience distress. We have developed emotions for a reason. At times, negative emotions have been portrayed as always requiring treatment or change. If we can carefully assess our client's response and put it into the context of their life experience, we can sometimes help by *not* suggesting any change. Listening to and sharing experiences and emotions and consoling can be more useful than needing to help our client change.

The second aspect is the importance of using a structured and transparent approach in our interaction with the client. Eliciting feedback at the beginning of our meetings, using objective written measures of progress and setting an agenda for our meeting can be useful tools to use our time with clients most effectively. This aspect also helps us to focus on the client's real needs rather than assuming that we know what the client may need.

The third aspect is how we talk to our client. CBT uses a collaborative approach where both client and practitioner agree to work together in the spirit of trying to find out about the client's mind through experimenting and trying things out. Putting the client's discovery of widening the perspective at the centre of the interaction can be both rewarding and effective.

The final aspect is the use of behavioural and cognitive strategies to empower the client to learn for him or herself how to influence mood and emotional reactivity. The beauty of CBT lies in its practical usefulness and its simplicity. It is not rocket science, but is still highly effective.

It is hoped that this practical guide will create interest in the practitioner to explore CBT and its uses in mental well-being further.

References

American Psychiatric Association (1994) *Diagnostic and Statistical Manual of Mental Disorders, Fourth edition (DSM-IV)*. Washington, DC: American Psychiatric Association.

Beck, A.T., Rush, A.J., Shaw, B.F. and Emery, G. (1979) *Cognitive Therapy of Depression*. New York: Guilford Press.

Cosmides, L. and Tooby, J. (2000) 'Evolutionary Psychology and the Emotions.' In M. Lewis and J.M. Haviland-Jones (eds) *Handbook of Emotions*. Second edition. New York: Guilford Press.

Gilbert, P. (2000) *Overcoming Depression: A Self-Help Guide Using Cognitive-Behavioural Techniques*. London: Robinson Publishing.

International Federation of Social Workers (2000) *Definition of Social Work*. Available at http://www.ifsw.org/en/f38000138.html, accessed on 10 December 2009.

Jacobson, N.S., Dobson, K.S., Truax, P.A., Addis, M.E. *et al.* (1996) 'A component analysis of cognitive-behavioural treatment for depression.' *Journal of Consulting and Clinical Psychology 64*, 295–304.

Keller, M.B., Lavori, P.W., Lewis, C.E. and Klerman, G.L. (1983) 'Predictors of relapse in major depressive disorder.' *Journal of the American Medical Association 250*, 3299–3304.

LeDoux, J. (1994) *The Emotional Brain*. London: Weidenfeld and Nicholson.

von Glasersfeld, E. (1995) *Radical Constructivism: A Way of Knowing and Learning*. London: The Farmer Press.

Chapter 8

Reflective Practice Using Systemic Family Therapy

Judith Lask

Introduction

Social workers have played a key role in the development of systemic work across social care and mental health provision. This is not surprising as systemic theories provide an extremely useful map for thinking about the complexities of the work undertaken by social workers. Increasingly government policy stresses the importance of seeing children and adults in the context of their relationships and a systemic approach is essential to do this effectively.

In systemic work, the word 'family' is used in a very flexible way and refers to the significant relationship networks or systems to which someone belongs. This includes family in many different forms: 'family of choice', network of friends and sometimes helping professionals. The family or system included is defined in collaboration with the client or clients and this discussion forms part of the first phase of work.

There are a whole range of systemic approaches and interventions and many will be referred to in this chapter. The theories of change underlying these approaches are different and there is an emphasis on choosing an approach that fits for the problem, the clients, the agency context and the competence and skill of the therapist. Family interventions in psychosis and parenting approaches are examples of interventions that fall within the systemic domain but focus largely on the more behavioural aspects of systemic work. Earlier models tended to focus on the system as a whole but the past 20 years have seen the development of narrative and social constructionist approaches that focus on the way in which discourses at every level of society shape personal narratives. An example of this is the way in which racist and gender discourses in the media, education and society can impact on personal education choices and opportunities. Personal narratives not only reflect lived experience but also shape the way we live our lives. In addition, a systemic approach does not rule out other approaches and interventions. For example, systemic family work may be carried out at the same time as individual cognitive behavioural therapy (CBT) – the systemic perspective enabling understanding of the impact of the individual work on other relationships and the opportunity to address issues that may be standing in the way of change. A number of books give a good overview of the field (e.g. Carr 2006; Dallos and Draper 2005; Vetere and Dallos 2003).

Systemic family therapy in mental health social work

In mental health social work with children and families, systemic work is a common ingredient in the delivery of services. It is generally recognised that it is essential to involve families and carers in any interventions with a child or adolescent, and that family and carers provide the most significant context for a child's development. There is good evidence to suggest that family approaches are effective in a range of child-focused difficulties including eating disorders, behavioural problems and depression. Carr (2009) provides a good summary of the current evidence.

The application of systemic ideas and work with families has been less widespread in adult mental health services. Family interventions in psychosis (Kuipers 2006), based on a psychosocial and behavioural model, is an approach with a secure evidence base. However, the evidence is that many people trained in this approach did not use it with clients with families because the expertise was not there to support it. Somerset Partnership Trust and Oxleas Mental Health Foundation Trust in south-east London have both developed a systematic plan of training staff to work with families (Stanbridge, Burbach and Leftwich 2009). At the basic level mental health practitioners are trained to be family sensitive and family focused. There is a pyramid level of training with the more complex work, service development, continued professional development and supervision being supported by fully trained systemic family therapists. Carr has also produced a useful review of the evidence for family work and family interventions in adult settings and confirms that it is an important psychosocial intervention across all mental health services (Carr 2009).

Reflective practice in systemic family therapy

Reflective practice is central to systemic family therapy and there is a strong emphasis on personal and professional development which focuses on the connections between personal self, professional self and the systemic work undertaken. This includes the identification of personal resources and constraints, including trigger families and situations that give rise to feelings and reactions that may get in the way of the work. These reflections are from a philosophical position that recognises a multi-verse[1] and the validity of a range of perceptions and views that will be shaped by many influences. The term 'self reflexivity' is frequently used. This is a process of identifying those influences, reflecting on them and then feeding that new understanding into the work. This is a continuous process. 'Relational reflexivity' refers to the process of reflecting more specifically on the relational aspects of the work and is done in a relational context. For example therapists might ask clients if they are being active enough or having sufficient opportunities to voice their concerns. The therapist then adjusts the therapy in response to feedback whilst also reflecting on themselves in the process. The inclusion of other viewpoints may be added through the literature, supervision and the use of consultation. It is essential to take a position of 'curiosity' – being open to new ideas and information and hypothesising about a range of possibilities.

Reflections on a case

Case Study 8.1 is chosen because it involves people of different ages and cultures and particularly because it is a family with small children being seen within an adult service. This is made possible because the therapist is trained to work across age ranges. It was also seen in a team context. There is a danger that this could make it seem less relevant for the many practitioners who work on their own. However, the advantage of describing a case in this setting is that it gives the opportunity to raise particular issues and to demonstrate more ways of reflective practice. Many of these reflective processes are transferable to work by a single practitioner. However, there are challenges in working alone with a

---

1   A multi-verse is a world where there are many different perspectives on, and experiences of, the same events.

family and those less experienced may want to think about the value of co-working at least part of their work. All names have been changed to preserve anonymity.

CASE STUDY 8.1 *THE RODGERS FAMILY*

Referral and agency context

Paul Rodgers was referred for family work to a Psychological Interventions Service by a liaison psychiatrist in the local hospital. The referrer explained that Paul, aged 38, had been severely injured in a 'hit and run' road traffic accident two years previously. He had been hospitalised for almost a year following the accident and suffered injuries to his back which left him with impaired mobility. He also suffered a head injury and continues to experience severe headaches, impaired vision and sometimes struggles to find words. The psychiatrist had been asked to see Paul because he seemed depressed. The psychiatrist confirmed that Paul was depressed and also had panic attacks and anxiety. Medication was prescribed. He considered CBT but as Paul had not engaged with a previous course of CBT this was not suggested. There is also good evidence that couple therapy is effective in the treatment of depression (Jones and Asen 2000). During the discussion with Paul and his partner, Lena, the psychiatrist heard that there were some difficulties in their relationship. Lena welcomed the opportunity to be seen together for some counselling. Paul and Lena have three children – a son, Eric (12), and two daughters, Celina (ten) and Sofia (six months). Eric was having some problems in school and Lena thought Celina might be depressed.

The family and couple therapy team was multi-disciplinary and comprised one white Greek female psychiatrist, one white British female psychologist and two social workers. The most senior member of the team was a black social worker of African Caribbean heritage who had worked in both adult- and child-focused mental health settings. The second social worker was a white British man who had worked mainly in adult psychiatry. The way that the team worked was that all members saw clients and usually worked on their own with the rest of the team watching the session via a video link. All members of the team had some systemic training and were directly involved in thinking about and contributing to the work, sometimes in the form of a 'reflecting team', which is described elsewhere in this chapter. The team has been described in detail because of the importance systemic practitioners give to characteristics such as gender and culture and the part they play in shaping the way we see the world. They are two of the many power and difference issues that impact on the work.

Convening the family and reframing the problem systemically

Contact with a family is often made on the telephone but the forming of the therapeutic relationship probably begins before that. In this case, it was potentially threatened by the fact that the referral was to a large psychiatric hospital with its associated stigma. Paul's family position was that problems are best dealt with within the family and he was unsure about seeking help from outside professionals. He also felt disadvantaged in talking settings as a result of his brain injury.

It was decided that Tom, a social worker, would see the couple as it was thought that Paul, who was probably the least eager for therapy, might find it easier to feel understood with a male therapist.

Tom made his first telephone contact and Lena answered the telephone. She was pleased to be offered an appointment but because Tom was concerned that Paul might feel differently he arranged to speak with Paul. Tom explained that the clinic was focused on relationships and gave some explanation of the way of working. The conversation ended with Paul agreeing to come along for one session to see if it would be helpful.

First session and the therapeutic relationship

As planned, the first session was with Lena and Paul, with Tom as the therapist. The room was arranged to ensure a good light source for Paul because of his impaired vision. Tom worked hard at the therapeutic relationship, noticing that Lena seemed pleased when he focused on engagement with Paul. Tom had initially been concerned that as there were two men in the room she might feel marginalised. (Watching, observing, making sense and responding to the feedback from clients are essential elements of systemic work.) Tom wanted to gather some systemic information to help him and the team map out the wider context of the family. One aspect of the family that was clear from the beginning was that Lena and Paul came from different cultural backgrounds and very different families. Lena came to England from Poland 14 years ago when she was 20, whereas Paul was Black British with an African Caribbean background.

Reflections prior to offering a first appointment

Systemic therapists place great importance on a process of reflective thinking before a client is seen. Developing a good therapeutic relationship or therapeutic alliance (Escudero *et al.* 2008) is crucial and appears to be a key factor in the common factors that account for a large part of therapeutic effect (Flaskas 1997; Sprenkle and Blow 2007). This initial process is designed to:

- identify key issues that may affect the therapeutic relationship

- develop ideas about the fit for client in relation to approach, model and therapist, taking account of research and clinical experience

- identify personal and group prejudices – strong ideas that may shut down curiosity and exploration (Cecchin, Lane and Ray 1992)

- identify any ethical and safeguarding issues to be taken into account including considering issues such as gender, race, religion, age, ability, culture, class, education, sexuality, spirituality and any implications for anti-discriminatory practice

- track the referral route and try to identify any strong beliefs and differences in relation to views of problem or usefulness of being referred

- use systemic ideas to develop some lightly held ideas or hypotheses that help to promote curiosity and organise some initial lines of questioning.

In relation to different levels of engagement there were concerns that Lena might be more of a 'customer' for the family work than Paul and this could have implications for building a therapeutic relationship. Solution-focused brief therapy (SFBT) (Berg 1994) has identified categories of 'customers' who are eager for change and involvement in therapeutic work; 'complainants', who recognise difficulties but are unsure about wanting to change; and 'visitors', who are often there because someone else has forced them to be there. It is important to identify the level of motivation that clients have and not assume that they see this in the same way as the therapist or referrer. One challenge in working with more than one person in the room at the same time is that a close alliance with one person can create more of a distance with another (changes in one relationship affect other relationships). It would therefore be important for the therapist not to make assumptions but to ask questions like 'Whose idea was it to come for help?' Systemic work includes the view that change rarely comes about by instructive interaction and more energy is put into change if the client is motivated and involved. One of the themes throughout systemic therapy is to ensure the therapist is working in this collaborative way and is in tune with how clients want their lives to change.

In our pre-therapy discussion concerns arose relating to anti-discriminatory practice, mainly around Paul's disabilities. Would he be able to get into the therapy room? What time of day would suit him best? And how would the therapist take account of his difficulty in finding words? There were also concerns that the disability was such a large issue that Lena's voice might be silenced. In thinking about involving the children there were discussions about the need for appropriate play materials, the use of child-friendly language and non-verbal approaches (Wilson 1998).

We also thought about who should be invited. As the couple issue had been identified, it was decided to invite the couple initially with the possibility of family meetings in the future. Systemic work usually holds the possibility of inviting other family members (and others) into the work at different times. This clearly raises issues of confidentiality which have to be discussed in detail with clients.

The team contained expertise relating to brain injury and there was some personal experience of having a father with disability. It was agreed these resources would be helpful but care would be taken to avoid making too many assumptions based on that personal experience.

Two initial hypotheses were developed. Systemic hypotheses attempt to involve all significant people in the hypothesis to ensure that the focus is on relational aspects as well as individual issues. There is a debate about how useful it is to generate hypotheses and some would argue that there is too much danger that the therapist becomes 'wedded' to them. However by generating more than one and holding on to them lightly while they are explored, they can help bring out assumptions and prejudices and generate curiosity (Jones 1993).

Byng-Hall (2008) uses attachment ideas to conceptualise therapy as a 'secure base'. He recognises that change is difficult and requires experimentation with new ways of thinking and behaving. Just as a small child needs a secure base from which to move away and experiment, it is essential that the therapist works to provide a secure base for clients. It is important to reflect on what might create a secure base and what might threaten it. We know that an effective therapeutic alliance usually includes the following elements:

- an agreement between therapist and client about the goals of treatment

- an agreement about the therapy tasks needed to accomplish those tasks

- an emotional bond developed between the therapist and client that allows the client to make therapeutic progress (Escudero *et al.* 2008).

Important positive characteristics of the therapeutic relationship in any therapy include empathy, being non-judgemental, ability to listen, sense of safety, confidentiality, reliability, clear boundaries and self-determination. There is debate about how much common factors account for the impact of therapy but they certainly form a significant part (Sprenkle and Blow 2007).

In systemic therapy as well as in social work the concept of 'collaborative practice' is frequently discussed. It is an ethical position and not just one that is strategic in helping clients to feel listened to. It involves valuing the important knowledge and contributions of family members and practitioners and using them in the work. It also involves being sensitive to imposing solutions, which do not 'fit' for clients, and always being aware of their preferences in relation to living their lives.

Systemic assessment and formulation

The systemic approach assumes there are multiple ways of seeing and understanding things so the whole assessment and formulation format does not easily fit with this approach. Some deal with the issue by using the concepts of 'domain of production' and 'domain of explanation'. The 'domain of explanation' refers to the multiple ideas that may be held around an issue and supports curiosity and exploration. The 'domain of production' is where a snapshot is taken and an assessment or formulation made.

Psychosocial practitioners within a mental health setting will be required to make assessments which can themselves become narratives that shape people's lives, sometimes in unhelpful ways. For example a diagnosis of personality disorder can severely affect the chances of someone obtaining effective help. However, assessments can also be helpful. For example a diagnosis of Asperger Syndrome may help a young person get more appropriate education and other support. Making sense of challenges and difficulties in a way that helps someone move forward is very important and formulations are key in this process. They should be done in as collaborative and transparent a way as possible and shared and discussed with clients.

A systemic formulation has a number of features:

- There is clarity about the intention and basis of the formulation.
- The formulation has many dimensions and sources of information.
- It includes a focus on strengths and resilience.
- It gives a steer for future interventions and development.
- It includes information about relevant contexts.
- It has a relational as well as an individual, couple or family focus.

Tom, with input from the team, developed a formulation after two sessions with the couple. At this point he had not seen the children so knew that this formulation would need to be revised as the work progressed. In the process he critiqued his own assumptions. For example, he formed the initial view that Paul had an unusually 'enmeshed' relationship with his family of origin (Minuchin 1974) because he would often go and stay for a few days following a row with Lena. The senior social worker in the team who shares a similar heritage to Paul was of the view that the family's loyalty to Paul, and wish to offer a refuge for him, was culturally very common and that after the severity of his accident it is understandable that they would want to support him as much as they could. She also understood how this dynamic could be problematic for Lena and their relationship. This illustrates the importance in systemic work of trying to understand the logic behind people's actions and not be ready to label them in a negative way. Tom revised his views about this and positioned himself in a less critical position in relation to Paul's family which helped him later in the work when he had a session with Paul, Lena and Paul's parents and sister. Working with clients from different cultures presents particular challenges and demands a high level of reflective practice (Mason and Sawyer 2006).

In developing his formulation, Tom used information from a number of sources including the sessions themselves, conversations with the team, his own past practice experience, research and literature relating to the family and the difficulties they were experiencing. He used the following systemic interventions to gather information from the sessions.

1. Genogram

An important part of formulation is to draw a rudimentary genogram, or family tree, as a way of mapping family and relationships over time.

Genograms can also be used as an intervention later in the work. The genogram (Figure 8.1) showed clearly that Lena and Paul's families were very different. Lena's older brother Adam died when she was 11 and this left her as an only child. Her parents separated soon afterwards and she lost touch with her father. Her mother became depressed and used alcohol to soothe her pain. Lena escaped from home as soon as she could and made her way to England. She made some friends but since Paul's accident has lost touch with most of them. On the other hand, Paul has three sisters and a brother and is the youngest in his family. His parents are retired and very involved with their children and grandchildren.

Genograms and other relationship maps can be usefully extended to include other support networks including professionals. It helped Tom to see how many different professionals the family had been in contact with and he wondered how this felt for Paul who had the belief that problems should be managed in the family.

2. Observation

With more than one person in the room it is essential to observe interaction carefully. It may be possible to notice subtle non-verbal clues to how individuals are feeling or reacting to others. For example in the couple interview Lena seemed to become distracted when Paul talked about his pain. Also, when the parents and children were seen together at a later stage it was observed that Celina tried to distract them when the couple disagreed. Although it is important not to jump to conclusions from little information this may be an important part of the jigsaw.

3. Pattern and process

In addition to content, it is also important to observe process. In the above example Tom observed a pattern of behaviour. For example Paul often said how much he worried about the effect of the accident on Lena (content), but during the sessions he did not give her space to speak (process). This difference was pointed out and Paul began to talk about the guilt that seemed to prevent him from being supportive to Lena. Patterns of communication and capacity to resolve difference can be particularly important.

4. Circular questions

Circular questions are a core technique in systemic work and most systemic and narrative models use varieties of these questions which

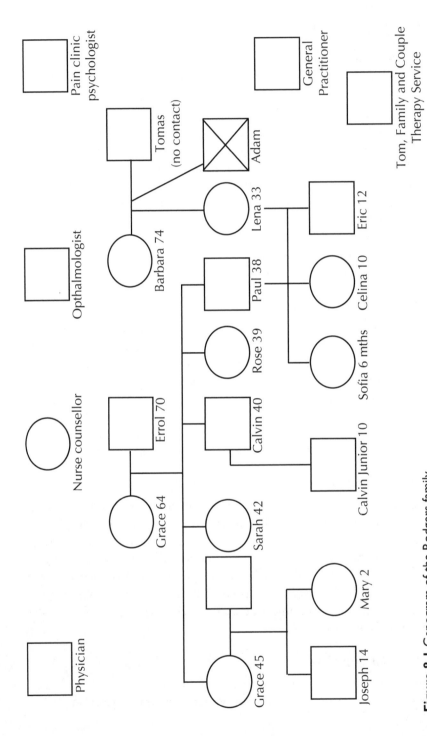

Figure 8.1 Genogram of the Rodgers family

Physician

Nurse counsellor

Opthalmologist

Pain clinic psychologist

General Practitioner

Tom, Family and Couple Therapy Service

Grace 64 — Errol 70

Barbara 74

Tomas (no contact)

Adam

Sarah 42 — Calvin 40 — Rose 39 — Paul 38 — Lena 33

Grace 45

Joseph 14

Mary 2

Calvin Junior 10

Sofia 6 mths

Celina 10

Eric 12

were originally developed by the Milan Group (Tomm 1987). They are circular in a number of ways:

- They elicit information about systemic relationships.

- They draw out information that links beliefs, behaviour, relationships and emotions and the connections between them.

- Different questions are asked of all members of the family present in turn so that everyone is heard.

- The therapist works in a circular fashion on feedback so the next question links to the answer that was given to the previous question.

Questions can be used to elicit the views of family members and others not present, for example 'What would the children say if they heard you say that?' They can also be used to ask one member what they think someone else might say, for example 'Lena, what do you think Paul would say if I asked him what he misses most about his old life?' Future-oriented questions can be very helpful in finding out how clients would like their life to be and helping clients look beyond the current challenges, for example 'Paul, how would you like to see your relationship with the children in eight years time?' Hypothetical questions can be helpful and inform thinking about possible ways forward. For example, Tom asked Paul 'What would happen if the next time you and Lena argued you did not go to your parents but stayed and talked about the problem after you had both calmed down?' The questions can also bring new information into the room and reveal significant differences that need to be addressed. Circular questions are also useful in the promotion of reflective practice. For example, Tom might ask himself 'If I felt less irritated with Paul what different questions might I ask?'

Areas covered in formulation and subsequent interventions

Holding a systemic frame around the work creates a necessary coherence when drawing from different models. In order to avoid drawing from a haphazard toolkit it is important to develop a map that gives a sense of direction to the work. Some interventions focused on behaviour, some on narratives and beliefs and some on relationships. Some interventions happened in the room through action and others through conversation. Most sessions were with the couple, others with the parents and children and another session with the couple and Paul's parents. Each of these pieces was negotiated carefully and related to an overall aim stated by the couple that they wanted to get on better, reclaim some of the fun they used to have and be better parents to the children. The children also wanted fewer arguments and more fun in their lives. The depression, pain and anxiety were always part of the discussion but they gave way to other concerns as the therapy proceeded and seemed to dominate family life much less by the end of the work.

1. Family structure and organisation

Minuchin (1974) developed a model for understanding families, based on structure and organisation. There are criticisms to be made of this model as it can sometimes lead to the application of an inappropriate normative model of family that does not take sufficient account of difference. However, if the core idea of 'structure fitting purpose' is taken on board it becomes much more widely applicable.

Minuchin and others developed a language to describe dimensions of family life. They focused on closeness/distance and the quality of boundaries (sets of rules that differentiate one sub-system from another). Rigid boundaries may prevent families changing when it is required, and diffuse boundaries may lead to chaos and lack of security. Together with communication patterns these dimensions appear to be good measures of family functioning.

In looking at the information Tom had gathered he thought that the rather rigid boundary between Lena and Paul's parents was probably unhelpful and meant that they did not really have a chance to communicate and get to know one another. At times there was a coalition between Paul and his parents against Lena which helped Paul to avoid facing up to some of their problems and Lena's unhappiness.

Tom also formed the view that Celina was triangulated between her parents in the sense that she became the peacemaker and sought to support whichever of her parents seemed most vulnerable. Tom was sensitive to this as it had been a position he had taken in his own family of origin and so he checked out the views of his colleagues who also felt that this was the case and was important to explore further. Being caught up in a parent's conflictual relationship can be very distressing for a child and hamper their emotional development so attending to this also had a 'damage limitation' and safeguarding aspect.

Minuchin (1974) suggested that many 'stuck' forms of family organisation arise because of the lack of capacity to resolve conflict and this seemed to fit well with this family. Rows usually led to a period of separation and coming back together without addressing the issues. Tom was also mindful of the way in which structural ideas of closeness and distance connected with attachment (Vetere and Dallos 2008) and he was interested in pursuing this area further.

Tom also wondered if the parents had a strong enough alliance to work together to help Eric with his behavioural difficulties. Tom helped Paul and Lena to talk together in the session about problems with Eric. At first they wanted to involve Tom but he kept supporting them to continue the conversation in the safe space of the therapy and they discovered that they could do this without it degenerating into argument and recrimination. A meeting was arranged between Paul's parents and the couple and encouragement was given to open the boundaries and discuss difficult issues.

2. Family life cycle

Family life cycle ideas have been developed by a number of authors but most notably by Carter and McGoldrick (1998). The assumption is that families have to continually change their beliefs, behaviour and relationships to meet the changing needs of family members as they develop and to fit with the changing demands of the outside world. Two kinds of stressor are identified: horizontal stressors which include the demands of normal developmental processes and unexpected events, and vertical stressors which relate to family functioning. The theory is that the more there are demands for change, the more stress there is on the system and the more likely problems will arise. Tom and the team felt that these ideas were helpful in thinking about this family. The unexpected event of the accident had demanded huge amounts of unexpected change and Lena's isolation made the impact greater. Eric was at a point when he would normally be moving more outside the family but this was very difficult when there was so much conflict and unhappiness. Conversations about the way families have to change over time helped the couple to appreciate that some of the struggles were not about the accident. Tom talked to Paul and Lena about their own growing up and helped them make links with the experience of their children. Conversations with the children and parents helped those needs to be articulated further. For example the children drew pictures, which showed how they would like their family to be, and discussed this in the session.

3. Important beliefs and narratives

The idea that beliefs drive behaviours and relationships is a central idea in systemic work. For example in the work with this family, it emerged that Paul's family had a strong belief that he should have married within his own community and that Lena, as a white Polish woman, would not value their close family ties. In addition they were concerned that she did not have any religious belief whereas Paul's family were active Christians. Their concern that Lena would not be a good enough partner for their son, led Paul's parents to be more protective than they otherwise would have been.

It became clear Lena had a narrative in which she expected to be let down and felt 'not good enough' most of the time. This narrative had been supported by her childhood experiences, including poverty, and emphasised again by the negative discourses in the press about the immigration of Polish people to England. This made it more difficult for Lena to challenge the negative view of Paul's parents or assert herself in discussions. The narrative model helps to identify beliefs that act as constraints to taking alternative courses of action (Morgan 2000).

4. Gender, culture and power issues

There were a number of issues to take into account but an important one was Paul's cultural narrative about being a man. For him this included physical strength, ability to provide for his family, enjoyment of an active sexual life and being a strong role model for his son. He felt all these had been taken away and it left him feeling very lost in relation to his role within his family and society. Time was taken for the whole family to mourn the loss of what they had planned for the future but then alternative futures and alternative ideas of manhood and fatherhood were discussed. For example Paul decided that he would learn to play chess so this was an activity he and Lena could do together. They also enjoyed films and made arrangements to have video evenings in together. The couple were also encouraged to seek help with the sexual issues relating to the disability, which the team felt was outside their knowledge and skill.

5. Relationship of diagnosis to family relationships

It was important to remember that Paul was depressed and anxious and this had to be taken into account in the formulation and planning of work. It became clear that Lena also had low mood and other depressive symptoms and Celina had fears and phobias which seemed directly related to tensions at home. Eric had behavioural problems at school and some problems with anger control. Although a close eye had to be kept on the severity of the symptoms carried by individuals and appropriate action taken, it seemed likely that there was a connection and that work with the family might benefit everyone.

Illness will of course affect families (Altschuler and Dale 1997) and it was important to know how they functioned before the accident. Typically families close down and attend less to things outside the immediate need. Other relationships can suffer and this had been the case with Paul and Lena. Not only had they given less attention to their own relationship but also the needs of the older children had been put on hold. However, family relationships can also affect the course of an illness and interpersonal stress certainly exacerbated Paul's pain and low mood. Identification of areas that were potentially under the control of family members links in with the next area for consideration.

6. Strengths, resilience and solutions

Systemic work also involves building on strengths and resilience and identifying times when family members have been able to lessen the effect of the problem. It is clear that good functioning in school is a protective factor for children in adversity and this prompted Tom to make sure he liaised with the children's school to ensure that appropriate help was in place. It also helps if it is possible to develop a narrative which is coherent and does not include self-blame. Individual sessions with Lena enabled her to identify the external events and relationships that had supported the idea of 'not measuring up'. This was a process of deconstructing the old story which contained a view that she should have prevented all the things that happened to her family and a move towards understanding that she was very young and others had responsibilities to her which they did not fulfil. She was also able to identify and remember that her parents had loved her but for reasons of their own could not cope. These understandings helped Lena to appreciate her success in moving her life forward and helped her to be more positive about what she could achieve in the future.

One important intervention undertaken in the couple work was to 'externalise' the problem of low mood that affected most of the family in different degrees. By talking about it as an entity of its own it was possible to explore the impact of low mood on the family and then to explore the times when it did not affect them so much. This led to an identification of successes in the fight against low mood (Parry and Doan 1994). For example if Lena gave Paul a cuddle when he complained of pain he felt more relaxed and able to manage. Lena said that if she went for a walk when she felt cross it helped her to calm down. This was helpful as Paul thought she was just running away. This led them to work together to fight low mood rather than blame one another and this brought a more positive flavour to discussions.

There were a number of sessions where the team came into the therapy room and discussed their thoughts and observations in front of the family but without involving then (Anderson and Jensen 2007). Paul and Lena found this useful as they were surprised how much the team had noticed about their struggles and how well they were able to identify their successes. They acted as an important witness group for their success.

7. Ethical and risk issues

Initially there had been concerns that Paul might self-harm as he seemed so angry and desperate but this was assessed carefully and this concern reduced. There was continued discussion about the effects on the children but as the work progressed these also became less. Good liaison with the school and GP helped support the work. Another issue was confidentiality and this was carefully discussed. An issue arose relating to therapist competence in relation to some interventions and it was decided that discussion of sexual difficulties should be done with a specialist team.

Outcome and reflections on reflections

All of the issues brought to therapy improved and it was decided after ten sessions that the family was moving forward in a good way. Life was still a struggle but the family was working together and Lena was more integrated with Paul's family, who appreciated more what she had done for their son. It was expected that the strong feelings of sadness and grief would sometimes be overwhelming and, for example, Celina may have found it difficult to totally relinquish the helping role. However the family identified the danger areas and developed strategies to overcome them. They also had a positive experience of therapy and would seek help in the future. Tom and the team learned a lot about the struggles of family life and the nature of resilience, which they will take into their future work. They also reflected on what they might have done differently and agreed that seeing the whole family in the beginning would have helped them tune in more quickly to the children's needs.

In the final session the family discussed what they had learned from the work, what had been more and less helpful and how they will predict backward sliding and deal with it. Tom and the team also had a useful reflection in front of the family about what they had learned from them and how that would help them in their work. The team wrote a follow-up letter to the whole family in which they acknowledged everyone's strengths and successes and wished them well for the future. This provided a tangible account of the work which could be an inspiration at times of challenge and difficulty.

Concluding thoughts: systemic reflective practice and social work

The social work task is complex, essential and challenging. Systemic reflective practice is about thinking things through from many angles and many perspectives. It includes self-reflection and exploring the way in which context gives meaning to conversations and actions. The ability to hold different possibilities is crucial and in serious case investigations there is often a suggestion that the situation is taken at face value and there is not enough curiosity and exploration (Laming 2009). If a social worker enters a family in an investigative capacity it is inevitable that family members will tell the story of what has happened in a particular way and the challenge is to ask the most useful questions, speak to the most useful people and observe process and relationship as well as listening to the content of what is said. The use of a variety of systemic models and frameworks can be very helpful in guiding the work and provide a language for communicating about complexity. This articulation is a key part of reflection whether it is articulation to oneself or discussion with colleagues. Unless there is a shared language useful discussion is very difficult. A better focus on wider family and systems can help identify resources as well as difficulties. Social work practice deals all the time with issues of power and difference and it is essential that these are taken into account in the building of an effective relationship, consideration of anti-discriminatory practice and decisions relating to particular interventions. The use of appropriate frameworks and language may also help society to appreciate more fully the complexity of the social work task.

References

Altschuler, J. and Dale, B. (1997) *Working with Chronic Illness: A Family Approach.* London: Macmillan.

Anderson, H. and Jensen, K. (eds) (2007) *Innovations in Reflecting Practices: The Inspiration of Tom Andersen Around the World.* London: Karnac.

Berg, I.K. (1994) *Family Based Services: A Solution Focused Approach.* New York: Norton.

Byng-Hall, J. (2008) 'The crucial roles of attachment in family therapy.' *Journal of Family Therapy 30*, 129–146.

Carr, A. (2006) *Family Therapy: Concepts, Process and Practice.* Chichester: John Wiley.

Carr, A. (2009) 'The effectiveness of family therapy and systemic interventions for adult focused problems.' *Journal of Family Therapy 31*, 46–74.

Carter, B. and McGoldrick, M. (eds) (1998) *The Expanded Family Life Cycle: Individual, Family and Social Perspectives.* Boston: Allyn and Bacon.

Cecchin, G., Lane, G. and Ray, W. (1992) *Irreverence: A Strategy for Therapists' Survival.* London: Karnac.

Dallos, R. and Draper, R. (2005) *An Introduction to Family Therapy and Systemic Practice.* Second edition. Milton Keynes: Open University Press.

Escudero, V., Friedlander, M., Varela, N. and Abascal, A. (2008) 'Observing the therapeutic alliance in family therapy: associations with participants' perceptions and therapeutic outcomes.' *Journal of Family Therapy 30*, 194–214.

Flaskas, C. (1997) 'Engagement and the therapeutic relationship in systemic therapy.' *Journal of Family Therapy 19*, 263–285.

Jones, E. (1993) *Family Systems Therapy: Developments in the Milan-Systemic Therapies.* Chichester: John Wiley and Sons.

Jones, E. and Asen, E. (2000) *Systemic Couple Therapy and Depression.* London: Karnac.

Kuipers, E. (2006) 'Family interventions in schizophrenia: evidence for efficacy and proposed mechanisms for change.' *Journal of Family Therapy 28*, 73–80.

Laming, Lord (2009) *The Protection of Children in England: A Progress Report.* London: The Stationery Office.

Mason, B. and Sawyer, A. (eds) (2006) *Exploring the Unsaid: Creativity, Risks and Dilemmas in Working Cross Culturally.* London: Karnac.

Minuchin, S. (1974) *Families and Family Therapy.* London: Tavistock.

Morgan, A. (2000) *What is Narrative Therapy? An Easy to Read Introduction.* London: Brief Therapy Press.

Parry, A. and Doan, R.E. (1994) *Story Re-Visions: Narrative Therapy in the Postmodern Times.* New York: Guildford.

Sprenkle, D. and Blow, A. (2007) 'The role of the therapist as the bridge between common factors and therapeutic change – more complex than congruity with world view.' *Journal of Family Therapy 29*, 109–113.

Stanbridge, R., Burbach, F. and Leftwich, S. (2009) 'Establishing family inclusive acute inpatient mental health services: a staff training programme in Somerset.' *Journal of Family Therapy 31*, 233–249.

Tomm, K. (1987) 'Interventive interviewing: Part 11: reflexive questioning as a means to enable self-healing.' *Family Process 26*, 167–183.

Vetere, A. and Dallos, R. (2003) *Working Systemically with Families: Formulation, Intervention and Evaluation.* London: Karnac.

Vetere, A. and Dallos, R. (2008) 'Systemic therapy and attachment narratives.' *Journal of Family Therapy 30*, 374–385.

Wilson, J. (1998) *Child Focussed Practice: A Collaborative Systemic Approach.* London: Karnac Books.

Chapter 9

Reflective Practice Using Attachment Therapy

Felicity de Zulueta

Introduction

It is as a result of reviewing the research literature relating to human violence, that I came upon the close links that exist between attachment behaviour, destructive behaviour and psychological trauma, especially when experienced in childhood (de Zulueta 2006a).

It was through meeting Dr Bob Johnson that I became aware of an even closer connection between destructive human behaviour and childhood traumatic attachments. This finding opened up an important new way of understanding why certain individuals cling to their destructive patterns of behaviour and can be so resistant to change in therapy. It has also resulted in a new approach in the treatment of complex cases of post-traumatic stress disorder (PTSD) or borderline personality disorder and other dissociative disorders (de Zulueta 2006b).

In this chapter, I will outline our findings in relation to the traumatic attachments individuals tend to develop when they are abused or neglected in childhood and the implications of these findings in terms of the way we understand and treat these individuals (de Zulueta 2006c).

Attachment therapy

Bowlby (1988) stated that in understanding each individual personality development, 'it is as necessary to consider the environment in which each individual develops as well as the genetic potentials with which he is endowed' (p.64). A principal variable in this development is 'the pathway along which his attachment behaviour comes to be organised and further that the pathway is determined to a high degree by the way his parent-figures treat him' (Bowlby 1988, p.64).

Bowlby goes on to say:

> A principal means by which such experiences influence personality development is held to be through their effects on how a person construes the world about him and how he expects persons to whom he might become attached to behave, both of which are derivatives of the *representational models of his parents that he has built up during his childhood.* Evidence suggests that these models tend to persist relatively unmodified at an unconscious level and to be far more accurate reflections of how his parents really treated him than traditional opinion has supposed. (Bowlby 1988, p.65; my emphasis)

When writing about the therapeutic treatment of patients, Bowlby was equally specific when he wrote:

> A therapist applying attachment theory sees his role as being one of providing the conditions in which the patient can explore his representational models of himself and his attachment figures with a view to reappraising them and restructuring them in the light of the new understanding he acquires and the new experiences he has in the therapeutic relationship. (Bowlby 1988, p.138)

In order to apply attachment theory in the way Bowlby suggests, a practitioner needs to have a basic understanding of the main findings relating to child development from an attachment perspective. He or she will also have to be able to explore in some way the representational models that their patients have both in terms of themselves and their attachment figures.

I will attempt to first provide a brief synthesis of the work in the field and illustrate how these findings can help us as practitioners to understand some of our patients' behaviour and difficulties and I will then focus on the problems that may arise in attempting to identify patients' representational models.

1. The role of attachment and fear during development

We sometimes forget that attachment behaviour is activated in infants when they feel frightened or helpless. At such moments the human baby, like other primates and mammals, is genetically predisposed to want access or proximity to an attachment figure, particularly when they are frightened. Thanks to the research carried out by Bowlby (1969, 1973, 1980) and his followers (Ainsworth *et al.* 1978; Main and Hesse 1992), they were able to establish that, when separated from their carer, the human infant behaves in ways similar to that shown by Harlow's (1974) monkeys. His research showed that the longer and the earlier these infant monkeys were separated from their mothers, the more anti-social their behaviour was in adulthood. It is now known that the psychobiological substrate of attachment behaviour in humans involves a great part of the right hemisphere and the supra orbital area of the brain which is crucial in the development of empathy and the capacity to form satisfying social relationships. When mammalian infants feel threatened by separation from their attachment Figure their threatened sense of security will express itself through a characteristic sequence of behaviours: protest, despair and detachment (Bowlby 1973).

Human infants are born particularly helpless and have been found to be unable to modulate their high levels of arousal nor can they gratify their emotional needs or even maintain a psycho-physiological homeostasis. The caregiver's role is to modulate the infant's emotions; this sensitive response to the infant's needs is referred to as 'attunement' and is normally provided by the mother but can be by another caring adult. In so doing the adult will also be protecting her infant from any external danger. This process of attunement between infant and caregiver is now known to be extremely important as it is through this matching of inner states between mother and infant, most aptly described by Stern as 'affect attunement' (Stern 1985), that the infant develops the capacity to modulate emotions. It is achieved by the parent responding to the infant's signals through holding, caressing, feeding, smiling and, in addition, giving meaning to the infant's different experiences. These daily interactions between the infant and his or her attachment figures also provide the infant brain with interactive memories that it synthesises into 'internal working models' (Bowlby 1988, pp.129–133). These models become 'internal representations' of how the attachment Figure is likely to respond to the child's attachment behaviour.

The development of the secure attachment

Whilst attunement is taking place between caregivers and their infant and internal working models are being developed, the infant's sense of self is also developing, closely intertwined with the 'internal representations' of his or her attachment figure(s). The resulting sense of self will be very dependent on whether a satisfactory attunement process has taken place between caregiver and infant. If such an experience has taken place it will translate into a sense of security for the child whose mental representations will involve an expectation of being taken care of in times of trouble.

Securely attached children will tend to feel confident and capable of empathising with others, thereby forming good attachments. This type of attachment, according to Schore (1996, 2000), becomes a primary defence against trauma-induced psychopathology in later life. However, in adolescence, peer group attachments become much more important. According to Mead, as the social self develops this will be 'constituted... by an organisation of the social attitudes of the social group...to which he (or she) belongs' (Mead 1934, p.158). In certain cultures this form of identity is much more prevalent than in our individualistic society. For example, according to the Zulus in South Africa 'You are what others make you feel you are'. This view of self dominates most non-Western cultures such as Muslim, African and Far Eastern societies where *shame* plays a major role in the development of an individual's sense of identity.

A similar and yet different social sense of self may be developing in young people in the West whose identity appears more and more consumer led leading to intense competition and insecurity.

Reflective functioning

As we mentioned earlier, in the process of attunement the caregiver of a secure child is both giving meaning to and anticipating his or her behaviour: this process of having the child's mind in his or her mind has been defined as 'reflective functioning' (Fonagy and Target 1997). This experience is then internalised by the infant and enables him or her to make sense of other people's mental states. It is also seen as central to developing a sense of agency and continuity as well as enabling the growing child to interact successfully with others (Siegel 2001).

The development of insecure attachments

When infants do not have a responsive caregiver in times of need they develop different strategies to gain access to their caregiver in order to survive. Ainsworth and her colleagues (1978) recognised two types of insecure attachment behaviours using the Strange Situation, a separation test carried out on one-year-old infants.

GROUP C: 'RESISTANT' OR ANXIOUS AMBIVALENT TYPE (ABOUT 12 PER CENT OF THE POPULATION)

The caregivers of these infants are inconsistent so these children have to make their presence known so as not to be ignored; this leads to a clinging angry behaviour after separation. According to the long-term prospective Minnesota study, such children are likely to develop anxiety disorders in the future (Sroufe 2005).

GROUP A: AVOIDANT TYPE (ABOUT 20–25 PER CENT OF THE POPULATION)

The caregivers are rejecting of their infants when they need to be comforted or supported. As a result these 'avoidant' infants learn to act as if they have no need for comfort by avoiding eye contact with their parent in the Strange Situation but they maintain some proximity to their rejecting caregiver. Their elevated heart rate when separated betrays their insecurity. To achieve such a state of detachment, these one-year-olds have learnt to deny and, later, denigrate the love and care they need when faced with fear, helplessness or loss. According to the Minnesota study, these children are likely to develop conduct disorders in childhood. In the same study, both resistant and avoidant attachments were moderately correlated with depression in later life (Sroufe 2005).

GROUP D: DISORGANISED TYPE (ABOUT 15 PER CENT OF THE POPULATION)

This group was identified later by Main and Hesse (1992). During the Strange Situation, these one-year-old infants display an unpredictable response in relation to their caregiver after a short period of separation, a mixture of both A and C behaviour. In addition, they are also seen to freeze in trance-like states. This behaviour can be understood as that of an infant suffering from PTSD as a result of being very frightened of their caregiver. These caregivers can be frightening either because they have abused their child, or because they themselves suffer from PTSD. Such a phenomenon can be observed in women who have been raped and whose children can sometimes be the trigger that reminds them of their abuser by having the same eyes as the man who raped them or by the presence of male genitalia in a boy. At such moments the mother is overwhelmed, both mentally and physically, by the terrible memories of what she experienced at the hands of her assailant and is unable to respond to her child's desperate need for comfort and reassurance. The child faces a mother in a state of terror and possible rage: she is no longer there for her young one.

Infants subjected to such terrifying behaviour from their caregivers are left in a state of 'fear without solution' since the 'secure base' represented by their attachment Figure has become their source of terror (Main and Hesse 1992). As a result, these infants develop what we describe as a 'traumatic attachment' to their caregiver.

Attachment and dissociation: the development of the 'traumatic attachment'

When in a state of 'fear without solution', the infant's autonomic response to danger comes into play involving the 'fight–flight or freeze' responses we share with other mammals (Schore 2001).

The 'fight–flight' response is mediated by the sympathetic component of the autonomic nervous system resulting in an increased heart rate, blood pressure, respiration and muscle tone as well as hyper-vigilance. The infant expresses its distress. The thyroid system is stimulated as is the Hypothalamic Pituitary Axis. Such states are referred to as 'kindling states' by Perry *et al.* (1995) due to the high levels of nor-adrenaline and adrenaline which trigger the release of glutamate, a major excitatory transmitter in the brain's limbic system. Symbolic processing is not possible in such states with the result that these traumatic experiences are stored in sensory, somatic, behavioural and affective states (Perry *et al.* 1995).

However, if the 'fight–flight' reaction is not possible, a parasympathetic dominant state takes over and the infant 'freezes', as mammals do in similar circumstances in order to conserve energy or feign death and thereby foster survival (Nijenhuis, Vanderlinden and Spinhoven 1998). In this state, endogenous opiates are released to produce numbing of pain as well as immobility. There is also a suppression of vocalisation so that, in the wild, the threatened animal does not attract the predator's attention by calling his mother. A similar process takes place in terrified children who become mute in relation to severe traumatic experiences.

This phenomenon is present in adults suffering PTSD when reliving their traumatic experience under Positron Emission Tomography (PET scanner) (Rauch *et al.* 1996).

In traumatic states of utter helplessness, both responses can be hyper-activated which results in the human infant experiencing 'an inward flight' from the source of danger, in this case the threatening caregiver. It is in this process that the 'dissociative' response is developed. Children, and later adults, who have lived in fear of their caregiver undergo a splitting of the mind in order to survive. As Schore put it, these children will:

> Maintain their attachment to their desperately needed caregiver by resorting to dissociation; in other words, they will develop an idealised attachment to their parent by dissociating off their terrifying memories of being abused. The resulting working models are those of an idealised attachment relation and that of a dysregulated self in interaction with a mis-attuning and frightening other. (Schore 2001, p.240)

As a result, the self of such individuals lacks self-continuity and is split into different representations of themselves in relation to their caregiver. Bowlby (1980) referred to this process as 'segregated different states' achieved through a process of 'defensive exclusion', which we would now call 'dissociation' (p.70). This phenomenon is evident in individuals who suffer from a borderline personality disorder (de Zulueta 1999; Ryle 1997) and in other dissociative disorders (Ogawa *et al.* 1997).

Clearly, these affected individuals tend to live in a state of fearfulness in relation to the outside world, without the security provided by either an internalised loving caregiver or by the presence of such a caregiver. Such an infant will tend to react defensively to threatening situations with little evidence of any reflective functioning (Fonagy and Target 1997). They will also tend to hold on to what Fairbairn (1952) called the 'moral defence' with desperation because by blaming themselves for their suffering they retain some sense of control and power in the face of overwhelming helplessness. This defence also helps them preserve the cherished hope that one day, especially if they are 'good', they will get the parenting they never had and desperately yearn for (Fairbairn 1952). Unfortunately, the resulting sense of guilt and culpability only reinforces their identification with the abusing parent in their minds.

The psychobiology of childhood neglect and abuse

Over-stimulation or under-stimulation of the neuronal circuits at critical periods of brain growth due either to neglect or to abuse can lead to stress-induced unregulated glucocorticoid and neurotransmitter secretions. This results in damage to the right hemisphere cortical and sub-cortical limbic circuits and other long-term alterations in brain functioning and other maladaptive changes with damaging implications for mental health later in life (Sapolsky 1997). For example, the reduced hippocampal volume reported in female survivors of childhood sexual abuse (Bremner *et al.* 1997) may lead to reduced encoding and retrieval of explicit memory. Similarly, a reduction in cortisol secretion during later stressful episodes can lead to increased vulnerability to PTSD in later life (de Zulueta 2006a; Henry 1997; Yehuda 1997).

Van der Kolk (1989) believes that it is the resulting loss of ability to regulate intense feelings that is the most far-reaching effect of early trauma and neglect. This results in a failure to modulate sympathetic dominant affects like terror, rage and elation, or parasympathetic-dominant affects like shame, disgust and hopeless despair.

Shame is a particularly important emotional reaction in individuals with a vulnerable sense of self and is particularly powerful in individuals whose sense of self has been totally invalidated such as victims of chronic neglect or abuse. The importance of shame lies in its capacity to trigger dissociation and violent behaviour. As one of Gilligan's (1996) homicidal patients said 'Better be bad than not be at all'. In addition to the state of chronic high arousal in individuals exposed to so much trauma, many of these individuals have a reduced ability to use symbols and fantasy to cope with stressful situations. This limitation is ascribed by Henry (1997) to a functional dissociation between the two hemispheres and is called alexithymia.

The triangle of abuse

As a result of these different psychobiological changes in interplay with their internalised working models, traumatised individuals will tend to respond through action rather than thought, often recreating their past abusive experiences from the perspective of either the victim, the abuser or the 'colluder'/bystander, depending on their social context. For example, an adult survivor of child sexual abuse may find herself in a relation with a man who ends up abusing her children in the way she was abused. In such a case, her daughter becomes victim to her mother's partner as a result of the mother's failure to protect her: the survivor parent has become the observer or colluder in the triangle of sexual abuse much as her mother probably was in relation to her own abuse.

The triangle of abuse is an important part of the internalised world of traumatised individuals and should play a part in their therapeutic journey, despite their initial understandable reluctance to be seen as other than a victim or survivor. As van der Kolk (1989) says: 'These victimised people neutralise their hyperarousal by a variety of addictive behaviours, including compulsive re-exposure to situations reminiscent of the trauma' (p.401).

Trauma-induced self-destructive behaviour can be found in veterans who enlist as mercenaries, in sexually abused children who become prostitutes (Welldon 1988), in physically abused children who recreate their violent abuse with their partners in adulthood and many violent offenders (de Zulueta 2005, 2006b; Fonagy and Target 1997; Gilligan 1996).

2. The identification of the traumatic attachment in the assessment and treatment of 'difficult' patients

Therapists working with individuals suffering from a borderline personality disorder or complex PTSD are very familiar with the repeated experience of finding their therapeutic work sabotaged by their patients. The latter may take an overdose after what appeared a good therapeutic session or end treatment just at the point when change was beginning to take place. For these individuals, there appears to be huge resistance in making the painful leap between what the Kleinians refer to as the 'paranoid-schizoid position' to the 'depressive position' (see Chapter 6). What we don't really understand is why there is such a resistance to change in this group of people, especially as most of them have presented for treatment with the specific intention of using the therapy to change their lives and overcome their symptoms and difficulties.

The problem is: how much of the patient is on board during the treatment? And the answer is: it all depends on how traumatically attached they still are to their childhood caregivers in their minds.

CASE STUDY 9.1 *A TRAUMATICALLY-ATTACHED PATIENT*

A female adult patient is referred for an assessment for psychotherapy. She has a past history of child abuse, a current history of self-medication to cope with difficulties in her interpersonal relationships, cutting and suicide threats.

The referrer notes that this patient is requesting psychotherapy although some members of the psychiatric team do not agree with the referral as they believe that she is not really ill and is simply playing up to get attention. There therefore appears to be some evidence that the patient has aroused a splitting in her treating team.

On assessing this 35-year-old woman, what she communicates very strongly is her conviction that she is to blame for all that has happened to her in her childhood and that she feels very guilty about it: she therefore has a strong 'moral defence'. In addition, despite having been exposed to repeated sexual abuse as a girl and teenager, her mother, who failed to protect her then, is seen as a 'good' parent whom the patient contacts three times a week for a chat. Could this patient be idealising her mother in order to continue to have some semblance of mothering in the present? The patient has been in therapy before; when asked why she stopped the therapy, she said that she did not feel understood by her therapist.

The woman in Case Study 9.1 fulfils the three criteria that indicate a likely traumatic attachment to at least one of her caregivers:

- a strong 'moral defence'
- idealisation and splitting
- resistance to change.

We are left with the likelihood that she may also show high levels of dissociation. In order to identify these the assessor looks for the following:

- discontinuities in train of thought: she appears to jump from subject to subject
- inexplicable shifts in affect during the interview, being upset one minute and then laughing or being suddenly angry and critical
- changes in facial appearance, speech and mannerisms: the latter are not always easy to detect during a first interview
- apparently inexplicable behaviour: the patient reports finding herself for no apparent reason in a police station having done something she does not remember doing

- somatic dissociative phenomena: she has pains and difficulties relating to the genital area.

The tendency to dissociate can be checked using the Dissociation Experiences Scale (DES) (Bernstein and Putnam 1986), a 28-item self-rating questionnaire measuring dissociation. It is a reliable and valid instrument that is able to distinguish between people with a dissociative disorder and those without. An update on this scale is provided by Carlson and Putnam (1993).

If we now return to Bowlby's view of what therapy should consist of we are reminded that the role of the therapist is to 'provide the conditions in which the patient can explore his or her representational models'. How can a patient whose view of his/her true nature of his/her attachment Figure is strongly idealised at a conscious level be able to access the true nature of his or her attachment figures?

Bowlby was well aware of the role of an idealised attachment in maintaining a life-giving attachment to the neglectful or abusing parent. He wrote that such children will consciously maintain a wholly favourable image of a parent but 'at a less conscious level he nurses an image in which the parent is represented as neglectful, rejecting or as ill-treating him' (Bowlby 1980, p.71).

He was also aware of the price they later pay for this. Of the many possible consequences there are two major ones, each with certain contingent consequences. First, one or more behavioural systems within a person may be deactivated, partially or completely. When this occurs one or more other activities may come to monopolise the person's time and attention, acting apparently as diversions. An example of such behaviour is provided in Case Study 9.2.

CASE STUDY 9.2 *ABUSE OF AN 18-MONTH-OLD BY A MOTHER WITH DISSOCIATIVE IDENTITY DISORDER*

A patient of Turkish origin was referred on account of her 18-month-old son who appeared emotionally frozen and showed signs of abuse. The patient did not understand why she needed to be assessed nor did many of the staff involved in her care as she appeared to be functioning well and, when visited in her tidy home, she seemed to be loving towards her son. It was not until a full trauma history was elicited from his mother that she revealed – in the incoherent way people with a disorganised attachment speak when talking about traumatic experiences – that she had often experienced him as her childhood abuser right from the time he was born. As a result, she had found herself rejecting him, shouting and hitting him and had herself been reduced to reliving the horror of her abuse at the sight of his male genitalia. It also became clear that she was not usually aware of this abusive behaviour which belonged to another dissociated 'self-other state' of mind. Her score on the DES was high, compatible with that of a dissociative identity disorder. Many similar cases of severe child abuse are probably being missed because their parent's potential for abuse would not be diagnosed in a standard psychiatric or social work interview.

The second consequence resulting from dissociation is that a response, or a set of responses, a person is making may become disconnected cognitively from the interpersonal situation that is eliciting it, leaving him unaware of why he is responding as he is. When that occurs the person may do one or more of several things, each of which is likely to divert his attention away from whomever, or whatever, might be responsible for his reactions. He may mistakenly identify some other person (or situation) as the one who (which) is eliciting his responses. For example, a man who has problems at work with his seniors in positions of authority may not be aware of the fact that he is experiencing these men as he experienced his authoritarian and abusive father.

Bowlby (1980) argued that he may divert his responses away from someone who is in some degree responsible for arousing them and towards some irrelevant Figure including himself. An example of such behaviour is provided by Case Study 9.3.

CASE STUDY 9.3 DISPLACEMENT OF A CHILD-LIKE NEED ONTO A CURRENT PARTNER

A war veteran suffered neglect at the hands of his mother in childhood. In adulthood, he became very dependent on his wife whilst suffering from PTSD following active service. He blames his wife and complains that she is not there for him despite her many attempts to attend to his needs. She notes that he is behaving like her third child, the other two being in their teens. On carrying out the Traumatic Attachment Induction Test (described below), he becomes physically aware of how much he still yearns for his mother and is able to see very clearly how he displaces this need onto his wife.

Bowlby went on: 'He may dwell so insistently on the details of his own reactions and sufferings that he has no time to consider what the interpersonal situation responsible for his reactions may really be' (Bowlby 1980, pp.64–65).

Freud's (1917) paper on 'Mourning and Melancholia' describes cases who, overwhelmed with their different physical and psychological symptoms, fail to identify the cause of their troubles. He described the ego of the 'melancholic' as being split to form a 'critical agency' or 'conscience' which he later renamed the 'super-ego'. The remaining ego he saw as identified with the lost object. As a result of this process, he concluded: 'In this way an object-loss was transformed into an ego-loss and the conflict between the ego and the loved person into a cleavage between the critical activity of the ego and the ego as altered by identification' (Freud 1917, p.249).

Freud also notes that these patients still succeed:

> by the circuitous path of self punishment, in taking revenge on the original object and in tormenting their loved one through their illness, having resorted to it in order to avoid the need to express their hostility to him openly. After all, the person who has occasioned the patient's emotional disorder, and on whom his illness is centred, is usually to be found in his immediate environment. (Freud 1917, p.251)

Later Freud postulated the existence of internalised relationships when he described the 'super-ego', otherwise known as our conscience, as a 'successful instance of identification with the parental agency' (Freud 1933, pp.63–64). He subsequently moved on to his theory of instincts.

Bowlby concluded by noting that the people for whom this defensive exclusion plays a part 'are handicapped in terms of their dealings with other human beings compared to people for whom it plays only a minor part' (Bowlby 1980, p.72). They are also difficult to treat precisely for the reasons Bowlby outlined so clearly. However, with the help of Johnson, my colleagues and I in the Maudsley Hospital have found a way of eliciting, in most of their abused adult patients, a response that bears many of the hallmarks of a 'working model' or 'internal representation'. By using a semi-structured interview during which they are asked to imagine themselves separating from their imagined caregiver, patients have experienced a tightening of the chest and throat and a churning feeling in their stomachs and have expressed varying degrees of fear and/or arousal.

This clinically induced experience has been described and recorded in patients who have a history of child abuse and what I have referred to earlier as having 'traumatic attachment' in relation to their caregiver. Johnson (1999) first published a description of this test as exemplified in Case Study 9.4, which describes a session he held with Lenny.

CASE STUDY 9.4 *INDUCING 'TRAUMATIC ATTACHMENT' IN A SESSION*

Lenny was a 43-year-old single Caucasian man who was in a high-security prison for killing his mate whilst out stealing in the countryside. On being interviewed by Dr Johnson, Lenny gave a history of being 'battered' by his mother when a child. He also admitted that he was frightened of her and was beginning to make links between his fear and his violent behaviour.

In this session, the doctor noticed this fear and tested it by asking Lenny: 'Say your mother was sitting over there, what would you say to her?' The prisoner replied 'I'd say "Mother, you can't hit me any more. I am an adult".' He then slumped in his chair, looked down and then brought his hand to his face with an accompanying fearful and wary expression – just like the disorganised infants on the return of their caregiver in the Strange Situation Test as described by Solomon and George (1999).

Dr Johnson continued: 'And you believe that?' 'Yes, partly,' said his patient.

The therapist says 'You partly believe it and you partly don't?'

Lenny, still looking frightened, says 'Yes. I don't know whether I could say it to her.'

'What would stop you?' asks the doctor.

'Fear' replies the big man in front of him.

'Fear of what? What is she going to do?' asks his therapist.

'Well, she might get up and clout me.'

The doctor continues questioning: 'Might she?'

Lenny, still looking apprehensive, replies 'Well, she might.'

Even after admitting that his mother is now 85 years old and only five feet two inches tall compared to his six feet three inches, when the doctor asked him: 'And she is going to do you an injury, is she?', Lenny replied 'Oh, she is still lively!' He also admitted that he can't disagree with her, let alone hit her.

This large 43-year-old adult is speaking and behaving like a small boy. Even though he does seem aware, at some level, that to be frightened of his old mother is irrational, the fact is that at that moment in time, faced with the idea of his mother, the mother in his mind, he could only admit to being scared like the child he once was, terrified of being battered.

It is then revealed that Lenny battered his mate to death when the latter, who had been out stealing with him, insisted that they spend the night in the comfort of his mother's house and 'mouthed' Lenny when he refused.

Some guidelines on how to elicit the traumatic attachment using the Traumatic Attachment Induction Test (TAIT)

We are currently in the process of refining the use of the TAIT which has been described in detail in an earlier paper (de Zulueta 2006c). Whilst the test is still in the process of being developed and refined, the following guidelines describe to some extent how the traumatic attachment can be elicited using the TAIT and in what context it has to be done in order to make it both safe and meaningful for the patient. It is essentially a way of enabling patients to become physically and emotionally aware of the nature of their attachments to their caregivers prior to and during their therapeutic journey so that they can, as Bowlby advised, reappraise them and restructure them in the light of the new understanding they acquire and the new experiences they have in the therapeutic relationship.

What we have noticed, however, is that therapists who are still traumatically attached to their internal attachment figures, often cannot make use of this test in a meaningful way with their patients. It should therefore be carried out under the supervision of an experienced therapist who is working in this field.

The TAIT is a short semi-structured intervention during which several parameters need to be in place:

1. It is designed to be carried out within a therapeutic context and be preceded by a thoughtful dialogue that focuses on the individual's attachment figures.

2. The relationship between the therapist and the patient needs to be one of mutual trust so that the patient feels able to share what he or she experiences when attempting to carry out the TAIT. The patients are in fact in control of the situation inasmuch as they can choose whether to divulge their experiences when carrying out the TAIT (since they are the ones to feel their body reacting to the imaginary situation, not the therapist). As such an unexpected physical response to an imaginary situation could make many patients feel embarrassed or humiliated, the therapist

needs to be very sensitive to this and offer to turn his or her head away or ask the patient to speak in his head, though this may reduce the impact of the response.

3. This test pre-supposes the existence of an 'adult self' in the patient and it is the adult self who is invited to consider expressing his or her independence in relation to his or her imagined caregiver. The value of the experience lies in the fact that the adult self finds that what he may have thought would be easy, such as telling an imaginary mother that he no longer needs her as he did as a child, turns out to be almost impossible. This is because of the autonomic response it elicits in the patient leading to an increased heart rate, stomach churning, tightening of the chest and the voice possibly disappearing.

4. What is experienced by the patient doing the TAIT is an autonomic response in relation to either (a) the fear of losing the parent due to their traumatic attachment or (b) a parallel fear of being once again a victim of that parent's destructiveness: both experiences reinforced the attachment to the caregiver during childhood.

5. The TAIT is not a 'role play', Gestalt-type experience whereby the adult is invited to imagine himself as a child talking to his attachment figure, as is done in certain types of psychotherapy. This can retraumatise or induce a dissociative response in traumatised patients and is not part of the TAIT as the adult self must be present throughout the process.

6. The timing of the actual TAIT is important. That is, the patient's attempt at facing the imagined parent whilst attempting to inform him or her that s/he no longer needs him or her should not take more than one or two minutes.

7. After patients have carried out the TAIT, the practitioner invites them to speak about their experience and to give an indication of how disturbing they found the experience in terms of body sensations. For example, a woman who had been adopted was very surprised to find that she responded with a great yearning to the possibility of letting go of her biological mother. She had always thought that her problems were all related to her relationship with her adoptive mother.

8. The degree of autonomic arousal can be measured as Subjective Units of Distress (SUDs) varying from nought (no response) to ten (a very high response).

9. The patient's thoughts and associations in relation to the TAIT are the most important aspect of the entire process since it can usually lead them to develop their own understanding of why they feel and behave as they do, thereby initiating the process of change. Case Study 9.5 illustrates this. If the practitioner has not had a similar therapeutic experience, they will find it difficult if not impossible to both elicit such responses and follow them through to their natural conclusion.

CASE STUDY 9.5 *USING TAIT TO DEVELOP SELF-UNDERSTANDING*

A young woman with a history of severe neglect and the symptoms of an eating disorder found herself quite unable to tell her mother that she did not need her during the TAIT. Even though she realised that she would have to give up this deep-seated yearning for the mother she never had when undergoing therapy, she told the assessing therapist that she wanted to take up the treatment being offered. However, when the therapist suggested that a part of her was terrified of the idea of 'getting better' because this would make it less likely for her to be able to elicit her mother's attention and love, she smiled ruefully. The therapist then asked her: 'How will this little one, who still yearns for mother and fears losing her, express her needs during therapy?' The patient replied: 'By not eating.' This enabled both therapist and patient to plan for an involvement with the eating disorders unit during her therapeutic journey.

---

10. The TAIT can be carried out in relation to either of the individual's parental figures and, as we would expect, produce differing responses. However, it is not recommended to do the TAIT in relation to two caregivers in the same session as this could be overpowering for the patient.

Conclusions

It is in the act of imagined separation from their caregiver during the Traumatic Attachment Induction Test that abused and neglected individuals can discover their 'traumatic attachment' with all that this implies in terms of fear and unrequited longing. Such an attachment can be understood as the internalised product of repeated experiences in which these children have felt both terrified and – paradoxically – desperately in need of their caregiver whose protection is felt as essential for their survival.

The TAIT has so far proved to be a powerful tool in revealing some of the psychopathology underpinning dysfunctional and violent behaviour in individuals with a history of childhood abuse. It has the additional merit of making people aware of their traumatic attachments in a very concrete and physical way, through their fear response. This act of self-discovery has the potential to provide individuals with the necessary insight to understand why they behave and feel as they do and to explore the possibility of change in the future. Both the extent of their reaction and their response to the TAIT can give practitioners and patients an indication as to how difficult that change might be. Not all individuals have the internal and external resources to let go of their 'traumatic attachments'; not all individuals are prepared to give up their childhood longing for love and care – whatever the cost to themselves and to others.

In the field of forensic mental health, the TAIT could play an important role in the assessment of risk in terms of predicting an individual's potential for violence and in assessing change during and after treatment. It could be particularly effective in measuring change and outcome in the treatment of patients suffering from a borderline personality disorder, which shares so many features with what is referred to as complex PTSD (de Zulueta 1999, 2009).

In the therapeutic field it can be used as an assessment tool, as illustrated above, and subsequently to measure degrees of change during treatment and at the end of therapy.

Whether the 'traumatic attachment' that is revealed through the TAIT is in fact the manifestation of a 'working model' or an 'internal representation' needs to be clarified. What we do observe is an individual reacting physically and emotionally to an imagined internal representation of a caregiver from whom he is attempting to separate, very much as disorganised infants behave in relation to their caregiver in the Strange Situation (Main and Hesse 1992). This is in itself an important breakthrough in the study of human behaviour and one that highlights the importance of traumatisation during childhood and its impact on the human attachment system in the genesis and transmission of violence.

References

Ainsworth, M.D.S., Blehar, M.C., Waters, E. and Wall, S. (1978) *Patterns of Attachment: A Psychological Study of the Strange Situation*. Hillsdale, NJ: Lawrence Erlbaum Associates.

Bernstein, E.M. and Putnam, F.W. (1986) 'Development, reliability and validity of a dissociation scale.' *Journal of Nervous and Mental Disease 174*, 727–735.

Bowlby, J. (1969) *Attachment and Loss. Vol. 1: Attachment*. New York: Basic Books.

Bowlby, J. (1973) *Attachment and Loss. Vol. 2: Separation: Anxiety and Anger*. London: Hogarth Press.

Bowlby, J. (1980) *Attachment and Loss. Vol. 3: Loss, Sadness and Depression*. London: Hogarth Press.

Bowlby, J. (1988) *A Secure Base: Clinical Applications of Attachment Theory*. London: Routledge.

Bremner, J.D., Licinio, J., Darnell, A., Krystal, J.H. *et al.* (1997) 'Elevated CSF corticotrophin-releasing factor concentrations in post-traumatic stress disorder.' *American Journal of Psychiatry 150*, 624–629.

Carlson, E.B. and Putnam, F.W. (1993) 'An update on Dissociative Experiences Scale.' *Dissociation 6*, 1, 16–27.

de Zulueta, F. (1999) 'Borderline personality disorder as seen from an attachment perspective: a review.' *Criminal Behaviour and Mental Health 9*, 237–253.

de Zulueta, F. (2005) 'Violence from an attachment perspective.' *Criminal Justice Matters 61*, 1, 20–21.

de Zulueta, F. (2006a) *From Pain to Violence: The Roots of Human Destructiveness*. Second edition. Chichester: John Wiley and Sons.

de Zulueta, F. (2006b) 'The treatment of PTSD from an attachment perspective.' *Journal of Family Therapy 28*, 334–351.

de Zulueta, F. (2006c) 'The role of the traumatic attachment in the assessment and treatment of adults with a history of childhood abuse and neglect.' *British Journal of Forensic Practice 8*, 4–15.

de Zulueta, F. (2009) 'Post traumatic stress disorder and attachment: possible links with borderline personality disorder.' *Advances in Psychiatric Treatment 15*, 172–180.

Fairbairn, R. (1952) *Psychoanalytic Study of the Personality*. London: Routledge and Kegan Paul.

Fonagy, P. and Target, M. (1997) 'Attachment and reflective function: their role in self organisation.' *Development and Psychopathology 9*, 679–700.

Freud, S. (1917) 'Mourning and Melancholia.' *The Standard Edition of the Complete Psychological Works of Sigmund Freud, Vol 14*. London: Hogarth Press.

Freud, S. (1933) 'The Dissection of the Psychical Personality. Lecture 31. New Introductory Lectures on Psycho-Analysis.' *The Standard Edition of the Complete Psychological Works of Sigmund Freud, Vol 22*. London: Hogarth Press.

Gilligan, J. (1996) *Violence, our Deadly Epidemic and its Causes*. New York: G.P. Putnam's Sons.

Harlow, H.F. (1974) *Learning to Love*. Second edition. New York: Jason Aronson.

Henry, J. (1997) 'Psychological and physiological responses to stress: the right hemisphere and the hypothalamic-pituitary-adrenal-axis, an inquiry into problems of human bonding.' *Acta Physiologica Scandinavica 161*, 164–169.

Johnson, B. (1999) *Building a Violence-Free Society. Conference Proceedings.* York: James Nayler Foundation.

Main, M. and Hesse, E. (1992) 'Disorganised/Disorientated Infant Behaviour in the Strange Situation, Lapses in Monitoring of Reasoning and Discourse During the Parent's Adult Attachement Interview, and Dissociative States.' In M. Ammanati and D. Stern (eds) *Attachment and Psychoanalysis.* Rome: Gius Laterza and Figli.

Mead, G.H. (1934) *Mind, Self and Society from the Standpoint of a Social Behaviourist.* Chicago: University of Chicago Press.

Nijenhuis, E.R.S., Vanderlinden, J. and Spinhoven, P. (1998) 'Animal defensive models as a model for trauma-induced dissociative reactions.' *Journal of Traumatic Stress 11*, 243–260.

Ogawa, J.R., Sroufe, L.A., Weinfield, N.S., Carlson, E.A. and Egeland, B. (1997) 'Development of the fragmented self: longitudinal study of dissociative symptomatology in a non clinical sample.' *Development and Psychopathology 9*, 855–879.

Perry, B.D., Pollard, R.A., Bajer, W.L., Sturges, C., Vigilandte, D. and Blakley, T.L. (1995) 'Continous heart rate monitoring in maltreated children.' *Proceedings, Annual Meeting of the American Academy of Child and Adolescent Psychiatry, New Research 21*, 69.

Rauch, S.L., van der Kolk, B.A., Fisler, R.E., Alport, N.M. *et al.* (1996) 'A symptom provocation study of post traumatic stress disorder using positron emission tomography and script driven imagery.' *Archives of General Psychiatry 53*, 380–387.

Ryle, A. (1997) *Cognitive Analytic Therapy and Borderline Personality Disorder: The Model and the Method.* Chichester: John Wiley and Sons.

Sapolsky, R.M. (1997) 'Why stress is bad for your brain.' *Science 273*, 749–750.

Schore, A.N. (1996) 'The experience-dependent maturation of a regulatory system in the orbital pre-frontal cortex and the origin of developmental psychopathology.' *Development and Psychopathology 8*, 59–87.

Schore, A.N. (2000) 'Attachment and the regulation of the right brain.' *Attachment and Human Development 2*, 1, 23–47.

Schore, A.N. (2001) 'The effects of early relational trauma on right brain development, affect regulation and infant mental health.' *Infant Mental Health Journal 22*, 201–269.

Siegel, D.J. (2001) 'Toward an interpersonal neurobiology of the developing mind: attachment relationships, 'mindsight' and neural integration.' *Infant Mental Health Journal 22*, 67–94.

Solomon, J. and George, S. (eds) (1999) *Attachment Disorganisation.* New York: Guildford Press.

Sroufe, A.L. (2005) 'Attachment and development: a prospective longitudinal study from birth to adulthood.' *Attachment and Human Development 7*, 349–367.

Stern, D.N. (1985) *The Interpersonal World of the Infant.* New York: Basic Books.

van der Kolk, B.A. (1989) 'The compulsion to repeat the trauma: re-enactment, re-victimisation and masochism.' *Psychiatric Clinics of North America 12*, 389–411.

Welldon, E.V. (1988) *Mother, Madonna and Whore.* London: Free Association Books.

Yehuda, R. (1997) 'Sensitisation of the Hypothalamic-Pituitary Axis in Post Traumatic Stress Disorder.' In R. Yehuda and A.C. McFarlane (eds) *Psychobiology of Post Traumatic Stress Disorder.* New York: New York Academy of Sciences.

Chapter 10

Towards a Working Group

Applying Theory From Group Dynamics and Group Analytic Psychotherapy

Caroline Grimbly

Introduction

From the 1940s onwards S. H. Foulkes developed a theory of the group that suggested we must reverse the traditional view that the individual is the primary unit, and instead see the group as the primary unit of consideration. So-called inner processes in the individual then become internalisations of the forces operating in the group to which he or she belongs (Foulkes 1990). Foulkes proposed a theory of mind in which mind is 'not a *thing* which exists but a series of events, moving and proceeding all the time' (Foulkes 1990, p.224). In relationships with others in a group, instead of thinking in terms of a number of interacting systems (individuals), we should think of 'interacting processes in the unified field, the matrix of the group' (Foulkes 1990, p.214). Foulkes stressed that this was not to deny the phenomenon of mind or individual as a coherent entity and as a whole person who interacts with whole people, but that what occurs in a group is 'selective interaction that goes on impersonally, instinctively, intuitively, basically unconsciously, in accordance with the inner constellation and predispositions of those concerned and which determine their interaction' (Foulkes 1990, p.228). This is also placed within the social context, with society *inside* the individual, as well as outside. Given that social work takes place within the context of groups – the family, social networks, the community, the social work team, the multi-disciplinary team, the organisation and so on – how can we use theory from group dynamics and analytic group psychotherapy to inform practice? This Chapter considers how paying attention to group dynamics can contribute to successful achievement of a task, which can otherwise be undermined by unconscious group processes.

To illustrate this approach I will present a case study (10.1), the setting for which is an MSc course for experienced social workers. As part of the learning on the MSc programme, there is a group to which each student brings a recording of a piece of clinical work. The group is used as a consultation forum, focusing on the relevance of theory and research and on power dynamics and anti-discriminatory practice. Material from this group is later presented to a viva panel for examination. Within Foulkes' framework, the case consultation group would be seen not only as a series of individuals presenting to other individuals, but primarily as a web (of interactions) woven from the social context, the individuals' histories and psyches and the emerging communications – conscious and unconscious. Details have been altered, in order to preserve the anonymity of those involved.

CASE STUDY 10.1 A CASE CONSULTATION GROUP FOR PRACTITIONERS

The MSc programme had been running for some 30 years when a decision was made to double the number of available places. There was recognition amongst the existing staff that it was a positive move to expand the course and there was considerable excitement about this. Alongside this was some anxiety about change. The case consultation group tutor was a practitioner with many years experience in the field and as a tutor on the course. An additional tutor (the author of this chapter) was engaged, close to the beginning of the new academic year, to run a second, parallel case consultation group. The two consultation groups consisted of seven and six students. The long-standing tutor, a man, facilitated the larger of the two. The other group was facilitated by the new, female tutor (the author). Within a few weeks, the only male student in this group was forced by work circumstances to withdraw from the course, leaving a mixed gender group and an all female group. The year got underway with little joint working between the two group facilitators and few opportunities to meet as a whole group.

On reflection, the staff team gave insufficient thought to how the real and perceived differences between the two group facilitators would impact on the student groups. The students were aware of the difference in experience of teaching on the course. In addition, the long-standing tutor gave lectures to the whole group, led the whole group session introducing the practice module and even had the larger room. Gender may also have contributed to the power differential. The system therefore set up a dynamic in which one group was perceived as having a powerful, safe 'parent', who could hold the group, whereas the other had a 'new mother' who carried the anxiety about potential failure. Amongst other things, splitting the two tutors in this way minimised the risk of destructive rivalry between the 'parents'.

Although all students were of the same profession, they worked with a range of groups of people, split particularly between children and adults, and in a range of settings, including rural and urban, public and private. The model of learning was consistent with that explored by Abercrombie in the 1950s, incorporating insights from group analysis (see Thompson 1999), which emphasised autonomous learning (rather than receiving information), student and tutor as co-operating explorers of knowledge, and relationships between peers as a powerful medium for collaborative learning. Seating was, as in a psychotherapy group, in a circle and, as such, did not privilege the tutor's position. However, the role of tutor as examiner was inevitably in the matrix from the start.

The smaller group, on which we will focus, settled fairly quickly to work, united perhaps, in the enthusiastic expectation that all would be solved by the acquisition of new knowledge (Thompson 1999). However, although all the students were experienced in their field, there was expressed anxiety about 'exposure' to other group members in presenting their clinical material. For adults returning to learning, earlier educational experiences will colour the process. Both regression to 'adult/child' ways of interacting and anxiety related to exposure and competition will be very present, in much the same way as in a therapy group. Thompson (1999) argued that intellectual and emotional growth cannot be kept altogether separate. If, as she asserts, learning involves the rearranging of knowledge and past experience and is often painful, the emotional is likely to have a significant influence on the potential of individuals and the group to achieve the stated task. König (1992) reflects that, in new situations – particularly complicated social structures experienced at school and work – similarities to previous situations are looked for, with the early mother–infant situation the most primary. He suggests that the need for familiarity may be dealt with by projecting onto the whole group an image of 'mother' as experienced at the earliest developmental stage. As group members get to know more about each other, the group may be experienced as sub-divided and the tendency is for members to project members of their nuclear family onto group members, 'thus obscuring the group's complex reality' (König 1992, p.153).

It is reasonable to suggest that in common with entering group therapy, each student was attempting to manage a high level of anxiety:

> Each participant [...] has expectations that are unconscious, or possibly even conscious, that the therapist will be able to cure him... The gaps between expectations and what will actually take place in the group, and the projections and the struggle within to attack these projections are what causes the group to move through its various phases of development. (Agmon and Schneider 1998, p.134)

I was perhaps expected to teach them all they would need to know, rather than 'cure' them.

The student members were, overtly, patient with the need for me to check details, particularly around assessment of the various modules. I took the line that pretending to know everything would disempower the students further, but it did mean they were left holding some anxiety about my own experience as 'new mother' and thus my capacity to 'feed' them. There were early complaints that this group had the smaller of two rooms, indicating a level of envy directed towards the other group, who not only had the larger room, but the 'larger' tutor. Where conflicts did arise in the group in the early days, they tended to find a focus in the material presented, often in the form of different perspectives on who needed the most support, protection or understanding: who is the most in need? Much of the material presented was of a distressing nature, including the story of the death of a child. As Thompson (1999) suggests, the nature of the topic in a 'discussion' group may increase the level of stress and: '...this is likely to be reflected in a strengthening of disruptive, as opposed to cohesive, forces in the group as a whole' (Thompson 1999, p.103).

Thompson (1999) points to the possible sense for adult learners of narcissistic hurt involved in acknowledging a teacher. Authority and dependency issues loom large. Foulkes and Anthony (1957) suggest that conflict over authority, dependency, conformity and change is evident in manifest or latent forms in every group situation.

CASE STUDY 10.1 *(CONTINUED)*

As the first term progressed, conflicts began to arise more frequently in the group. I was beginning to receive complaints in individual tutorials that there was a lack of respect amongst certain individuals and that the feeling of safety was being compromised in the group. At around this time, the group received news that one of our members had been attacked at work by a female patient and she was off work for a number of weeks. During the consultation group the week she returned, there was a heated disagreement between two group members, related to events that occurred in the group. One member of the group felt disrespected, whilst the other felt she responded aggressively. This exchange was particularly difficult to witness for the member who had been attacked at work.

I attempted to respond in a way that would demonstrate that I was robust enough to both set boundaries and also survive this attack on the group, in the hope that this would contain the group's destructive feelings. Melanie Klein, in 'Notes on some schizoid mechanisms' (1946), writes about the process whereby the individual develops. She states that the early ego (or 'I') lacks cohesion and that the infant has a tendency to alternate between a sense of integration and disintegration. Fear of annihilation, separation anxiety and the frustration of bodily needs lead to anxiety that is experienced as being caused by parts of the self or parts of other people ('objects', in Klein's terms). The infant responds to this anxiety by feeling persecuted by these 'objects', which they have taken into their self-image, and this reinforces their fear of their own destructiveness. Fear of retaliation by the 'object' leads to further anxiety and this is dealt with by splitting up the 'I' and projecting parts out onto others. In normal development, this phase is transitory and is balanced by repeated positive experiences of good 'objects'. Considering this theory in relation to the group, the risk at this stage was that anxiety regarding survival would lead to individuals projecting their more destructive feelings, either onto group members or onto the group as a whole, and that this would leave the group feeling like a dangerous place to be. This could lead either to individuals leaving or to an inability to use the group effectively. The accidental death of a child and the stories of disturbed women were powerful stories in the group matrix. Would I enable my children to thrive or would I retaliate?

The group suffered an early loss, but it was the assault against one of the members that appeared to be particularly traumatic and allowed the cracks to become open wounds. Brought into the room was the reality of murderousness: the assailant had been convicted of murdering an older woman – perhaps, at least in fantasy, her mother? Winnicott (1949) wrote of the importance of the mother managing her own hateful feelings and surviving the hate of the infant towards her; in this scenario there is no survival and no way to deal with anger. To follow Klein (1986), anxiety attached to the fantasy of retaliation by the mother will not be defused – and that way madness lies. Foulkes and Anthony (1957) note that, to defend against such disturbing content or affect, the group might defend itself collectively, perhaps by developing defence mechanisms that reflect individual members, with the defences of dominant members predominating. In this group at *this* time, in Bion's terms, the defence fight/flight became pervasive.

Wilfred Bion (1989) described the individual as a 'group animal at war, not simply with the group, but with himself for being a group animal and with those aspects of his personality that constitute his "groupishness"' (Bion 1989, p.131). Group phenomena for Bion do not appear when people get together – 'groupishness' is primitive and no individual can be regarded as outside the group. He developed a theory of 'basic assumption groups', in which primitive emotional drives are expressed in group processes. The group defends itself against anxiety by behaving in ways consistent with one of the three 'basic assumptions' – namely, dependency, fight/flight and pairing. In these terms, in this student group we can see a group consistent with basic assumption dependency and basic assumption fight/flight. The group's initial strategy for managing the conflicts was to bring them up individually with me in tutorials. This appeared to be a continuation of the dependency dynamic – I would hold the pain and anxiety, dispense justice and solve the problem. Agmon and Schneider (1998) suggest that to ward off regressive feelings of emptiness and hopelessness, related to the passive-dependent relationship to the 'mother', there are defence mechanisms of flight into health, denial of the problem or projection of the problem onto others in the group. When these actions do not lead to serious consequences: '...the group members transfer their trust to the conductor to see what he or she can do for them. *They create a unity around an unconscious oral-dependent wish*' (Agmon and Schneider 1998, p.137; my emphasis).

Avoidance of discussion as a group enabled individuals to maintain the fantasy that everything would be all right if they depended on me and, by implication, ignored the other group members. However, as Klein (1946) notes, the risk of projecting all the 'good' (the sense of agency) onto the object is that it can lead to an impoverished ego (or 'I'). The notion of disrespect, where 'respect' is from a Latin root meaning 'to look', implied a process of not noticing the other. If there is a fear of a failure in the source of nurturance through neglect, annihilating any rivals could ensure your survival. Equally, should the fear be of *attack* by the carer, it would be vital to unhitch one's destructive rage from the carer onto an other, on whom you did not depend. As Foulkes and Anthony suggest (1957) the scapegoat is attacked when the group fears attacking the person on whom feelings are really focused.

When I presented the conflict to the group as a dilemma to be thought about together, the group drew up a list of 'group rules', resorting to what may be deemed stereotypes of the profession they held (e.g. 'respect difference'). Relationships were mediated through a professional role. Although outwardly this appeared to be an attempt to cohere as a group, it by-passed any attempt to process the emotions raised by the conflicts or to understand what might be occurring in the group. Feelings still ran high and were acted out in ways such as absence or withholding feedback to each other in the consultation group – there was still a reluctance to 'look at' the other. According to Bion (1989) a relative lack of verbal exchange indicates the continuation of basic assumption behaviour – communication is debased in the basic assumption group, whereas verbal exchange is a function of the work group.

The group dynamics presented me with two particular dilemmas. First, whilst the students had in a sense contracted to reveal something of themselves, implied in the emphasis on reflective practice, the group was not a therapy group. I was not at liberty to bring into the group material brought into individual tutorials, nor to necessarily encourage it into the group, in the way one might when working therapeutically with individuals who are in concurrent individual and group therapy (see, for example, de Zulueta and Mark 2000). Second, there was a balance to be struck between paying attention to the process and driving through the task. As the group tutor, I felt it my responsibility to hold the completion of the task in mind, as a boundary to which we must keep. At the same time, I was aware that the task was being compromised by the group dynamics: the group was operating at a basic assumption level, not as a work group (Bion 1989).

Towards a work group

At the beginning of this chapter, we noted the impact of wider organisational dynamics on the development of the group, related to the evolving course structure. We moved on to consider in particular the resulting anxiety in the group associated with the fear of environmental ('mother') failure, reflecting in part the anxiety of the wider system. The hypothesis is that, in this group, this anxiety was experienced as a threat to survival and was reinforced by the content of the clinical material present in the group matrix and by a potentially deadly traumatic event. To manage this anxiety, the group diverted its rage from the primary mother object, in the person of the group tutor, and onto split-up parts of the group, in the persons of individual group members.

Having identified the impact of the organisation on the group, it was important to bring the second consultation group, along with its tutor and the programme leader, into the frame. Roberts and Obholzer (1994) note that 'troublesome' individual behaviour must be perceived and treated as an indication of a problem in the group: the unconscious suction of individuals into performing a function on behalf of others, as well as themselves, can usefully be regarded as a response to the unconscious needs of the institution – in this instance, concerned with managing anxiety in relation to change. They suggest that an intervention focusing on the institutional process could serve to draw all members back into role and enable them to resume work on the primary task. By focusing on the institution and the whole group, we aimed to avoid a parallel process, whereby the small, all female group would become the 'troublesome' failing group. It was also hoped that, by opening out the discussion to involve the whole system, individuals would feel less persecuted and anxious and more able to think. As Rogers (1987) notes: 'Attention paid to both the content and the nature of the communication is more frustrating for the [patient], but will move the culture of the group towards using more dialogue [and less projective identification]' (Rogers 1987, p.101).

As a staff group, we aimed to present ourselves as a united 'parental' unit. The purpose was to provide the students with a sense of what Bion (1991, 1993) terms containment. For Bion, the mother must resist being overwhelmed by anxiety in the face of her infant's powerful (and sometimes destructive) feelings. She must retain the capacity to think, in the sense of identifying the baby's feelings and presenting them back to the baby in a manageable form ('there, there, I know it hurts, it'll be all right'). In this arena, this translated as making feelings available to the group as 'food for thought'. We hypothesised with them that the group was responding to changes in the organisation, which might include rivalry between my colleague and me, anxiety from both of us about my ability, and issues of gender and power. Agmon and Schneider (1998) define the purpose of such an interpretation or intervention in group therapy as allowing:

> Group members to identify with him or her [the conductor] and see him or her as a more stable and adequate superego. This allows healthier identifications with the conductor to develop, and allows for a re-differentiation in group structures – a healthier and more mature superego and ego…as well as internalization of good and bad elements. (Agmon and Schneider 1998, p.137)

Moreover, the intervention may be seen as an example of what Agmon and Schneider describe as the 'median point between the ideal response and a paranoid response' (Agmon and Schneider 1998, p.152) – that is, one that neither implies that the course tutors have the answers and can solve the students' problems (as the split-off 'good objects'), nor one that involves becoming part of a persecutory response to a split-off 'bad' part of the group (either by defending or blaming one part of the group or another).

In addition to this meeting, we built in a future session looking, as a whole group, at theoretical material on groups, thus presenting a framework for more developed thinking. We looked at Jon Stokes' (1994) paper on Bion's basic assumptions and unconscious group processes in the workplace and James Zender's (1991) paper on projective identification in group psychotherapy, offering the opportunity to approach the subject from either a more or less affect-laden perspective and to focus either on the experience of the group as a group, or on work-based relationships. The group was particularly interested in Stokes' suggestion that different professions may predominantly operate within particular basic assumption modes. Stokes suggests that social workers tend towards basic assumption fight/flight, which in sophisticated mode could translate into a productive fight against injustice and in a degenerate mode could translate into a 'demand for our rights' and the projecting of responsibility for change onto others. Taking Bion's (1993) concept of learning, persisting with the whole group in being curious enhanced the opportunities to develop *thinking*:

> Where unacceptable feelings evacuated by projective identification are given back to the child/patient [student] by the mother/analyst [tutor] in a more tolerable form, a thought and thinking process can develop, stimulating the impulse to be curious on which all learning depends. (Rogers 1987, p.104)

Within the small group, I continued to offer containment through persisting in keeping a focus on the task, continuing to name difficulties in the group and paying attention to individual needs in tutorials. As a group, the students also took on a containing function, by completing work as required and participating more freely in discussions. There was a sense in which the group worked through some of its difficulties via the clinical material. For example, there was intensive discussion about a client who split her workers into 'good' and 'bad' and depended heavily on the student (perhaps reflecting the splits in the group and dependence on the tutor), and sensitive exploration of a family in which twin sisters (the two groups?) were treated differently, but the parents did their very best.

There is a temptation to either over-manage processes in the group or to ignore processes, in the hope that they will 'go away' if you press on with the task. As Thompson (1999) suggests, the alternative is to facilitate an understanding:

> So facilitation does not mean moving impediments in the way of development so much as helping a group to recognise and address the impediments for itself. When the group is able to do this, impediments can be reframed as opportunities. (Thompson 1999, p.117)

Rogers asserts that, in order to move on from what she terms an 'oral-dependent' phase '...the group needs to learn to bite...to say what it thinks, and to carry on doing so' (Rogers 1987, p.102). It was important to ensure that we had time as a group to consider our ending and, when we came to our final session, it was possible to name many of the difficulties the group had encountered and to also acknowledge the growth and learning that had taken place over the year. This end of year evaluation by the students suggested this was still a 'work in progress', with complaints still being raised about the difference between the two group tutors – and, indeed, one must accept both the reality *and* the fantasy involved in this. However, the experience of the latter part of the year indicated that the group was more able to operate independently and to manage conflict. Sound outcomes in the examinations provided evidence that the task had been successfully completed.

Concluding remarks

In this chapter, a case has been made for practice that engages the reflecting part of each group member in developing the ability to understand and deal with the powerful emotions engendered in the group by regressive transferences (König 1992). This group had moved on from feeling unsafe and riddled with aggression, towards a point where it may be said that:

> Altruism and group co-operation, the ability to individuate and to make constructive emotional attachments, point to growth in object relations... The group has developed from a dependent one upon the conductor to a group that functions fairly autonomously and can evaluate itself and decide how to use its skills and resources. (Agmon and Schneider 1998, p.154)

In social work practice we are constantly confronted by situations in which complex tasks are to be completed, whilst balancing individual needs and risks within systems comprising configurations of many groups. Each assessment of an adult with mental health problems, for example, takes place within a group context of family, social network, wider society, multi-disciplinary team, social work team and department, and so on. The work can be facilitated or hindered by the unconscious or unexpressed dynamics of the various groups. As an advanced practitioner, a willingness to explore and reflect on these processes as an individual worker and within groups may be crucial in ensuring that the service user is met with practice that is containing, thoughtful and constructive.

References

Agmon, S. and Schneider, S. (1998) 'The first stages in the development of the small group: a psychoanalytic understanding.' *Group Analysis 31*, 131–156.

Bion, W.R. (1989) *Experiences in Groups and Other Papers.* London: Routledge.

Bion, W.R. (1991) *Learning from Experience.* London: Karnac Books.

Bion, W.R. (1993) *Second Thoughts.* London: Karnac Books.

de Zulueta, F. and Mark, P. (2000) 'Attachment and contained splitting: a combined approach of group and individual therapy to the treatment of patients suffering from borderline personality disorder.' *Group Analysis 33*, 4, 486–500.

Foulkes, S.H. (1990) *Selected Papers: Psychoanalysis and Group Analysis.* London: Karnac.

Foulkes, S.H. and Anthony, E.J. (1957) *Group Psychotherapy: The Psychoanalytic Approach.* Harmondsworth: Penguin.

Klein, M. (1946) 'Notes on some schizoid mechanisms.' *International Journal of Psychoanalysis 27*, 99–110.

Klein, M. (1986) *The Selected Melanie Klein.* Harmondsworth: Penguin Books.

König, K. (1992) 'Basic Assumption Groups and Working Groups Revisited.' In M. Pines (ed.) *Bion and Group Psychotherapy.* London: Routledge.

Roberts, V.Z. and Obholzer, A. (eds) (1994) *The Unconscious at Work.* London: Routledge.

Rogers, C. (1987) 'On putting it into words: the balance between projective identification and dialogue in the group.' *Group Analysis 20*, 99–107.

Stokes, J. (1994) 'The Unconscious at Work in Groups and Teams: Contributions From the Work of Wilfred Bion.' In V.Z. Roberts and A. Obholzer (eds) *The Unconscious at Work.* London: Routledge.

Thompson, S. (1999) *The Group Context.* London: Jessica Kingsley Publishers.

Winnicott, D.W.W. (1949) 'Hate in the counter-transference.' *International Journal of Psychoanalysis 30*, 66–79.

Zender, J.F. (1991) 'Projective identification in group psychotherapy.' *Group Analysis 24*, 117–132.

Part III

Advanced Reflective Practice in Action

Chapter 11

Psychosocial Mental Health Practice in Children and Family Services

Rebecca Peters

Introduction

The Children Act 1989 requires Local Authority Children's Social Care (CSC) services to safeguard and promote the welfare of children 'in need'. Inevitably, CSC services limit their interventions to children with a high level of unmet need – children in families with parental mental ill health, learning difficulties, drug and alcohol misuse and domestic violence (Cleaver, Unell and Aldgate 1999). Referred children often exhibit emotional and behavioural difficulties. Families tend not to self-refer and, initially at least, do not work voluntarily with CSC.

Rightly, government expectations for children and families, as set out in the *Every Child Matters: Change for Children* (Department for Education and Skills 2004) programme and the White Paper *Care Matters: Time for Change* (Department for Education and Skills 2007) are high. Therefore, the challenges facing social workers involved in case management are great. Guidance such as *Working Together to Safeguard Children* (Her Majesty's Government 2006) and the *London Child Protection Procedures* (London Safeguarding Children Board 2007) encapsulate good procedural practice but provide relatively little guidance on effective interventions. A doctor treating a patient with asthma can consult an up-to-date guideline, and largely 'follow the recipe'. In social work, there is rarely a scientifically validated intervention that can be applied 'off the shelf'.

Enquiries into cases where children known to CSC have died reveal that workers often feel overwhelmed and fail to be thoughtful and emotionally engaged. In such cases, social workers often describe the family's situation accurately, and record a great deal of relevant information, but they implement few effective interventions.

Recently, prompted by the death of 'Baby Peter', a child known to CSC and killed by his carers, Lord Laming undertook a review of child protection services in England. The review recommended more support for children's social workers and a practice-focused post-graduate qualification (Laming 2009).

This Chapter argues that a key element in effective support for social workers is the development of a research tradition that rivals medical research in its scope and ambition – the mantra 'evidence-based medicine' translated into 'evidence-based social work'.

The case examples described below are chosen to show that even the sparse research literature that is currently available is already helpful in the day-to-day caseload of the CSC Service in the London Borough of Hackney. In the future, as modern research techniques are increasingly applied to the social sciences, the research literature will become even more productive.

Evidence-based practice in Hackney

In Hackney, a diverse and deprived inner London local authority, a *Reclaiming Social Work* change agenda has been initiated by Isabelle Trowler, assistant director of CSC, and Steve Goodman, deputy director of children and young people's services. A key element in these changes is to provide an environment where practitioners can implement evidence-based interventions to help families change.

Social work teams are being replaced by small multi-disciplinary units led by a consultant social worker. Working with them are a second social worker, a children's practitioner, a unit co-ordinator and a clinician (clinical psychologist or systemic family therapist). Cases are discussed at weekly unit meetings. Sharing the burden of work in this way means families benefit from a reduced likelihood of drift; work continues despite the absence of any individual, and workers benefit from the support of colleagues.

Clinicians are funded by local Child and Adolescent Mental Health Services. Clinicians are embedded within units to undertake interventions, and to advise colleagues – hardwiring clinical thinking and clinical evidence within the units.

Promoting evidence-based interventions involves investment. For example, Hackney promotes the employment of systemic family therapy and social learning theory, based on strong evidence of their success in facilitating change in families (Brestan and Eyberg 1998; Carr 2000; Cottrell and Boston 2002). Staff therefore receive training in these core methodologies. Systemic family therapy suggests that problems originate within the family and its wider social network, rather than among single individuals. Social learning theory suggests individuals learn behaviours by observing people around them; learning is strengthened through reinforcement and punishment.

CASE STUDY 11.1 *INTERVENING EFFECTIVELY TO AVOID CARE PROCEEDINGS*

Debbie, aged 32, asked CSC to take her only child, Sarah, aged 13, into care. Sarah had become defiant and started running away from home. Both mother and child were angry; recently Sarah hit her mother when being physically prevented from leaving the home. The family were not previously known to CSC. Sarah's father does not know of her existence.

Debbie reported that as a child she was maltreated by her parents. In adolescence she herself often ran away from home.

Six months before, Debbie entered into a relationship with a male named James, who spent a great deal of time in the home but did not get involved in disciplining Sarah.

When interviewed by the children's practitioner, Sarah described her mother as controlling and preoccupied with James. Sarah was clearly unhappy, but reported that her relationship with her mother had been good, with no abuse.

There are risks associated with children being looked after (Department for Education and Skills 2006). Since Sarah reported no abuse, it was agreed attempts should be made to keep her at home.

Research-based social learning theory was employed in case formulation. Sarah, emotionally neglected, exhibited challenging behaviour in order to gain her mother's attention. This attention, though negative, was better than nothing. Social learning theory predicted that if Debbie gave Sarah more attention when she was not demanding it, and less attention when Sarah exhibited challenging behaviour, challenging behaviour should diminish.

Debbie often expressed herself in a child-like way and was insensitive to the needs of her daughter. She depicted herself as a victim tormented by Sarah, and expected Sarah to allow her as much time as she liked with her new partner. It was agreed that Debbie needed help to come to terms with her responsibilities as an adult (Berne 1964).

The unit considered that Debbie, Sarah and James should be encouraged to attend family therapy sessions, facilitated by the unit clinician and social worker. James declined to participate. Since he played little role in parenting Sarah it was agreed to leave out James unless he undermined progress.

Motivational interviewing techniques, shown in randomised controlled trials to help people change (Miller and Rollnick 2002), were used to enhance Debbie's motivation to address the relationship difficulties. Debbie was helped to explore the benefits and risks of her daughter becoming looked after; she soon acknowledged that Sarah being looked after would impact negatively on them both. Debbie was helped to define concrete objectives: less arguments with her daughter and her daughter running away less often.

The children's practitioner was assigned to work to persuade a reluctant Sarah to participate in family therapy sessions. The unit clinician assisted the children's practitioner in thinking through how to approach this work. The children's practitioner obtained more information about Sarah's life to inform the ongoing assessment and to help minimise the risks associated with Sarah running away.

To help mother and daughter regain a sense of perspective, they were encouraged to move from a problem-saturated narrative to a more balanced account. Describing enjoyable times together helped them realise that, until recently, they had got on well, each sensing a strong relationship.

Sessions were conducted in a style likely to be perceived as supportive; praise was given and strengths highlighted. Debbie was told it was impressive that despite feeling worn down, she still sought what was best for her daughter. Mother and daughter were encouraged to expand various brief emotional statements about how hard they were finding things. This allowed both to appreciate they were being given a sympathetic hearing.

Practitioners attempted to avoid defensiveness, employing a method described by Casement (1985), thinking all the time whether remarks might be interpreted as criticism. Practitioners frequently determined how mother and daughter reacted to their input.

Debbie described Sarah as 'testing her' but was unclear what exactly Sarah was testing. She was helped to understand that Sarah's behaviour was a response to feeling rejected. Debbie was asked about the impact of her daughter's behaviour. Debbie was also asked to remember her own adolescence, and to remember what she had been trying to achieve when she ran away from her parents. These conversations helped Debbie recognise that Sarah was in fact testing how much her mother cared about her, and that she was seeking attention. In sessions Sarah described her feelings during and after arguments. This helped Debbie understand how unhappy Sarah was feeling.

Sarah was asked why she thought her mother was imposing rules and disciplining her. This helped make Sarah aware that her mother was motivated by concern for her safety.

To help Debbie understand how she was contributing to and maintaining Sarah's challenging behaviour, specific behavioural sequences were examined. This revealed that Sarah's challenging behaviour often occurred when she felt ignored and the result was generally that Sarah received immediate attention. Debbie was encouraged to consider this overall pattern rather than dwell on the detail of individual arguments.

Debbie initially considered it appropriate that she should respond angrily to Sarah's outbursts. She considered her own parents had been too passive and had failed to protect her. When asked about the intended and actual outcomes of her behaviour, Debbie accepted that a better way to protect her daughter might be by improving the quality of the relationship, rather than simply attempting to assert control during conflict.

Support was provided to Debbie while she attempted to pay less attention to Sarah's challenging behaviour. Debbie was praised when she withdrew from conflict. When asked about the results of these tactical withdrawals, Debbie reported that conflicts were briefer and did not escalate.

After five sessions over a period of six weeks, mother and daughter reported enjoying time together and a reduction in conflict. Sarah had stopped running away and Debbie felt she could manage without CSC support.

CASE STUDY 11.2 *WORKING TOGETHER TO IMPROVE PARENTING SKILLS*

Tina, aged 28, and her son, Jake, aged two, were rehoused in Hackney. Jake had been known to a neighbouring local authority since birth due to chronic neglect and was the subject of a child protection plan. Jake was under-stimulated, sometimes not responded to when distressed, had severe untreated nappy rash and home conditions were very poor.

Jake had significant developmental delay in a range of areas. Tina had put little effort into effecting change. The previous authority had made clear their expectations of Tina but offered little therapeutic intervention. Observations suggested Tina suffered from depression and a learning difficulty, but specialist assessments had resulted in no formal diagnoses. Tina was supported by an adult sister and received some support at her church.

The Hackney unit was very concerned; research shows neglect at young ages causes serious and lasting impairment (Macdonald 2001), and Jake had already suffered harm. The case had drifted for two years before being referred to Hackney. The unit was aware social workers often fail to prioritise neglect, though they may act decisively on physical and sexual abuse (Taylor and Daniel 2005).

Given the need for urgent change, the unit planned a time-limited assessment of Tina's capacity to change when supported with evidence-based interventions. The consultant social worker clearly warned Tina that unless her care improved within three months, court proceedings would be initiated in order to attempt to secure an alternative permanent placement for Jake.

Risk to Jake was minimised during the assessment. A full-time nursery placement was secured because quality pre-school education promotes a range of good outcomes (Sylva 1994). Regular visits by professionals and repeated health and developmental checks ensured any deterioration would be detected.

Tina and her sister had been neglected as children and not exposed to models of good parenting. Social learning theory emphasises how many behaviours are learnt through exposure and modelling.

Tina and her sister suffered a striking lack of self-confidence. According to change theory Tina and her sister were at pre-contemplation stage (Miller and Rollnick 2002), only vaguely recognising the concerns of CSC and the need for change. The unit hypothesised Tina may have been 'in a bind': someone with low confidence, reluctant to consider the need for change because they perceived themselves unlikely to achieve change successfully.

Motivational interviewing techniques, shown in randomised controlled trials to help people change (Miller and Rollnick 2002), were employed to increase Tina's confidence and to help her realise the importance of change. The unit social worker undertook these interventions, helped in planning sessions by the consultant social worker and clinician.

Identifying changes Tina had made in the past, however small, led Tina to recognise she had shown the ability to change in certain circumstances.

Tina was praised for attending sessions with unit staff, and for coping with what must seem enormous pressure from CSC.

Miller and Rollnick (2002) showed that when a current situation is sufficiently discrepant from a desired ideal, people are motivated to reduce the discrepancy. Possibly Tina's enhanced confidence and the social worker asking open, neutral (non-blaming) questions such as 'What is going well?' and 'What concerns you?' enabled Tina to slowly open up, expressing clearly how she was caring for Jake and how she would ideally care for him.

Tina was offered a great deal of time in which to reflect and provided with considerable support with the process. With support, Tina was able to recognise links between the treatment she had endured as a child and its adverse outcomes; for example being bullied at school due to her poor appearance led her to leave school prematurely. Tina was clear she did not want Jake to be harmed by neglect – as she had been – and Tina hoped for a better future for her son. Tina was able to speak about the perceived advantages of improved mothering, and what she feared might happen if she did not improve.

Once Tina came to acknowledge the need for change she was helped to identify specific changes she might make.

Through discussions a plan for change began to emerge. SMART (specific, measurable, achievable, realistic, time-scaled) goals and plans were negotiated and agreed. To heighten her motivation Tina was asked to articulate in what way each goal would help achieve a particular value dear to her.

Tina attended sessions three times a week with the unit's children's practitioner, who demonstrated parenting skills. A schedule of desired behaviours was devised that included playing with Jake, taking him to nursery and tidying the home. Promoting behaviour in this way has been shown to be effective in treating depression and other disorders (Hopko, Ruggiero and Eifert 2003). Tina was asked to identify the benefits of her new behaviours, in the hope that recognising these benefits would reduce the need for prompting. Tina reported that playing with Jake made her feel 'like a good mum' and she was pleased the child had begun to seek her out more often. She reported that a cleaner, more organised home made her feel 'alive' and made it easier to attend appointments.

Tina and Jake were isolated, with only Tina's sister offering close support. *Care Matters: Time for Change* (Department for Education and Skills 2007) emphasises the importance of engaging the support of wider family and friends to support parents. Tina was able to identify acquaintances at her church that could possibly provide support. The unit shared the task of meeting these individuals to help prepare them to contribute constructively at a family network meeting. At the meeting they brainstormed creative ways to provide Tina with emotional and practical support. Tina was encouraged to share her plans for change at the meetings, because evidence shows commitment to a plan is enhanced by making it public (Miller and Rollnick 2002). At a later family network meeting, the network fed back positive changes they had noted in Tina. This helped her see herself as someone who could achieve positive change and parent Jake effectively.

Plans and support were reviewed and modified at family network and core group meetings. Given Tina's level of need, it is likely that ongoing support will be needed at different stages of Jake's childhood. However, within three months Tina showed considerable initial progress, meeting all Jake's needs and reporting improved confidence.

Part of the work in this case involved scheduling many appointments and meetings. The unit co-ordinator undertook this time-consuming work in order to allow the other unit members to focus on working directly with the family to facilitate change.

Reflection

CSC units actively managed these cases using those approaches most likely to achieve positive change. A clear formulation regarding what was causing and maintaining problematic behaviour helped devise effective interventions. Therapeutic relationships, in which family members felt empathy and support, helped foster engagement and allowed clients to reflect and consider alternative behaviours. Evidence-based family therapy and motivational interviewing techniques allowed unhelpful behaviour and beliefs to be challenged without arousing defensiveness. In Case Study 11.2, the unit threatened its statutory sanction of care proceedings to maximise the chances of a successful intervention. After this initial threat, subsequent interventions were reinforcing rather than punitive.

Conclusion

In the current climate, following massive vilification of social workers involved with 'Baby Peter', social workers may be particularly inclined to act defensively, undermining government aspirations to maintain children at home whenever possible (Department for Education and

Skills 2007). Over-reaction will only be avoided if social workers have professional confidence, based on managing risks and on thoughtfully implementing evidence-based interventions. The government's response to Lord Laming's recent review of England's child protection services emphasised its commitment to providing social workers with adequate training and support (Department for Children, Schools and Families 2009). The Social Work Task Force subsequently set in motion a comprehensive programme of reform for the social work profession (Social Work Task Force 2009). However, to ensure proposals are effective, the government must ensure training is sufficiently evidence-based.

Greater engagement is needed between social work practitioners and academics to ensure academics realise the practical problems facing social workers, and to ensure that practitioners make the fullest use of the evidence base that is already in place.

References

Berne, E. (1964) *Games People Play: The Psychology of Human Relationships.* New York: Grove Press.

Brestan, E. and Eyberg, S. (1998) 'Effective psychosocial treatments of conduct-disordered children and adolescents: 29 years, 82 studies, and 5,272 kids.' *Journal of Clinical Child Psychology 27*, 2, 180–189.

Carr, A. (2000) 'Evidence-based practice in family therapy and systemic consultation.' *Journal of Family Therapy 22*, 29–60.

Casement, P. (1985) *On Learning From the Patient.* London: Tavistock.

Cleaver, H., Unell, I. and Aldgate, J. (1999) *Children's Needs. Parenting Capacity: The Impact of Illness, Problem Alcohol and Drug Use, and Domestic Violence on Children's Development.* London: The Stationery Office.

Cottrell, D. and Boston, P. (2002) 'The effectiveness of systemic family therapy for children and adolescents.' *Journal of Child Psychology and Psychiatry 43*, 573–586.

Department for Children, Schools and Families (2009) *The Protection of Children in England: Action Plan. The Government's Response to Lord Laming.* London: The Stationery Office.

Department for Education and Skills (2004) *Every Child Matters: Change for Children.* London: The Stationery Office.

Department for Education and Skills (2006) *Care Matters: Transforming the Lives of Children and Young People in Care.* London: The Stationery Office.

Department for Education and Skills (2007) *Care Matters: Time for Change.* London: The Stationery Office.

Her Majesty's Government (2006) *Working Together to Safeguard Children. A Guide to Inter-Agency Working to Safeguard and Promote the Welfare of Children.* London: The Stationery Office.

Hopko, D.C.L., Ruggiero, K. and Eifert, G. (2003) 'Contemporary behavioral activation treatment for depression: procedures, principles, and process.' *Clinical Psychology Review 23*, 699–717.

Laming, Lord (2009) *The Protection of Children in England: A Progress Report*. London: The Stationery Office.

London Safeguarding Children Board (2007) *London Child Protection Procedures*. Third edition. London: London Safeguarding Children Board.

Macdonald, G. (2001) *Effective Interventions for Child Abuse and Neglect: An Evidence-Based Approach to Planning and Executing Interventions*. Chichester: Wiley.

Miller, R. and Rollnick, S. (2002) *Motivational Interviewing – Preparing People for Change*. Second edition. London: The Guilford Press.

Social Work Task Force (2009) *Building a Safe, Confident Future. The Final Report of the Social Work Task Force*. London: Department for Children, Schools and Families.

Sylva, K. (1994) 'School influences on children's development.' *Journal of Child Psychology and Psychiatry and Allied Professions 35*, 1, 135–170.

Taylor, J. and Daniel, B. (eds) (2005) *Child Neglect – Practical Issues for Health and Social Care*. London: Jessica Kingsley Publishers.

Chapter 12

Psychosocial Practice in Community Mental Health Services

Tony West

Introduction

After a long period following the violent death of Jonathan Zito in December 1992 (Ritchie, Dick and Lingham 1994), in which public debate about community mental health was disproportionately dominated by the notion of public safety, there have been more encouraging signs in public policy in recent years.

There has been an increasing recognition of the importance of mental health to the nation's welfare, as reflected in the influence of the recent work of Richard Layard and his colleagues at the London School of Economics (e.g. Centre for Economic Performance Mental Health Policy Group 2006; Layard 2005). It has led, for example, to the development of the Improving Access to Psychological Therapies programme, which aims to increase the provision of evidence-based treatment for anxiety and depression in primary care.

There is also a welcome, if belated, promotion of social models of mental health, emphasising the social inclusion and citizen rights of secondary mental health service users (see Chapter 4), and giving centre stage to the concept of recovery (e.g. National Institute for Mental Health in England 2005). Thus, for example, the early intervention teams that have developed in recent years (Department of Health 2001) have specifically sought to maintain the social roles, activities and relationships of young people first presenting to secondary mental health services. The personalisation agenda (Her Majesty's Government 2007), though not without its critics and as yet lagging behind in mental health compared to implementation in other service areas, does have the potential to lead to more creative care planning, in which the service user's voice is a much more potent presence than previously.

I will argue that this explicit official endorsement of new ways of working with service users offers an opportunity to create more empowering services, leading to better outcomes for users and greater fulfilment for professionals. However, implementing these new ideas is neither straightforward nor easy. There are significant impediments to doing so, both internal and external to services.

In this chapter, I will give a brief description of what I take to be a viable social model of mental disorder. I will then attempt to illustrate some of the complexities involved in its implementation through the use of a case study. I will end with a discussion of some of the obstacles to effective implementation.

A social model of working with mental disorder

In the box below I propose a plausible social model for working with mental distress, drawn largely from recent thinking and research. It is particularly influenced by the strengths model, developed in the School of Social Welfare at Kansas University during the 1980s and 1990s by Charles Rapp and his colleagues, as well as by the recovery movement, with which it shares many core beliefs.

It is a somewhat minimalist social model in that it does not require a denial of the reality of mental disorder (associated particularly with Szasz 1961, for example), nor does it imply any specific view about the causation of such mental disorder. However, it probably sits most comfortably with those models, such as the stress-vulnerability model (Chapter 3), which emphasise the causative role of social factors. This agnosticism about the aetiology of mental disorder is motivated by a pragmatic commitment to practice priorities. The model is based on a commitment to a form of value-based practice which is fundamentally user-centred. It is also underpinned by an attitude of optimism about the capacity of service users to make sense of their experiences, manage their own mental health and to find a niche for themselves in which they can contribute to society.

A social model of mental disorder

1. The intelligibility principle

The experience of those deemed mentally ill – even those with severe psychotic conditions such as schizophrenia – are not *sui generis*, utterly discontinuous from those of, or unintelligible to, 'normal' people. Psychotic experiences and paranoid ideation are much more common than is commonly assumed (Bentall 2003, 2009; British Psychological Society 2000; Freeman and Freeman 2008). Sometimes, what is construed as a symptom of psychopathology (e.g. negative symptoms) can be better understood as an understandable reaction to an environment which is not offering the individual hope or motivating options (Deegan 1996; Rapp 1998). Similarly, the behaviour and concerns of people with severe mental illness can often be strikingly similar to that of people with physical illnesses of comparable magnitude or persistence. For example, an intense preoccupation with religious or spiritual themes (Pritchard 2006). Also, though there are differences in recorded incidence of medication non-compliance for mental health and general health patients (Mitchell and Selmes 2007; Osterborg and Blaschke 2005), some of this may be explained by differing methods of accounting for non-compliance (Joyce, Cramer and Rosenbeck 1998).

2. The user expertise principle

The service user should be recognised as an expert on their own experience and potentially in their own self-management (Deegan 1996; Repper and Perkins 2003). The role of the worker is to understand that experience and to facilitate the development of relapse prevention and other self-management techniques. It is crucial to assist the service user in identifying his or her own personal goals, not least because these will best engage that person's motivation and will generally, as a by-product, lead to improvements in other areas of the person's mental health (Rapp 1998). There is an emphasis on the user's latent strengths and resourcefulness rather than on her/his deficits and weaknesses.

3. The recovery as social inclusion principle

The obstacles to recovery – where this is understood as recovery of meaning, purpose and sense of social inclusion rather than 'cure' – are much more social and environmental than psychopathological (Deegan 1996; Rapp 1998; Repper and Perkins 2003). There is a danger that community mental health services create for users – as did the old hospitals – social milieus which are entrapping rather than enabling (Rapp 1998). The role of mental health services should be to facilitate the tapping of naturally occurring opportunities within the social mainstream – such as employment, accommodation, education, recreational activities – whilst advocating for reasonable adjustments to enable social inclusion wherever necessary.

CASE STUDY 12.1 *THE SOCIAL WORK ROLE IN COMMUNITY MENTAL HEALTH SERVICES*

Selema was a 24-year-old undergraduate student who approached the local housing department to apply for public housing, claiming that she was being abused by her parents with whom she had been living. She was now staying temporarily with a friend after, she claimed, being hit across the face by her father. Records indicated that Selema had been admitted to a psychiatric ward outside the local area three years earlier due to a brief psychotic episode and she was therefore referred to the local community mental health team (CMHT) for assessment.

At interview, Selema presented as rational and calm though it was difficult to gauge the truth of her allegations against her family, and her account seemed consistent with a simple but acrimonious falling out with them. It was known that prior to her previous admission Selema had become extremely paranoid about her mother and father, seeing them as imposters who were holding her real parents hostage. There was no suggestion of such psychotic thought processes currently.

Initially, the work focused on helping her to clarify her plans and to process her housing application. With her explicit consent, the team also liaised with both her university (so that she could be supported especially as she faced her final exams in only four months time), and with her parents, who reluctantly agreed that it would be better for her to leave home and co-operated with her housing application.

However, over the coming weeks, Selema gradually became more guarded in manner, and there were reports from her parents that she had again been accusing them of being imposters and on occasion had been violent to them. This led to the police removing her from the family home to her friend's house. It then became impossible to see Selema as she stopped attending both college and CMHT appointments. It was when her family contacted the CMHT, extremely concerned that she had bought an air ticket to stay with her 'real' parents, that a Mental Health Act assessment was arranged.

Her care co-ordinator, who was also an Approved Social Worker (ASW) (as then was), undertook the assessment with a team psychiatrist. In contrast to her usual bright appearance, Selema was found to be in a self-neglected state, having visibly lost weight. She seemed disorientated, utterly passive and unable to give coherent responses to questions or to make simple decisions. It was decided to detain her under Section 2 of the Mental Health Act.

In hospital, Selema responded well and quickly to treatment. This included the resumption of anti-psychotic medication which, it transpired, she had ceased to take some weeks earlier. Interestingly, her mood, alertness and responsiveness noticeably improved before this medication would have been expected to take effect. As her mental state improved so did her relationship with her parents.

On discharge, the care co-ordinator was able to re-establish the trusting relationship that had previously existed with Selema and, in collaboration with the team clinical psychologist, was able to engage her in detailed relapse prevention planning. This identified pertinent stressors, various phases of the relapse process, and the appropriate actions to be taken by her or her circle of support at each stage. Whilst the timing of her admission made it necessary to postpone taking her exams, detailed plans were made with her and the college regarding her return to her studies. Selema also decided that, though she now saw her suspicions of her parents as unfounded, it would nevertheless be helpful to her to live independently of – but still relatively close to – them. This was subsequently arranged.

Discussion

With hindsight, it seems clear that when Selema (Case Study 12.1) was first referred she was already in the prodromal stages of a psychotic relapse, exhibiting subtle changes of mood and behaviour that were indicators of what was to follow. Though this possibility was entertained by the team, it was poorly placed to recognise and appreciate the significance of these specific signs given its very limited previous acquaintance with Selema. Nevertheless, by taking an initial user-focused approach to the work with her, in which she drove the agenda, the basis of a trusting and respectful relationship was formed. This was to prove invaluable in the work subsequent to her discharge, particularly that around relapse prevention.[1]

As indicated above, in this case the care co-ordinator, an ASW, carried out the Mental Health Act assessment. There is some controversy as to whether this is good practice, with some feeling that it may harm the therapeutic relationship (Hurley and Linsley 2006). There is probably no definitive answer to this question as it is likely to depend on the individual service user and the particulars of his or her relationship with the care co-ordinator. In this case, though, it certainly appeared to be right and appropriate. The novelist Clare Allen, herself a long-term user of specialist mental health services, appears to have respected her social worker for admitting her to hospital directly – and then remaining steadfastly in contact throughout the admission (Allen 2008). She has written with feeling of the importance of worker reliability and persistence, the benefit of having a consistently empathetic accompanying presence at all the stages of her mental health journey. Ryan and Morgan make the point that each episode of relapse needs to be seen as a further learning opportunity (Ryan and Morgan 2004). In Selema's case, it seems to have been positively helpful that the worker was actively involved throughout the whole early warning signs–crisis–post-crisis process. It enabled them to work more effectively together in understanding what was, albeit from very different perspectives, a shared experience.

One further point about relapse prevention work may be worth making. Ryan and Morgan remind us that an undue emphasis on signs of relapse can achieve the opposite of what the strengths model intends, causing service users greater anxiety rather than enhancing their confidence in themselves (Ryan and Morgan 2004). For a relapse prevention approach genuinely to help the user, it must be something which, though s/he may not initiate it, s/he must actively participate in and ultimately own. With this psychosocial intervention, as with others, it is at best unproductive (and likely counter-productive) if, imperceptibly perhaps, it becomes something a naively well-meaning worker *does to* rather than *with* the user. In this case, Selema did participate actively in the relapse prevention planning, and it therefore did promote her

---

1   I am, throughout this discussion, conscious of the evidence cited in Chapter 4 that service users are typically more positive about their experience of services in dialogue with professionals as opposed to, say, fellow users. Where statements or assumptions are made about Selema's experience, for example that she found the relationship with her care co-ordinator a trusting one, this is recognised as an interpretation, from an external perspective, rather than a bald statement of fact.

self-management, and respect her expertise about her own mental health (consistent with the user expertise principle above).

Of course, the decision to detain Selema seems, on the face of it, the most blatant breach of the principle of user expertise. In this case, I think a strong case can be made for arguing that the breach was apparent rather than real. That is, at the time of the assessment Selema was temporarily mentally incapacitated and the decision made was in her best interests (consistent with the principles of the Mental Capacity Act 2005), and was one which she appeared to endorse when she regained capacity.

Nevertheless, the worker had to be mindful not to push the process too forcefully, and to be sensitive to Selema's tendency to seek to please others when still feeling vulnerable. This underscores the point made by American user-advocate Patricia Deegan that professionals need to be discerning as to when service users have properly made the transition from a survival stage (when they are still too immersed in their distress to be able to reflect on it or to make meaningful plans for their future) to a recovery stage, if they are to offer appropriate help and support (Deegan 1996).

Finally, there was recognition of the need for Selema to maintain important pre-crisis relationships and activities to facilitate her recovery (the recovery as social inclusion principle). Thus, for example, apart from the work undertaken to secure her university place and to re-establish her relationship with her parents, it transpired that, as her mental health deteriorated, Selema had been barred from a young person's service she had used regularly. The worker assisted Selema in contacting this service and rebuilding bridges, so that she was able to return there and participate in mainstream activities as opposed, for example, to joining a mental health day centre. This service was also able to keep her in touch with an educational resource that would support her in preparing for the return to college. Selema and the worker also discussed strategies for resuming social contacts that had been disrupted during her relapse such as local friends and fellow students at the university she had socialised with.

Implementing social models of working

In a sense, much of the work described above seems familiar. There is little that is revolutionary about concepts such as relapse prevention planning or – to a lesser extent – the role of social networks and activity in recovery. For this reason, when training in the strengths model or the recovery model is provided, a familiar reaction from many in the audience is 'But we're already doing it!' Nevertheless, this claim does not seem sustainable as a general description of how modern community mental health work is typically done.

For example, the essence of this kind of social model is that it starts with the goals and aspirations of service users. But, asks Rapp, given that the users' lives and goals are so disparate, why are their care plans generally so homogenous (Rapp 1998)? This still seems applicable to the UK context too, and may indicate that care plans first and foremost reflect professional rather than individual user concerns – and that, like Tolstoy's happy families, such plans all resemble one another. Similarly, it is axiomatic within a strengths model approach that the assessment focuses heavily on what the user can, rather than cannot do: on qualities and abilities, that may be of potential benefit to others, rather than on deficits. Again, this is not reflected in reality. Though most assessment formats now have a section on user strengths, these are not usually completed in detail, or linked to user goals or external opportunities. At any rate, what is written in this section is usually dwarfed by the attention given to the user's illness and symptoms, distress, vulnerability, anxiety, poor functioning etc. – what Peter Morgan acerbically calls an entire 'alphabet of negativity' (Morgan 2004).

To point this out is to show how far there is to go; it is not to berate mental health professionals. It is, first of all, testimony to the enduring power of the traditional problem-solving paradigm, in which a problem (or pathology) is identified/diagnosed, and a treatment plan then drawn up to address it. It is typically the nature of such paradigms that their assumptions seem so natural that we are scarcely aware that we have them. Faced with an alternative paradigm, such as the strength or recovery model, it then becomes easy to fail to see it as such, to incorporate elements of it into our traditional practice, without understanding the inherent radical challenge. Such, I think, is the current position with regard to the adoption of these newer ways of doing community mental health.

However, there are also other factors which inhibit their spread, which reinforce tendencies to conservatism. I will mention two. First, whilst the public safety panic appears to have abated somewhat in recent years, it has certainly not disappeared. The response to the case of 'Baby Peter' in the field of child care is a reminder to mental health professionals, if indeed they needed it, both that a service is more likely to be judged on the basis of a single catastrophe than on an objective assessment of its overall performance, and of the potential consequences for individual professionals and managers associated with such a catastrophe. Inevitably then, this awareness encourages an attitude of risk aversion. By contrast, it is a fundamental tenet of a social model of working that risk-taking is necessary to promote individual growth. There will always be a tension in mental health practice between the goal of promoting rights and opportunities for the generality of service users on the one hand, whilst taking sensible precautions against the risks posed by a minority (alas, not always easily distinguishable) on the other. This tension can never be dissolved; it can only be managed through careful discrimination of risk, and judicious therapeutic risk-taking. The danger that needs to be guarded against is that all of our thinking becomes infected with a note of excessive, defensive caution.

There may be a second reason to think that this danger could re-emerge more forcefully. In Chapter 2, Paul Godin refers to the hypothesis that optimism in mental health, of the kind hospitable to more socially orientated and user-focused approaches, fluctuates with the economic cycle. In current circumstances, as we face the prospect of a prolonged retrenchment in public services, there are likely to be some corresponding tendencies to revert to more traditional, narrower models of practice, particularly where these are perceived as more cost-effective.

Conclusion

In recent years, progressive ideas about new ways of working with mental health service users have received important official backing. There have been some encouraging developments in practice, though the full implications of these new models have not yet been fully grasped or comprehensively implemented. If this was to be done, it could have very radical consequences in terms of the relationship between professionals and service users, and indeed between service users and society generally. Despite official government approval, there are countervailing influences, which probably reflect in part society's continuing ambivalence about serious mental disorder.

Important work has been done by a vanguard of practitioners, educators and service users in publicising and teaching these recovery and strengths models. It is crucial that this moment of opportunity is seized, and a new paradigm of practice – one that starts from the goals and strengths of service users, requiring relationship skills in eliciting and supporting these, rather than from a professionally defined deficit model – is firmly embedded in mainstream community mental health practice. Once this is done, there will still be much work to be done. There will inevitably be a backlash of some kind, both from within and without mental health professions. There will also be circumstances, which this brief piece has scarcely been able to touch on, in which the application of the new paradigm will be problematic and puzzling. However, if this new way of working and seeing is established as a lodestar amongst a critical mass of community mental health practitioners, these challenges, though difficult, should prove to be navigable.

References

Allen, C. (2008) 'In the thick of our mess, it's the social workers who clear up.' *The Guardian*, Society Section, 1 August, p 4.

Bentall, R. (2003) *Madness Explained: Psychosis and Human Nature*. London: Allen Lane.

Bentall, R. (2009) *Doctoring the Mind*. London: Allen Lane.

British Psychological Society. (2000) Understanding Mental Illness: Recent Advances in Understanding Mental Illness and Psychotic Experiences. Available at www.schizophrenia. com/research/Rep03.pdf, accessed on 9 May 2009.

Centre for Economic Performance Mental Health Policy Group (2006) *The Depression Report: A New Deal for Depression and Anxiety Disorders*. London: London School of Economics and Political Science.

Deegan, P. (1996) *Recovery and the Conspiracy of Hope*. The Sixth Annual Mental Health Services Conference of Australia and New Zealand, Brisbane, Australia.

Department of Health (2001) *The Mental Health Policy Implementation Guide*. London: Department of Health.

Freeman, D. and Freeman, J. (2008) *Paranoia: The 21st-Century Fear*. Oxford: Oxford University Press.

Her Majesty's Government (2007) *Putting People First: A Shared Vision and Commitment to the Transformation of Adult Social Care*. London: Department of Health.

Hurley, J. and Linsley, P. (2006) 'Proposed changes to the Mental Health Act of England and Wales: research indicating future educational and training needs for mental health nurses.' *Journal of Psychiatric and Mental Health Nursing 13*, 48–54.

Joyce, A., Cramer, B.S. and Rosenbeck, R. (1998) 'Compliance with medication regimens for mental and physical disorders.' *Psychiatric Services 49*, 196–201.

Layard, R. (2005) *Happiness: Lessons from a New Science*. London: Allen Lane.

Mitchell, A.J. and Selmes, T. (2007) 'Why don't patients take their medication? Reasons and solutions in psychiatry.' *Advances in Psychiatric Treatment 13*, 336–346.

Morgan, S. (2004) 'Strengths based practice.' *Openmind 126*, 16–17.

National Institute for Mental Health in England (2005) *NIMHE Guiding Statement on Recovery*. Available at www.psychminded.co.uk/news/news2005/feb05/nimherecovstatement.pdf, accessed on 19 July 2010.

Osterborg, L. and Blaschke, T. (2005) 'Adherence to medication.' *New England Journal of Medicine 353*, 487–497.

Pritchard, C. (2006) *Mental Health Social Work: Evidence-Based Practice*. Abingdon: Routledge.

Rapp, C. (1998) *The Strengths Model: Case Management with People Suffering from Severe and Persistent Mental Illness*. New York: Oxford University Press.

Repper, J. and Perkins, R. (2003) *Social Inclusion and Recovery: A Model for Mental Health Practice*. Edinburgh: Balliere Tindall.

Ritchie, J.H., Dick, D. and Lingham, R. (1994) *The Report of the Inquiry into the Care and Treatment of Christopher Clunis*. London: HMSO.

Ryan, P. and Morgan, S. (2004) *Assertive Outreach: A Strengths Approach*. Edinburgh: Churchill Livingstone.

Szasz, T. (1961) *The Myth of Mental Illness*. New York: Hoeber-Harper.

Chapter 13

Psychosocial Practice in Inpatient Mental Health Services

Paul Richards

Introduction

Social work in a medium secure hospital is multi-faceted, complex and challenging. There are a number of domains within which the work takes place and at times the roles can appear to be in conflict – such as promoting social inclusion by increasing access to mainstream education, but having to disclose information regarding an index offence that subsequently leads to the college excluding a client.

The best social work takes place in multi-disciplinary team (MDT) settings which are open, democratic and respectful. On a typical ward, the multi-professional team comprises nursing staff, medical staff, a clinical psychologist, an occupational therapist and a social worker. Decisions are not put to the vote and decision-makers are not bound by the views of others, but each profession should have their views heard and respected. Inter-professional disagreements should be productive and support good practice. For example, the responsible clinician may wish to recommend discharge because the patient's mental health has been stable for some time. However, the social worker may not support discharge because the client has just started having contact with their infant child and is due to have an assessment from Children's Social Care. A good outcome to the disagreement may be a conditional discharge that includes the patient having no unsupervised contact until the children and families team have completed their assessment.

Experience

The best hospital-based social workers come into the role from a strong background in community work. In today's finance-stretched world of community mental health care, the care co-ordinator is at the front line, with other support available only in emergencies or at the end of long waiting lists. It is sometimes a struggle to have the client reviewed by the Responsible Clinician within the one year minimum recommended timescale (Department of Health 2008). In a sense, the social worker in the community has to undertake all the other roles of the hospital-based MDT, albeit in a limited fashion. For example, the care co-ordinator is often responsible for: dispensing medication (nursing); mental state examination (psychiatry); counselling and support through difficult times (psychology); referring to day centres, education or vocational opportunities (occupational therapy); assessing and managing risk (clinical team); and assisting with benefits claims and bus pass applications (welfare rights).

Knowledge

Social workers have a unique and intrinsic knowledge that comes from working with people with mental health problems in community environments. This means they can offer motivational advice on what is necessary to enable the individual client to progress and move on to greater independence. The knowledge of community resources again relates to a number of domains, which includes family, statutory, voluntary, occupation and accommodation. The social worker will be able to draw upon at least some of the following in assessing the suitability of a potential placement:

- previous experience of working in residential care
- making funding arrangements
- an understanding of the inspection and regulation of registered care
- understanding of the training requirements for project workers
- experience of working with conditionally discharged patients in the community

- a sound knowledge of the client's history, including their strengths and vulnerabilities

- proximity to other support systems, e.g. family, day centres, etc.

Ideology

Often employed by the local authority, rather than the NHS, the social worker comes from a different ideological background than the majority of their health colleagues. In 2001 the British Association of Social Work adopted the International Federation of Social Workers' (IFSW) definition of the profession as quoted in the introduction to this book (see p.21). The IFSW also describes the value base as follows:

> Social work grew out of humanitarian and democratic ideals, and its values are based on respect for the equality, worth, and dignity of all people. Since its beginnings over a century ago, social work practice has focused on meeting human needs and developing human potential. Human rights and social justice serve as the motivation and justification for social work action. In solidarity with those who are disadvantaged, the profession strives to alleviate poverty and to liberate vulnerable and oppressed people in order to promote social inclusion. (International Federation of Social Workers 2000)

Anti-oppressive practice

The role of the social worker on the ward will include seeking to challenge the dominance of the medical model and to promote the social work agenda with its commitment to anti-oppressive and anti-discriminatory practice. Nathan and Webber (2010) refer to the 'bureau-medicalisation' of mental health care, with its emphasis on data gathering and 'bed management' decarceration. This is in tension with the psychosocial perspective that strives to look at an individual's needs and wider social circumstances. Nathan and Webber's (2010) view is that social workers need to confront psychiatric hegemony by maintaining a 'double identification' with both the institution they represent *and* with the service user, by ensuring that the voice of the service user is heard.

Approved Mental Health Professionals

Formerly known as Approved Social Workers (ASWs), the mental health social worker (MHSW), in this setting, will often be a qualified Approved Mental Health Professional (AMHP). The value of being an AMHP is the independence enshrined within the role by the Mental Health Act 1983 and its purpose includes challenging and redressing discrimination. There is also a requirement to work in partnership to 'articulate, and demonstrate in practice, the social perspective on mental disorder and mental health needs' (Schedule 2, The Mental Health (Approved Mental Health Professionals) (Approval) (England) Regulations 2008). Nathan and Webber (2010, p.24) neatly encapsulate this point:

> Within such an institutional framework the radical dimension encapsulated by the old ASW role, needs to be preserved and extended to the MHSW role. By so doing, MHSWs can provide an independent perspective, thereby mitigating the effect of clinical team collusion in decision-making and preventing service users' needs from taking second place to the requirements of institutional and psychiatric hegemony.

Even in medium security there are times when a patient may need a Mental Health Act assessment. As the potential applicant, therefore, the balance of power in the ward dynamic is with the AMHP. In practice this means that the consultant psychiatrist cannot assume an application will be made, but must argue and justify the views made in their medical recommendation. This gives the social worker greater latitude for ensuring that an admission, or continuance of detention, proceeds with social care needs high on the agenda, such as including systemic family work as part of the treatment plan (see Chapter 8).

Report writing

As a consequence of their position within the system the social worker brings a unique and independent view to the tribunal that does not necessarily accord with that of the Responsible Clinician (Tribunals Judiciary 2008). The social worker will be reporting on risks relating to discharge across a very broad range of circumstances. This will have been informed by their involvement with the client's family, carers and statutory agencies that may include probation, multi-agency public protection panels, victim liaison units, Children's Social Care services and community mental health teams. In practice this means that the decision-makers will be able to weigh up not only information from what has been observed by the mental health system, but also the perceptions of a wider array of stakeholders. This may lead, for example, to an exclusion zone that protects the rights of the victims, but the boundaries of which still allow the client to travel to an outpatient clinic or work opportunity.

Recovery

Modern psychiatry now acknowledges that it is not always possible or even desirable to completely 'cure' mental health problems. This is because the physical impact of the treatment is often perceived, particularly by the recipient or their family, to be worse than the symptoms of the illness itself. Side-effects such as weight gain, diabetes or more permanent iatrogenic disorders such as tardive dyskinesia can severely impinge on the quality of life of the service user. However, recent strategy on mental health (Her Majesty's Government 2009) appears to embrace recovery principles that will be second nature to most social workers: promoting hope, having control of one's life, finding meaning, empowerment, encouraging learning, valuing relationships and social inclusion.

Within forensic services there is an ongoing debate as to how much of this can apply to our clients when so much of what happens to them is in response to the need for public protection. Little choice is available to them in terms of the conditions of their discharge from hospital. The issue of 'decarceration' referred to by Nathan and Webber (2010) is less of a problem for forensic patients. However, those that do not fall under the remit of the Ministry of Justice, can still find themselves subject to the idiosyncratic vagaries of bed management pressures.

Principles of recovery have found their way into forensic services with more information being shared with clients, for example the clinical team's view of their risk of violence. Patients are often given a 'Recovery Folder' containing copies of Care Programme Approach minutes, risk assessments, course certificates and 'Wellness Recovery Action Plans'. However, there is a concern that, as 'recovery' becomes a 'model' within the mental health system, it changes fundamentally from its roots in the American user movement and becomes just another word for 'rehabilitation'. One of the challenges for the advanced social work professional is to ensure that the underlying philosophy of the recovery approach informs the work undertaken. The following case study shows how sustaining hope, supporting social inclusion and valuing relationships are crucial underpinnings to recovery.

CASE STUDY 13.1 *SOCIAL WORK IN A MEDIUM SECURE UNIT*

Background

Jessica is a 40-year-old Spanish woman who came to this country several years ago looking for work. Her index offence was the murder of one of her two children during the first presentation of an acute psychotic illness. The surviving child, Pedro, was also injured and went back to Spain to live with family there. Jessica was still very unwell when admitted to our ward, believing that some of the staff were demons only she could perceive. She had also assaulted staff at a previous medium secure unit in the private sector. Jessica was started on a newer neuroleptic medication and her mental health began to improve.

Work undertaken

An initial difficulty encountered was that of language as complex issues needed addressing with an interpreter. Jessica was also without funds and received a discretionary subsistence allowance from a hospital charity fund. The hospital welfare department were reluctant to apply for benefits as they were wary of making a false claim. I assisted her to apply for benefits as I knew her to be from a European country. The Department of Work and Pensions initially insisted on her original passport accompanying the application. Eventually they agreed to accept a photocopy as long as it was endorsed by the senior police officer holding the passport until the conclusion of the criminal proceedings. The initial application was declined so we asked for a review, which also failed. The requested 'explanation' of the decision was a dossier of unfathomable references to European Law. As there was documented proof of Jessica's employment in the UK prior to her illness, I assisted her to apply for a Benefits Tribunal. I was able to obtain the services of an advocate from a Law Centre who subsequently helped Jessica win her appeal.

As Jessica's mental health improved, she began to talk about her surviving son and eventually asked for help in re-establishing some form of contact. Before undertaking the following work, I spoke in depth to Jessica and the multi-disciplinary team about a range of issues including the possible impact on her son's well-being, about the stress it might place on Jessica's mental health and of the possible legal or moral objections to facilitating contact. Using an interpreter, I spoke to Pedro's father about his views on the matter.

He was generally supportive and with his consent I contacted services in Spain to request an assessment of Pedro. Local services already provided an allocated social worker and psychologist to Pedro due to the possible post-traumatic stress of the index offence. We agreed to permit telephone contact of limited duration and frequency, enabling the impact on Pedro and Jessica to be carefully monitored.

Following protocol, I presented Jessica's case to the local panel responsible for multi-agency public protection arrangements. The panel consists of senior officers from police and probation, as well as other key partners from social services, health services, education and housing. They endorsed our plans regarding Jessica but with the caveat that we re-present the case before considering face-to-face contact between Jessica and Pedro.

Reflection

Case Study 13.1 deals with two fundamentals of life that we often take for granted: income and family. Jessica's untreated illness led to the death of one of her own children. As the belief system that motivated the index offence diminished with successful treatment, it was replaced with grief and immense sadness (see Thomas, Adshead and Mezey 1994, for a discussion on traumatic responses to child murder). The nature of the offence led to vilification in the press at the time of her arrest, some of which resurfaced in the media at the conclusion of the court case. Additionally, Jessica was the occasional target of harassment by other women in the unit who knew of her offence.

A couple of years before working with Jessica I had undertaken the MSc in Mental Health Social Work with Children and Adults at the Institute of Psychiatry, King's College London. As well as benefiting from the opportunity of being in a learning environment with colleagues from both Children's Social Care and adult services, I also learned from a series of case presentation workshops how using psychoanalytic concepts could inform and encourage reflective practice in social work. In my early meetings with Jessica, I was wondering whether she was going to attack me or believe I was a demon. Considering my own counter-transference experience, as described by Jack Nathan in Chapter 6, I wondered if my feelings were indicative of the sort of experience Jessica was having, what is termed reflective counter-transference. From Jessica's point of view she could have perceived me as a white, male social worker and key member of the omnipotent team that was responsible for her detention. In addition to the potential for oppression inherent in the power dynamic, she may have been afraid that I would regard her as a 'demon' because of the nature of the index offence and because of her earlier media exposure. In other words, Jessica may have been projecting her own sense of herself as a demon, something that she found literally impossible to believe about herself.

Adopting an approach from the theories of cognitive behavioural therapy (CBT) for psychosis (such as Fowler, Garety and Kuipers 1995), I did not directly challenge Jessica's belief and was therefore able to empathise with how terrified by the demons she must have been, thereby validating her experience. Once Jessica realised that I was going to be open-minded and not confrontational or judgemental, she was able to be more open about her difficulties. This allowed me to say that although I had never perceived demons, I was aware that her perception was a common one, thereby normalising her experience. This is not an easy task and raises the kinds of conflicts I referred to at the beginning as, in these situations, it is incumbent on the practitioner not to collude with the client around issues of criminality. Without collusion, I was still able to acknowledge that the tragic outcome of the index offence was a tragedy for her as well as her family. Although I was not going to behave in a 'judgemental' manner, I would be making judgements at every stage of her recovery around areas such as risk to self and others, supporting applications for Section 17 leave and recommendations to tribunals (see Chapter 7 for a fuller explanation of 'empathic conversation' and a discussion of CBT in social work).

It could have been assumed that the nature of the index offence meant that Jessica had relinquished her right to a family life and that contact with her surviving son would never be appropriate. However, keeping an open mind about this and being prepared to explore the range of possibilities was a major factor in maintaining Jessica's hope about the future and commitment to recovery. Employing the 'miracle question' from solution-focused brief therapy, as described in Chapter 1, revealed that Jessica's preferred future was one that included her having an ongoing mothering role for her surviving son. In addition, the professionals in Spain felt that facilitating contact would also be in Pedro's best interests. Lord Laming makes the point that: 'ultimately the safety of a child depends on staff having the time, knowledge and skill to understand the child or young person and their family circumstances' (Laming 2009, p.10). Had a narrow-minded approach to contact been adopted, the welfare of Pedro could then have been negatively affected.

Conversely, working with Jessica, with Pedro's father and with services in Spain, meant that we were able to more effectively safeguard Pedro through having control of the situation.

The number of professions and agencies referred to in the case study highlights the often task-centred nature of the social work role, as well as the degree of in-depth emotional engagement and networking required to effect change. This key difference between the social work role and the other professions in the multi-disciplinary team is indicative of the importance of psychosocial interventions. As social workers we need to use an eclectic range of psychological skills and interventions to engage with the client, to work as advanced practitioners. However for us the engagement is not an end in itself, we are often struggling to achieve practical tasks that will make a real difference to the client's social milieu.

Every profession plays an important part in enabling the client to make progress and will play a greater or lesser part in their recovery, depending on the individual client. The psychiatrist finds the right medication to reduce symptoms, the clinical psychologist will work in a structured way to address internal distress, the nurses look after day-to-day needs and the occupational therapist encourages vocational work and groups. For Jessica, the issue of entitlement to benefits was crucial. Not being entitled to public funds meant that she would not be able to make progress beyond the subsistence of Section 117 of the 1983 Mental Health Act entitlement to aftercare. Therefore the apparently simple issue of benefits was also about rights, belonging and citizenship.

Whilst psychological work made progress on increasing Jessica's understanding of the index offence and looked at ways in which she could both accept what happened and live with herself, the task-oriented nature of the benefits appeal led to trust and a feeling that both she and her crime could be tolerated by society and that she could survive. Working through all the problems presented by obtaining benefits became a metaphor for her own journey towards recovery. For Jessica, the benchmark of this recovery was being able to provide a maternal role to her surviving son.

References

Department of Health (2008) *Refocusing the Care Programme Approach: Policy and Positive Practice Guidance*. London: Department of Health.

Fowler, D., Garety, P.A. and Kuipers, E. (1995) *Cognitive Behavioural Therapy for Psychosis: Theory and Practice*. Chichester: Wiley.

Her Majesty's Government (2009) *New Horizons: A Shared Vision for Mental Health.* London: Department of Health.

International Federation of Social Workers (2000) *Definition of Social Work.* Available at http://www.ifsw.org/en/f38000138.html, accessed on 10 December 2009.

Laming, Lord (2009) *The Protection of Children in England: A Progress Report.* London: The Stationery Office.

Nathan, J. and Webber, M. (2010) 'Mental health social work and the bureau-medicalisation of mental health care: identity in a changing world.' *Journal of Social Work Practice 24,* 1, 15–28.

Thomas, C., Adshead, G. and Mezey, G. (1994) 'Case report: traumatic responses to child murder.' *Journal of Forensic Psychiatry and Psychology 5,* 1, 168–176.

Tribunals Judiciary (2008) *Practice Direction. First-Tier Tribunal. Health Education and Social Care Chamber. Mental Health Cases.* London: Tribunal Judiciary.

Chapter 14

The Person on the Receiving End

Don Brand and Sarah Carr

> *…the trauma of falling into ruins offers us a post-traumatic chance to rise, to rebuild ourselves in a better way. We didn't ask for the trauma, we don't want it, yet if we look it in the face and live with it, we can become more than we are. (Berman 2007, p.11)*

Introduction

In the past 15 years, there has been increasing emphasis in mental health services on involving consumers in service monitoring and review (see Chapter 4). The intentions are good, the practice variable, the impact disappointing. There was significant user input to the National Service Framework (NSF) for Mental Health (Department of Health 1999), and service structures changed in line with the Framework. But there has been much less change in the unequal balance of power between clinicians and patients, the attitudes instilled in professional training which devalue the opinions of mentally ill people and the fragility of user organisations in this field.

In this chapter, two individuals from research and policy backgrounds reflect on their experience of mental illness, the case for a stronger social dimension in understanding and responding to mental health needs, and the challenges of working with a mental health condition.

Direct experiences of mental health services: Don and Sarah
Don

I was 34 and married with three children when I had my first depressive breakdown. The mood change was obvious to my wife for some time before I was able to admit there was anything wrong. I worked in a responsible senior position in a large social services department, and was normally able to carry a heavy workload without difficulty. I began to slow down and lose confidence, my work rate declined dramatically and I become increasingly anxious. Colleagues were sympathetic and concerned. They tried to help, but I couldn't accept their offers, and ground to a halt. In the end, I was sent home from work, deeply depressed, and had to be signed off by my GP.

The GP, friendly but normally taciturn, was supportive and helpful. He listened to my story, asked thoughtful questions, and summed up 'So your get-up-and-go has got up and gone?' He explained how depression worked, talked through the medication options, gave me a prescription and another appointment, and signed a certificate saying I was unable to work because of 'malaise'.

It seemed a long time before the depression began to lessen. I felt a fraud, my 'illness' a cover for incompetence. Being off work seemed wrong and at home I kept out of sight of passers-by for fear of being reported for malingering. Extreme anxiety made mountains out of getting dressed, routine shopping, signing a cheque. I was sure we were heading for bankruptcy. My family, my GP and a few close friends kept me going. Other people found my gloom and negativity hard to take and stayed away.

Eventually, when the medication seemed to have kicked in, and the clouds of anxiety and despair began to lift, I was euphoric. I rushed back to work, was full of energy, enthused about everything, launched into a host of old and new interests, became over-confident and excitable. My wife and I again consulted the GP. He referred me to a wise and understanding London psychiatrist, who diagnosed a bipolar disorder. He talked to us together about how best to manage the effects of the condition and pitfalls to look out for. With fresh medication, and after a further lurch into depression, things slowly got back on an even keel. My workload built up, and with renewed energy, confidence and creativity, I embarked on a busy, productive decade of senior management, development and partnership working in local and central government.

In the 30-odd years since that first breakdown, I've experienced four or five major depressive episodes. Each involved about three months off work and steady scaling back of medication levels over a further 9 to 12 months. Meeting people and dealing with social situations caused me acute anxiety. The pattern has remained constant: an abrupt and steep decline into deep agitated depression, which lasts for up to 10 or 12 weeks, and then, equally suddenly, lifts. Stabilising medication avoids the up-swing that would otherwise follow.

The other constants have been my wife, my GP, and in the latter years a knowledgeable and unconventional psychiatrist. This group has formed my psychosocial support and treatment team, all expertly playing their own part whilst respecting one another's contributions and working together to protect my autonomy. Like Moliere's bourgeois gentleman, who discovered he'd been speaking prose all his life, the GP and I were practising 'co-production' long before government discovered the term (Boyle, Clark and Burns 2006). He was non-directive almost to a fault in seeking my views and involving me in medication decisions, even when depression limited my capacity to contribute. The psychiatrist, appreciating the heavy burden carried by the spouse of someone with bipolar, also worked to the principle that the person closest to them holds the best evidence of their condition and progress. Through her evident respect and confidence in my wife's judgement, she was a source of great encouragement and support to us both.

Sarah

I have been in various parts of the NHS mental health system for nearly 20 years, as a young person and as an adult. If I were to assess the statutory mental health services I have received, the clinical notes would read: 'the patient appears to be fragmented, unstable and inconsistent: there is a conceivable risk of harm to self and others'. Despite reforms and the efforts of those promoting psychosocial understandings of mental health, the system exists within a structure which perpetuates the medical model with the single diagnosis and cure approach. As a patient, you find yourself being systematically processed, with the sole focus on symptoms, diagnosis and treatment. But if you're lucky you'll come across someone who treats you as a human being and resists clinical reductionism, an approach which reduces individual experiences of mental distress to standard symptoms and treatments.

In all those 20 years using mental health services, I never had consistent access to someone who had the time, capacity or resources to treat me as a whole person. If I have continuity and consistency in the practitioners I work with, this enables me to build a relationship with them, so I can be known as an individual with my own particular experience of mental distress and my own ways of managing it. I know this because the only continuous support I have had has been from a private psychotherapist I was able to choose myself; but I had to go outside the NHS mental health system to access her. Working with my therapist over a number of years, I have been able to build up a respectful and extremely supportive therapeutic relationship which enables me to develop insights necessary to manage the non-clinical aspects of my mental health. Sadly, the NHS has not been able to offer me this as part of standard mental health services. I am acutely aware that there are thousands of people who are not in an economic position to exercise the same choice and control as I have over their long-term care and support. As the health and social policy critic, Charles Leadbetter has noted, 'Services manage and process people and problems, but only rarely allow people to change their lives' (Leadbetter 2009, p.2).

There are good people in the statutory system practising with humanity despite the fact that they are working in what can be a dehumanising situation for both parties. I will always remember the positive human encounters: the gentle primary care nurse who dressed my arm after an episode of self-harm when the GP wouldn't see me; the duty doctor and nurse at the walk-in crisis clinic who joked with me as we used string and a ruler to measure the swollen bruising on my leg, because they didn't have a measuring tape; the humorous psychiatric ward manager who looked at the injury I'd inflicted on my leg and said 'Bloody hell, you pack quite a punch don't you, lass?'; and the insightful community psychiatrist who said 'You're having a shit time, aren't you?' and finally found medication that began to help.

All these people helped me because they treated me as a human being, but the system was helping neither of us. The majority of positive encounters were one-off, because I only got to see the person once. Even while receiving treatment at my local community mental health team for over two years, and very intensively for six months, I only saw the good consultant psychiatrist three times. I also saw four other psychiatrists of varying sensitivity, seniority and experience, none of whom got to know me. I was reduced to a case file, a set of symptoms, a couple of diagnoses and a prescription to be passed between busy practitioners.

Being discharged back into primary care has had its own perils. I compete for time with an even greater number of people in the general primary care system to see a doctor now. The new appointments system means I can't always get to see the same GP. Yet I have to get a GP appointment every two months to get my medication, with the assumption that it's going to be with the same doctor who is able to assess any changes in my condition. Sometimes I feel like disengaging, because I have to fight to access the basic support that should be helping me manage my own mental health and prevent a crisis.

Even though I've been through the system, recent changes in my locality mean that if I have a crisis again, I'll be even more lost than I was before. A while ago my local mental health trust decided to close the specialist crisis clinic and transfer the functions to general accident and emergency. An inner city accident and emergency unit is not where you want to present with a mental health crisis, particularly one which may have involved self-harm! So the current mental health system in itself can be an obstacle to recovery.

Advancing social models in mental health

There is a cliché that sometimes a breakdown can be a breakthrough. Sarah's most severe crisis landed her in a locked ward of a psychiatric wing of a general hospital in the heart of London.

> It was not what anyone could call a 'therapeutic environment'. As some offenders must do after a spell in prison, I left the hospital vowing never to go back. This was my breakthrough – I wasn't able to ignore the extent of my mental health problems anymore because I knew where doing that could lead. I finally faced up to being 'properly mad' (psychotic episodes can have that effect!) and became determined to manage my mental health, to recognise triggers and the effect of disabling environments and to be more open with people.
>
> But I am not cured. I am recovering my life. That is how I have come to understand the debated term 'recovery' (Social Perspectives Network 2007) in relation to long-term mental health conditions, which cannot necessarily be 'cured' in the medical sense. I am learning all the time about limitations and risks – then I am learning how to give myself permission to manage those things safely. I am aware that my condition is fluctuating, and the statutory mental health system is too

clinical, fragmented, inconsistent and inflexible to support me properly. The system is limited, and it has been up to me to discover the social, psychological, environmental and cultural influences on my mental health. I realise that I am in a relatively privileged position to do so. Unlike some people with long-term mental health problems who are socially excluded, I enjoyed a decent state education and now have a good job and accommodation; I have a circle of close friends and a partner who support me; I can share experiences with fellow service users/survivors.

Hierarchy and power

For a growing number of people using and working in mental health services, there is an urgent need to strengthen the social element in assessment, treatment and support. Clinical models have been dominant in this field, understandably given the way advances in medication have transformed treatments and services; but there has been a price, and not only in rocketing pharmaceutical costs to the NHS. The power imbalances – between professionals and people needing help, amongst the different and competing professional groups, between hospital-based and community-based services, between primary and secondary care – have continuing adverse effects on the efficacy of treatment programmes and the experience of people with mental health problems.

In the hierarchy of mental health services, mentally unwell people are at the bottom of the pile, by definition lower in status than paid professionals, expected to fit into a service-centred world, and liable in some circumstances to be deprived of liberty and compelled to accept treatment by those higher up the tree. Even as they recognise they desperately need help, many people feel demeaned and disempowered by having to accept it on these terms.

Strengthening the social dimension

The social model was developed by the disability movement. Proponents argued that disability was a product, not of deficiencies in the individual, but of the barriers and obstacles presented by disabling environments. Effective intervention and support involved helping the person and their family to identify the obstacles and find ways to remove and/or overcome them. The obstacles come in many forms – physical, environmental, social, economic, professional, political and legal. Although there is still much to do, this thinking has helped transform the position of disabled people in a variety of ways.

More recently, the Social Perspectives Network (SPN) has worked to promote application of the social model in mental health services (Tew 2005). This raises several issues. What are the equivalent barriers for people with mental health problems and the means to remove them? Can the model broaden the focus from treatment services and recovery to the centrality for people of a job, a home, a social life and a capacity for self-management? Can it support greater equality between individuals and professionals in co-production approaches? Can it revalue the roles of non-professionals in supporting people's mental well-being? Is it the way to *New Horizons* (Department of Health 2009)?

Sarah sums up the lessons from her experience:

> So what has helped? There are six main things that have helped me so far:
>
> 1. exploring how my diagnoses affect my identity
>
> 2. consistency and control in treatment
>
> 3. peer support
>
> 4. being known and accepted by friends and colleagues
>
> 5. a stable personal life
>
> 6. having meaningful occupation.
>
> Of course all of these things sound relatively straightforward: but maintaining these elements can be a huge challenge – particularly if you have an inherent tendency for suicidal self-loathing. If this is the case, you're often locked in a fight against the impulse that you're not really worth it, and struggling with what Erving Goffman (1959) called a 'spoiled identity'.

Working with mental health problems

As well as providing an income, employment is often a key source of social identity, human contact, organisational involvement, satisfying challenge and personal well-being. For most people between their twenties and their sixties, a job provides a structure to the week and, with holidays, a rhythm to the year. Grumbling about work is probably, after the weather, the most common conversational currency (Department of Work and Pensions 2006). Loss of a job, whether through retirement, or prematurely through redundancy or employer closure, often has an effect on people akin to bereavement or severe depression. It can take away the meaning from their lives and leave them wounded.

But work can also be an area of stress, difficulty and conflict for many people with mental health problems (Carr 2003). At any one time, a significant proportion of the workforce will be coping with various mental health conditions. For them, particular features of work may be more difficult to manage, or may exacerbate the conditions. Overload, lack of control, a mismatch of demands and skills, bad relationships, unsupportive management, limited development opportunities, poor working conditions – any or all these can affect people's competence, coping ability, levels of anxiety and depression, which in turn make situations worse (Social Care Institute for Excellence 2008).

Working through a depressive episode

There are different perspectives on the merits or otherwise of trying to continue working through a severe depression. For the individual, it may be hard to acknowledge the problem or its cause, despite the signs of diminishing capability and performance at work. The often intense feelings of guilt and anxiety make it hard to say 'This deadline I agreed, this commitment I accepted, this response I should be submitting – I'm not going to be able to deliver them, because I've slipped into an acute depression'. There's also a tendency to cover up the problem and keep going through the motions as long as possible. This makes it harder for others to intervene in a timely fashion.

Much also depends, however, on the response of employers, colleagues and close family members. A sympathetic and supportive employer is a godsend, but inevitably they also have to take a wider view of the needs of the organisation. 'You can afford one breakdown, but not two,' Don was told by one boss. Colleagues may have to cope with some of the fall-out from a breakdown, not only landing extra work, but also accommodating uncharacteristic behaviour, attitudes and moods. Partners and family members may worry about damage to the individual's reputation at work from actions or omissions during the breakdown period.

Work and the cycle of depression and recovery

The link between work and the cycles of depression and recovery is not a simple one. Pressures, demands and heavy responsibilities are not necessarily the main triggers for breakdown. Instead, with the onset of depression, tasks that would normally cost little or no effort – writing a note, taking a view, weighing up options and making choices – become impossible. In her memoir of depression, *Shoot the Damn Dog* (2008), Sally Brampton quotes her consultant. 'Depression, as my psychiatrist told me when…I complained at my inability to think myself out of it, depresses every cognitive process. Concentration, memory, logic, reason, even the interpretation of facts and actual events are all interrupted' (Brampton 2008). Once this line is crossed, the mix of collapsing confidence, rising anxiety, harsh self-judgement and fear of permanent failure creates a vicious circle.

Coming out about mental health problems

How open should we be about our own experience of mental health problems? This has to be a matter for the individual to decide. It also means assessing what information other people and groups can cope with. Overcoming residual feelings of guilt and shame by speaking openly from experience of mental distress can be a liberating and empowering experience. It can reduce the sense of isolation felt by others with similar problems, and help the relatives of people with mental illness, particularly parents of young adults, express their anxieties and shift perspective.

Attitudes among the health and care professions to a colleague with mental health problems can be particularly negative. A consultant in emergency medicine with bipolar disorder and associated conditions recently reported experiences of being criticised, marginalised, isolated and rejected by her peers. 'My colleagues do not want me back, they are frightened by a diagnosis that has existed for as long as I can remember, they do not want a psychiatrically diagnosed colleague, and two have even offered to resign. The stigmatisation, the effect loneliness and lack of support has had on my life and that of my family is indescribable' (Smith 2009).

Such experiences serve as a warning. But they do not detract from the positive benefits of speaking from user experience to mental health professionals about the more disempowering aspects of their practice; of describing first-hand the difference it makes when a GP or consultant genuinely treats a patient as an expert in her own right, with a distinctive contribution to make; of asking routinely in policy-making, planning and implementation processes, 'but do we know what the people using services think about the present arrangements, and have they got different perspectives on what needs to change?'

References

Berman, M. (2007) 'Introduction.' In M. Berman and B. Berger (eds) *New York Calling: From Blackout to Bloomberg.* London: Reaktion Books.

Boyle, D., Clark, S. and Burns, S. (2006) *Co-Production by People Outside Paid Employment.* York: Joseph Rowntree Foundation.

Brampton, S. (2008) *Shoot the Damn Dog: A Memoir of Depression.* London: Bloomsbury.

Carr, S. (2003) 'Duty of care: employment, mental health and disability.' *Journal of Mental Health Promotion 2*, 1, 6–23.

Department of Health (1999) *National Service Framework for Mental Health: Modern Standards and Service Models.* London: Department of Health.

Department of Health (2009) *New Horizons: Towards a New Vision for Mental Health and Wellbeing.* London: Department of Health.

Department of Work and Pensions (2006) *New Deal for Welfare: Empowering People to Work.* London: The Stationery Office.

Goffman, E. (1959) *The Presentation of Self in Everyday Life.* New York: Doubleday.

Leadbetter, C. (2009) (2009) 'State of loneliness.' *The Guardian*, Society Section, 1 July, p 2.

Smith, S. (2009) 'Stigma in the medical profession.' *Pendulum (Journal of MDF: The Bi-polar Organisation) 25*, 2, 5.

Social Care Institute for Excellence (2008) *Supporting People in Accessing Meaningful Work: Recovery Approaches in Community Based Adult Mental Health Services.* Knowledge Review 21. London: Social Care Institute for Excellence.

Social Perspectives Network (2007) *Whose Recovery is it Anyway?* Available at www.scie.org.uk/publications/misc/recovery.pdf, accessed on 15 September 2009.

Tew, J. (ed.) (2005) *Social Perspectives in Mental Health: Developing Social Models to Understand and Work with Mental Distress.* London: Jessica Kingsley Publishers.

Chapter 15

Challenges and Opportunities for Psychosocial Practice in Mental Health

Martin Webber and Jack Nathan

Over the last 30 years mental health services in the UK have witnessed a rapid expansion in community care at the expense of inpatient treatment. Many other developed countries have undergone similar transformations. These reforms have been hastened in the first decade of the twenty-first century in the UK by the *National Service Framework for Mental Health* (Department of Health 1999). This recommended the introduction of community-based assertive outreach, crisis intervention and home treatment services on the basis of research evidence of their effectiveness, mostly from the USA and Australia.

Mental health service reform, which is still ongoing in many places, has been accompanied by new ways of working for mental health professionals (Department of Health 2007). This, and changes brought in by the Mental Health Act 2007, have created opportunities for nurses to train to become prescribers alongside psychiatrists; nurses, clinical psychologists and occupational therapists to train as Approved Mental Health Professionals alongside social workers; and consultant psychologists and advanced social work professionals to train as Responsible Clinicians alongside psychiatrists. These reforms, however, have created considerable uncertainty for many professional groups. Psychiatrists, in particular, have been concerned that an increased focus on 'non-specific psychosocial support' in mental health services devalues traditional biomedical interventions and undermines their role (Craddock *et al.* 2008; St John-Smith *et al.* 2009). To ensure its survival psychiatry must move away from biodeterminism and embrace bio-psychosocial models (Pilgrim and Rogers 2009).

In the second decade of the twenty-first century, as the Government sets sail for *New Horizons* (Her Majesty's Government 2009) – a policy vision which adopts a psychosocial lifespan approach – social workers are well placed to provide professional leadership in mental health services. Social workers have been empowering mental health service users to actively participate in their care, promoting their inclusion in mainstream community life and working towards their holistic recovery long before these became government priorities. However, the profession needs to overcome a number of challenges and to clearly articulate its own unique discourse to enable it to truly fulfil its potential.

Mental heath social workers work with those who have the most complex needs in community mental health teams (Huxley *et al.* 2008). They report high levels of stress and emotional exhaustion and low levels of job satisfaction (Evans *et al.* 2006), often as a result of inadequate supervision, in contrast to consultant psychiatrists who have much more latitude in their decision-making and are less burnt out (Mears *et al.* 2007). Mental health social workers with statutory responsibilities in England and Wales effectively manage complex assessments involving a number of competing demands, inter-changeable roles and challenging dynamics (Quirk *et al.* 2000, 2003). However, they experience high levels of burn-out (Evans *et al.* 2005) and their numbers were in decline in the years leading up to the new Mental Health Act (Huxley *et al.* 2005). Unfortunately, this made a compelling workforce argument for the government to widen the Approved Social Worker role to other mental health professionals.

As we argued in Chapter 5, social work lacks a robust evidence base in contrast to other mental health professional groups, notably psychiatry and psychology. It consequently has a limited ability to influence clinical guidelines or service design. However, evidence is emerging which contradicts the assumed empirical strengths of biological and psychological interventions. For example, two large non-commercial trials of anti-psychotic drugs for people with a diagnosis of chronic schizophrenia in the USA and UK found that newer drugs neither were more effective nor had fewer side-effects than older ones (Lewis and Lieberman 2008). Additionally, a meta-analysis of unpublished findings of clinical trials of anti-depressant drugs (Turner *et al.* 2008) found that selective publishing of positive results gives the impression that these drugs are more effective than earlier thought. In spite of the vast expenditure on the development of new drugs, biomedical interventions for people with mental health problems do not appear to be becoming any more effective.

In terms of psychological interventions, a recent meta-analysis of high-quality trials of cognitive behavioural therapy found that it is no better than non-specific control interventions in the treatment of schizophrenia, it only has a small effect on major depression and it does not prevent relapse in bipolar disorder (Lynch, Laws and McKenna 2010). Echoing these findings, Cuijpers *et al.* (2010) reviewed 11 high-quality trials and found that the effectiveness of psychological interventions for depression has been previously over-estimated. They concluded that higher-quality trials found that psychological interventions were less effective than in poorer-quality trials.

These reviews call into question the effectiveness of biomedical and psychological treatments for mental disorders. Any investment in further developments of the evidence bases for medicine and psychology (and there seems no shortage of it at present) will bring proportionately fewer knowledge gains than equivalent investment in the development of the social work evidence base. In spite of calls for new investment in social science research in mental health (Huxley and Evans 2003), little has been forthcoming. Strengthening the professional basis of social work will help it to make a stronger case for funding to develop its research capacity and evidence base.

A further challenge to statutory social work in the UK is its susceptibility to government reform. Not all reform is necessarily harmful to the profession, but the shifting sands of political ideology have constrained the ability of social work to develop and define its own discourse. From the Younghusband Report (1959), through Seebohm (1968) and Barclay (1982) to the Social Work Task Force (2009a), social work has oscillated between genericism and specialisation. Whilst this appears to have been resolved in favour of retention of generic social work training with the acquisition of specialist skills and knowledge through continuing professional development after qualifying (Social Work Task Force 2009a), the lack of a consistent vision for the profession has stifled the development of a unique social work discourse. In multi-disciplinary contexts such as mental health services this has damaged social work as it struggles to define its own role.

Yet as we have argued in this book (Introduction and Chapter 1) and elsewhere (Nathan and Webber 2010) social workers are *the* professional grouping who possess the tradition, expertise and experience to challenge the creeping bureau-medicalisation of practice within mental health settings. Borne of a 'double identification' (Nathan and Webber in press), social workers play a key role in representing the institution they work for *and* putting service users at the centre of their practice ensuring that their voice is heard. No other professional body carries this unique role. By continuing to develop the social work discourse, and thereby refining its roles and tasks (Association of Directors of Adult Social Services, Skills for Care and Department of Health 2009; General Social Care Council 2008), practitioners will be better able to articulate their unique contribution. The Social Work Task Force (2009a) report makes specific reference to the need for 'stronger leadership and independence – with the profession taking more control over its own standards...and the contribution it makes to changes in policy and practice' (p.6). Advanced practitioners, in particular, are well placed to undertake this role providing just such leadership for the profession.

The Social Work Reform Board provides the opportunity to make this vision a reality by developing a national career structure for social work, which includes Advanced Social Work Professional (ASWP) status. For this to be a success, consistent national criteria for ASWP status need to be established. Some employers have their own career structures that may relate to achievements in the post-qualifying (PQ) framework (General Social Care Council 2005), other professional development such as Approved Mental Health Professional status, or passing an assessment centre process. In Children Social Care services, others have developed Consultant Social Worker roles (e.g. London Borough of Hackney) to provide professional leadership in social work and clinical teams (see Chapter 12). This model of 'reclaiming social work' enables practitioners to continue to see clients as well as provide high-quality supervision (something the Social Work Task Force (2009a) implicitly recognises has not been consistently available to date). In this way consultants will be able to claim a seniority that befits their experience and expertise, without being engulfed by the demands of management. For its part, the Children's Workforce Development Council is piloting a scheme of employer nomination of practitioners for ASWP status. A consistent pathway needs to be developed with clear evidence of continuing professional development through PQ awards to make the role meaningful and one to be respected. This career structure needs to be suitable for use by employers within the statutory, voluntary sector and private sectors.

The career pathway appropriately provides options for experienced practitioners to stay in front-line practice. However, social work academics currently lack career pathways that keep them in practice. Unlike health professionals there are no clinical academic pathways for social workers. In clinical psychology and medicine, joint appointments enable practitioners to also hold senior academic positions. Academic contracts for social work lecturers do not routinely include a practice component. To improve the synergy between practice, teaching and research in social work, there is an opportunity to develop a national clinical academic pathway for social workers equivalent to that for health professionals. This will both improve the quality of social work practice and the relevance of social work research.

ASWP status is best achieved through the PQ framework for social work (General Social Care Council 2005). Although there is strong support for the framework from universities, employers and practitioners, it has largely been sidelined in the Social Work Task Force's discussions about the continuing professional development of social workers (Ayres 2009). As Alan Rushton stated in the Foreword, this book has been developed from an advanced level PQ programme in the PQ framework. PQ programmes can hold the vision for the future of social work and develop advanced practitioners who can help to make the vision a reality through professional leadership in their agencies.

The PQ framework for social work is employer-led and the responsibility for funding PQ awards falls with employers. However, the main source of motivation to study the PQ award in advanced social work is intrinsic and originates in the practitioners' own desire for professional development, rather than a workforce development plan originating from employers (Nyandoro 2009). Funding for the PQ award in advanced social work comes primarily from the practitioners themselves. The majority of students on our programme at the Institute of Psychiatry (more than 80%) are fully self-funding. With no source of bursary funding, they have to take career development loans or build up credit card debts to afford their own professional development. Practitioners are prepared to do this because they are keen to advance their careers and develop the social work profession. More funding needs to be made available for the training of ASWPs within a revised continuing professional development (CPD) framework.

The former government's acceptance of Lord Laming's (2009) recommendation to develop a Master's in Social Work Practice supports our argument for the enhancement of the professional status of social work. Although the coalition government has dropped the plans for a Master's in Social Work Practice, it remains committed to providing opportunities for all social workers to acquire a Master's degree after qualifying. We would argue that existing good practice in the current PQ awards in advanced social work that focus on professional practice needs to inform the revised PQ framework.

The model, developed over the 30 years of our programme at the Institute of Psychiatry, essentially fits with the proposal put forward by the Social Work Task Force (2009b) which favours 'more specialist training being achieved at post qualifying level' (p.26). It has two essential elements: a lifespan approach and educational inclusiveness. The latter was specifically recommended in the Interim Report (2009b) which made clear that post-qualifying training has to be 'open to everyone in the profession and that it sits in the context of a much wider, more coherent framework for professional development' (p.42). On our programme, which recruits practitioners from across the spectrum of social work practice arenas, this not only means that practitioners from *all* social work arenas have a legitimate claim to being on the course, but that we also ensure that it is specifically tailored to the student's employer-based needs. In the first year they all participate in the intensive taught programme. This 'advanced generic' element delivers current research, policy and practice developments in all areas relevant to social work. In their own area of practice, students simultaneously pursue their 'specialism' in the two core building blocks of the programme: namely, casework practice and completion of their research project in the second year. By such means, no unnecessarily rigid distinction is made between genericism and specialism. One often overlooked and fundamental educational outcome is that students benefit from the richness of experience brought to the group. This is especially noticeable in the sometimes heated conversations that take place between those on the 'side' of parents in child care cases, usually mental health social workers, and children's social workers, who often have insufficient knowledge of parents with mental health problems. This professional cross-fertilisation leaves both parties the wiser and enhances the quality of social work provision in both arenas.

Beyond the Master's level proposals, the Social Work Task Force (2009a) report also indicates that the CPD framework may include Professional Doctorates in Social Work. The inclusion of Professional Doctorates within a CPD framework for social work will bolster the development of academic social work and provide practitioners with an accredited route to developing research skills that is lacking in the current framework (General Social Care Council and Joint University Council 2008). These need to be developed with robust funding plans and employer engagement to ensure their success. In addition to this, it is worthwhile considering establishing a bursary fund for PhDs in social work to further enhance the research capacity of the profession (Orme and Powell 2008). As we have discussed in Chapter 1, advanced practitioners in social work create new knowledge that contributes to the profession's evidence base and develops the discipline's discourse from within. Results of practitioner research could potentially be disseminated to a wider audience through systematic use of the Research Register for Social Care or via Social Care Online.

Looking forward

This book has presented an ambitious, but realistic, vision for social workers engaging with people with mental health problems across the life-course. Paul Godin has identified the social context of mental disorders (Chapter 2) and Tirril Harris has provided an overview of her work with George Brown on the social origins of depression in Chapter 3, indicating the tremendous potential for social work interventions in mental health. Pete Fleischmann's revealing insight into service user/survivor research knowledge (Chapter 4) reminds us of the social construction of knowledge and how social work must retain its close connection to the people it works with.

Advanced reflective practitioners have a range of theoretical and therapeutic traditions to draw on in their practice. We have selected just a few for inclusion in this book to provide practitioners with a taste of the richness and diversity of perspectives they have at their disposal to enrich their practice. Advanced reflective practice in mental health requires practitioners to draw upon insights from psychoanalysis (Chapter 6), cognitive behavioural therapy (Chapter 7), systemic family therapy (Chapter 8), attachment therapy (Chapter 9) and psychodynamic group work (Chapter 10) to promote change. Being at ease with a plurality of practice models is an enduring strength of social work and will ensure its survival in mental health care. This is ably shown in Chapters 11 through 13 where advanced practitioners have skilfully drawn upon a range of relevant paradigms to enrich their practice with children and adults.

In this book we set out to contribute to the definition of the discourse of mental health social work. Its unique ability to draw upon a range of perspectives is a strength, as is its unique position vis-a-vis the service user. In taking a lifespan perspective to mental health – so that it is the concern of practitioners working with children, adults and older adults – we suggest that all practitioners should become familiar with the intervention techniques we have introduced here. This will require the development of professional confidence and mastery in contrast to narrow competence-based approaches.

The process of reform we are undertaking at the start of the second decade of the twenty-first century provides us with an ideal opportunity to develop advanced reflective practitioners in social work. As this book clearly demonstrates there is a wealth of knowledge, experience and expertise to draw on, the potential of which has not to date been fully realised within the profession. There is now a growing commitment to repositioning social work so that we finally claim the clear voice and professional leadership that the Social Work Task Force (2009a) envisages. If we are at this progressive moment, and not retreading another passing pipedream, then we – practitioners, employers and educators – must all play our part in rising up together and seizing this moment.

References

Association of Directors of Adult Social Services, Skills for Care and Department of Health (2009) *The Roles and Task of Social Work in Adult Services under 'Putting People First': A Statement for Consultation.* London: ADASS, Skills for Care, Department of Health.

Ayres, S. (2009) *What to do about PQ.* Available at http://shirleyayresconsulting.co.uk/post-qualifying-learning-and-education/what-to-do-about-pq, accessed on 16 December 2009.

Barclay, P.M. (1982) *Social Workers: Their Roles and Tasks.* London: Bedford Square Press.

Craddock, N., Antebi, D., Attenburrow, M.-J., Bailey, A. *et al.* (2008) 'Wake-up call for British psychiatry.' *British Journal of Psychiatry 193*, 1, 6–9.

Cuijpers, P., van Straten, A., Bohlmeijer, E., Hollon, S.D. and Andersson, G. (2010) 'The effects of psychotherapy for adult depression are overestimated: a meta-analysis of study quality and effect size.' *Psychological Medicine 40*, 2, 211–223.

Department of Health (1999) *National Service Framework for Mental Health: Modern Standards and Service Models.* London: Department of Health.

Department of Health (2007) *Mental Health: New Ways of Working for Everyone: Developing and Sustaining a Capable Flexible Workforce. Department of Health Progress Report.* London: Stationery Office.

Evans, S., Huxley, P., Webber, M., Katona, C. *et al.* (2005) 'The impact of 'statutory duties' on mental health social workers in the UK.' *Health and Social Care in the Community 13*, 2, 145–154.

Evans, S., Huxley, P., Gately, C., Webber, M. *et al.* (2006) 'Mental health, burnout and job satisfaction among mental health social workers in England and Wales.' *British Journal of Psychiatry 188*, 1, 75–80.

General Social Care Council (2005) *Post-Qualifying Framework for Social Work Education and Training.* London: General Social Care Council.

General Social Care Council (2008) *Social Work at its Best: A Statement of Social Work Roles and Tasks for the 21st Century.* London: General Social Care Council.

General Social Care Council and Joint University Council (2008) *Research and the PQ Framework*. Available at http://www.gscc.org.uk/NR/rdonlyres/74CB0243-6F7B-4A47-A31E-6FD7AA3C0664/0/Research_guidance_JUCSWECandGSCC.pdf, accessed on 14 Dceember 2009.

Her Majesty's Government (2009) *New Horizons: A Shared Vision for Mental Health*. London: Department of Health.

Huxley, P. and Evans, S. (2003) 'Social science and mental health.' *Journal of Mental Health 12*, 6, 543–550.

Huxley, P., Evans, S., Webber, M. and Gately, C. (2005) 'Staff shortages in the mental health workforce: the case of the disappearing approved social worker.' *Health and Social Care in the Community 13*, 6, 504–513.

Huxley, P., Evans, S., Munroe, M. and Cestari, L. (2008) 'Mental health policy reforms and case complexity in CMHTs in England: replication study.' *Psychiatric Bulletin 32*, 2, 49–52.

Laming, Lord (2009) *The Protection of Children in England: A Progress Report*. London: The Stationery Office.

Lewis, S. and Lieberman, J. (2008) 'CATIE and CUtLASS: can we handle the truth?' *The British Journal of Psychiatry 192*, 3, 161–163.

Lynch, D., Laws, K.R. and McKenna, P.J. (2010) 'Cognitive behavioural therapy for major psychiatric disorder: does it really work? A meta-analytical review of well-controlled trials.' *Psychological Medicine 40*, 1, 9–24.

Mears, A., Pajak, S., Kendall, T., Katona, C. *et al.* (2007) 'Consultant psychiatrists' working patterns.' *Psychiatric Bulletin 31*, 7, 252–255.

Nathan, J. and Webber, M. (2010) 'Mental health social work and the bureau-medicalisation of mental health care: identity in a changing world.' *Journal of Social Work Practice 24*, 1, 15–28.

Nyandoro, G. (2009) *An investigation into factors which motivate qualified health and social care professionals to undertake part-time post-qualifying education at MSc level*. MSc thesis. London: Institute of Psychiatry, King's College London.

Orme, J. and Powell, J. (2008) 'Building research capacity in social work: process and issues.' *British Journal of Social Work 38*, 5, 988–1008.

Pilgrim, D. and Rogers, A. (2009) 'Survival and its discontents: the case of British psychiatry.' *Sociology of Health and Illness 31*, 7, 947–961.

Quirk, A., Lelliott, P., Audini, B. and Buston, K. (2000) *Performing the Act: A Qualitative Study of the Process of Mental Health Act Assessments. Final report to the Department of Health*. London: Royal College of Psychiatrists' Research Unit.

Quirk, A., Lelliott, P., Audini, B. and Buston, K. (2003) 'Non-clinical and extra-legal influences on decisions about compulsory admission to psychiatric hospital.' *Journal of Mental Health 12*, 2, 119–130.

Seebohm, F. (1968) *Report of the Committee on Local Authority and Allied Personal Social Services*. London: HMSO.

Social Work Task Force (2009a) *Building a Safe, Confident Future: The Final Report of the Social Work Task Force*. London: Department for Children, Schools and Families.

Social Work Task Force (2009b) *Facing up to the Task: The Interim Report of the Social Work Task Force*. London: Department for Children, Schools and Families.

St John-Smith, P., McQueen, D., Michael, A., Ikkos, G. *et al.* (2009) 'The trouble with NHS psychiatry in England.' *Psychiatric Bulletin 33*, 6, 219–225.

Turner, E.H., Matthews, A.M., Linardatos, E., Tell, R.A. and Rosenthal, R. (2008) 'Selective publication of antidepressant trials and its influence on apparent efficacy.' *New England Journal of Medicine 358*, 3, 252–260.

Younghusband, E.L. (1959) *Report of the Working Party on Social Workers in the Local Authority Health and Welfare Services*. London: HMSO.

Contributors

Don Brand is a consultant and advisor to the Social Care Institute for Excellence (SCIE), and a trustee of the Joseph Rowntree Foundation. He has spent 40 years in social work and social care, including 20 years in local authority social work, training, policy and senior management in Oxford and Kent. From 1989 to 1996, he was Deputy Chief Inspector in the Social Services Inspectorate at the Department of Health. He moved to the National Institute for Social Work, led development work on the General Social Care Council and its UK counterparts, and worked with the Department of Health on establishing SCIE in 2001. He has helped SCIE to put service users at the heart of its work and build partnerships with user-led organisations, and has himself been a user of mental health services. He has worked on SCIE's contributions to government policy, including the Green Paper *Independence, Wellbeing and Choice*, the *Putting People First* personalisation programme, the Adult Social Care Workforce Strategy, the joint Social Work Task Force, the Green Paper on the long-term funding of care and support, and initiatives in Wales and Northern Ireland. He is a trustee of the Residential Forum, and has been a trustee and board member of voluntary organisations providing services for older people, people with learning disabilities and those with mental health problems.

Sarah Carr is a senior research analyst at the Social Care Institute for Excellence (SCIE), currently leading on the organisation's personalisation work and advising on the policy at a national level. She has also worked for the National Institute for Social Work, Oxleas NHS Trust and at the Sainsbury Centre for Mental Health in research and information roles. In addition to her post at SCIE, Sarah is currently an honorary fellow at the Faculty of Health at Staffordshire University, an Executive Committee member of the Social Perspectives Network (SPN) and a board member of the National Development Team for Inclusion (NDTi). She is a long-term user of mental health services and has written on her own experiences as well as general mental health practice and policy, LGB welfare and equality issues, service user empowerment and participation.

Felicity de Zulueta is a consultant psychiatrist in psychotherapy heading the Traumatic Stress Service in the Maudsley Hospital, London, and an honorary senior clinical lecturer in Traumatic Studies at the Institute of Psychiatry. She studied biology at the University of East Anglia prior to doing medicine at Cambridge University. She created and led the department of psychotherapy at Charing Cross Hospital. She is a group analyst and a systemic family therapist whose main interests lie in the study of attachment and psychological trauma as well as bilingualism. She is author of *From Pain to Violence, the Traumatic Roots of Destructiveness* (John Wiley and Sons, second edition, 2006) and many chapters on the subject. She is also a founding member of the International Attachment Network.

Pete Fleischmann leads the Social Care Institute for Excellence's (SCIE) participation work. This covers commissioning good practice guidance around participation issues and managing SCIE's internal participation activity. Pete has experience of using mental health services. Pete was development worker and then co-ordinator of Brent Mental Health User Group (BUG) from 1991 to 1996. Until 2004 when he joined SCIE, Pete worked as an independent consultant.

Paul Godin teaches sociology at City University. He has undertaken ethnographic and participatory research studies in mental health care.

Caroline Grimbly is a practising social worker and Approved Mental Health Professional who is currently working within a specialist inpatient unit for people who self-harm. She is a group psychotherapist and a tutor on the MSc in Mental Health Social Work with Children and Adults at the Institute of Psychiatry.

Tirril Harris divides her time between clinical work in private practice with adults and research in social psychiatry with George Brown in the Health Service and Population Research Department, Institute of Psychiatry, King's College London. The Brown-Harris model of depression, which has emerged from this colleagueship of some 30 years, succeeds in blending ideas from both medical sociology and psychoanalytic thought and in collecting data to verify these insights about the mutual influence between outer and inner worlds. She is a member of the London Centre for Psychotherapy and is also a member of the Research Committee of the United Kingdom Council for Psychotherapy.

Judith Lask is programme leader for the Family Therapy programmes at the Institute of Psychiatry, King's College London. She trained originally as a social worker and worked within child and adolescent mental health settings for 20 years before training as a family and systemic psychotherapist. For the past 15 years she has combined clinical practice with course delivery and development. She is an ex-chair of the Association for Family Therapy and is currently involved in policy development. She has taught extensively in the UK and internationally and is particularly interested in the application of systemic ideas in developing family sensitive practice in all mental health related professions.

Jack Nathan qualified as a social worker in 1980. On becoming a social work manager at Maudsley Hospital in 1989, Jack began teaching on the MSc in Mental Health Social Work with Children and Adults as a tutor running the advanced case consultation groups. He is now a senior lecturer in social work at the Institute of Psychiatry. Jack went on to qualify as a psychoanalytic psychotherapist at the London Centre of Psychotherapy. He also works as a consultant psychotherapist in the Maudsley Psychotherapy Service and Self-Harm Out-Patients Service. Jack has dedicated much of his thinking and teaching into 'translating' the profound insights of psychoanalysis as tools to help social work practitioners in their everyday work. This is reflected in his publications that have concentrated on making psychoanalytic concepts practitioner-friendly. In addition, Jack's more recent publications have focused on his specialist interest in self-harm and group work with people who experience severe mental health problems.

Rebecca Peters is a social worker particularly interested in parenting and preventative interventions. She is a graduate of the MSc in Mental Health Social Work with Children and Adults programme and is currently head of the London Borough of Hackney Children Social Care's Access and Assessment service.

Paul Richards is a social worker and Approved Mental Health Professional. He is currently the social work team manager at a medium secure unit within the South London and Maudsley NHS Foundation Trust. Paul is also an advanced practice assessor on the MSc in Mental Health Social Work with Children and Adults at the Institute of Psychiatry, King's College London.

Florian Ruths is a consultant psychiatrist at the Maudsley Hospital, London, and holds a Postgraduate Diploma in CBT from King's College London. After further CBT training at the Centre for Anxiety Disorders and Trauma he developed his interest in CBT for anxiety and depression. Florian is the consultant lead for the Mindfulness Based Cognitive Therapy Groups at the Maudsley Psychotherapy Service. He teaches CBT on two MSc courses at the Institute of Psychiatry, and he has published in the areas of anxiety and depression. Florian has appeared on TV and radio commenting on CBT for anxiety.

Martin Webber is a registered social worker and programme director of the MSc in Mental Health Social Work with Children and Adults at the Institute of Psychiatry, King's College London. He has research interests in social capital and mental health, social interventions and social work practice. He is author of *Evidence-Based Policy and Practice in Mental Health Social Work* (Learning Matters, 2008) and has authored and co-authored several papers and chapters on social capital or social work.

Tony West qualified as a social worker in 1989. Since then he has worked in a variety of practice and management roles, mainly in adult mental health. These include the roles of Approved Social Worker (now Approved Mental Health Professional), community mental health team manager and borough lead social worker for mental health. More recently, he has been doing some project work on the mental health needs of people with learning disabilities. He is a graduate of the MSc in Mental Health Social Work with Children and Adults programme.

Subject Index

Author Index